Introduction to Help Desk Concepts and Skills

Susan M. Sanderson

McGraw-Hill Technology Education
New York Chicago San Francisco
Lisbon London Madrid Mexico City
Milan New Delhi San Juan
Seoul Singapore Sydney Toronto

McGraw-Hill Technology Education

Introduction to Help Desk Concepts and Skills

Published by McGraw-Hill Technology Education, an imprint of The McGraw-Hill Companies, Inc. 1333 Burr Ridge Parkway, Burr Ridge, IL, 60527. Copyright © 2004 by The McGraw-Hill Companies, Inc. All rights reserved. No part of this publication may be reproduced or distributed in any form or by any means, or stored in a database or retrieval system, without the prior written consent of The McGraw-Hill Companies, Inc., including, but not limited to, in any network or other electronic storage or transmission, or broadcast for distance learning. For information on translations or book distributors outside the U.S.A., please see the International Contact Information page immediately following the index of this book.

    10 QDB/QDB 11
ISBN 978-0-07-223159-5
MHID 0-07-223159-9

Publisher
  Brandon A. Nordin

Editor in Chief
  Bob Woodbury

Editorial Director
  Linda Bruton

Sponsoring Editors
  Cynthia Baule
  Chris Johnson

Developmental Editors
  Cristina Di Battista
  Laura Stone

Editorial Development
  Chestnut Hill Enterprises, Inc.

Project Editors
  Barbara Everett
  Jennifer Malnick

Composition
  Maureen Forys,
  Happenstance Type-O-Rama

Illustrator
  Chestnut Hill Enterprises, Inc.

Cover Series Design
  Greg Scott

This book was composed with QuarkXPress 4.11 on a Macintosh.

About the Author

Susan M. Sanderson is senior technical writer for Chestnut Hill Enterprises, Inc., and has developed successful products for McGraw-Hill for more than ten years. She has authored all Windows-based editions of *Computers in the Medical Office*. She has also written *Patient Billing, Capstone Billing Simulation*, and computer simulations for other programs. Susan has experience in working with instructors to site-test materials and has provided technical support to McGraw-Hill customers. Previously, Susan worked in IT Training and Support for a major Wall Street firm.

A member of the Help Desk Institute, Susan has completed Help Desk Institute and HelpSTAR training programs. She is a graduate of Drew University, with further study at Columbia University.

About the Series Editor

Michael Meyers is the industry's leading authority on A+ and Network+ certification. He is the president and cofounder of Total Seminars, LLC, a provider of PC and network repair seminars, books, videos, and courseware for thousands of organizations throughout the world. Mike has been involved in the computer and network repair industry since 1977 as a technician, instructor, author, consultant, and speaker. Author of several popular PC books and of A+ and Network+ courseware, Mike is also the series editor for the highly successful Mike Meyers' Certification Passport series as well as the new Mike Meyers' Computer Skills series, both published by McGraw-Hill/Osborne. Mike holds multiple industry certifications and considers the moniker "computer nerd" a compliment.

About the Peer Reviewers

A number of people contributed to the development of *Introduction to Help Desk Concepts and Skills*. For insightful reviews, criticisms, and helpful suggestions we would like to acknowledge the following:

Barb Axmark
Computer Information Systems Department Chair
Rockford Business College
Rockford, IL

Debbie E. Karl
Assistant Program Chair, Computer Information Technology
Texas State Technical College
Abilene, TX

Hunter Hopkins
Director of Information Technology
ICM School of Business Careers
Pittsburgh, PA

Dr. Albert Taccone
Dean of Instruction
Cuyamaca College
El Cajon, CA

Acknowledgments

This book is in your hands today thanks to the many people who believed in the need for an introductory help desk book that blended technical content and interpersonal and communication skill-building. Too many times these "hard" and "soft" skills are separated, and the emphasis is on technical competency, with soft skills suffering as a result. It is my belief, and the belief of those who supported me during the writing of this book, that the two sets of skills are inseparable, and that more emphasis needs to be placed on the skills required to work with people—especially listening and communicating.

Before my writing began, instructors at schools and colleges throughout the country were surveyed to discover just what should be included in an introductory help desk book. The outline for this book was developed based on the survey results, and content was reviewed by survey respondents throughout the book's development.

I would like to thank Gary Schwartz for being the first one to believe in the project; Cynthia Baule for picking up the ball midstream and running with it; and the group of supportive people at McGraw-Hill Technology Education, including Chris Johnson, Laura Stone, and Jenny Malnick.

A special thanks to Help Desk Technology for providing a version of their HelpSTAR software program for use with this book. Thanks to their efforts, this book contains numerous computer-based exercises in which students gain real-life experience using help desk software to enter service requests, respond to problems, move requests from dispatch to queue, and so on. The opportunity to build these skills in such a powerful way is invaluable.

The staff at Chestnut Hill Enterprises, Cynthia Newby in particular, made everything possible. Without them, this book would simply not exist.

Finally, I would like to thank my family—Cindy, George (the first and second), Jack, and Marie—for suffering through day after day of my writer's block, dealing with last-minute changes of plan due to the ever-present deadlines, and believing that I could indeed write such a book.

About This Book

Important Technology Skills

Information technology (IT) offers many career paths, leading to occupations in such fields as PC repair, network administration, telecommunications, Web development, graphic design, and desktop support. To become competent in any IT field, however, you need certain basic computer skills. The Mike Meyers' Computer Skills series builds a foundation for success in the IT field by introducing you to fundamental technology concepts and giving you essential computer skills.

Feature Sidebars put concepts into industry and career contexts.

Example Scripts and **Rephrase Suggestions** promote good communication skills.

Computer Practice and **Audio Exercises** tie to HelpSTAR software and audio examples on the CD-ROM.

HELP *desk* **In Action**

Finding the Best Support Specialists

A typical help desk analyst is expected to play all of the following roles:

* **Team member**
  Cooperating with other support staff members to ensure that the help desk meets its goals

* **Problem-solver**
  Not only solving problems but also eliminating their root causes and preventing their recurrence

* **Communicator**
  Exchanging information with users and with others on the help desk

* **Marketer**
  Encouraging users with technical problems to turn to the help desk as a first resort

* **Researcher**
  Gathering data from users and consulting reference materials and other sources about problems and how to solve and prevent them

* **Expert**
  Possessing a depth of knowledge and instinct about how to solve and prevent problems

* **Customer service representative**
  Providing prompt, professional, and courteous help to customers and internal users

  To ensure that the people they hire can fill those roles, managers look for these qualities:

  * Focus on the help desk's goals
  * Problem-solving skills
  * Initiative

* Communication skills
* Technical aptitude and skills
* Customer relations skills

In addition to information from resumes, job applications, school transcripts, tests, and reference checks, whether candidates have the necessary skills and traits. Managers often invite other members of the help desk staff to participate in interviews of candidates, and sometimes they invite users. The screening process often includes a series of interviews, one of which may be conducted by telephone so the manager can check the candidate's telephone manner.

APPLYING SKILLS

1. Explain why each of the traits managers look for in technical support candidates is important for a help desk worker to have.

2. Write a one-page assessment of how well your own skills and personality traits match the requirements for working on a help desk. Indicate which of the required traits and skills are your strongest and which you feel you need to develop further.

46 Introduction to Help Desk Concepts and Skills

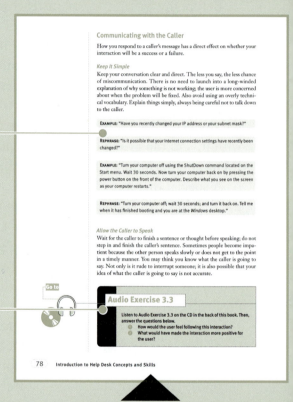

Communicating with the Caller

How you respond to a caller's message has a direct effect on whether your interaction will be a success or a failure.

Keep It Simple
Keep your conversation clear and direct. The less you say, the less chance of miscommunication. There is no need to launch into a long-winded explanation of why something is not working; the user is more concerned about when the problem will be fixed. Also avoid using an overly technical vocabulary. Explain things simply, always being careful not to talk down to the caller.

EXAMPLE: "Have you recently changed your IP address or your subnet mask?"

REPHRASE: "Is it possible that your Internet connection settings have recently been changed?"

EXAMPLE: "Turn your computer off using the ShutDown command located on the Start menu. Wait 30 seconds. Now turn your computer back on by pressing the power button on the front of the computer. Describe what you see on the screen as your computer restarts."

REPHRASE: "Turn your computer off; wait 30 seconds; and turn it back on. Tell me when it has finished booting and you are at the *Windows* desktop."

Allow the Caller to Speak
Wait for the caller to finish a sentence or thought before speaking; do not step in and finish the caller's sentence. Sometimes people become impatient because the other person speaks slowly or does not get to the point in a timely manner. You may think you know what the caller is going to say. Not only is it rude to interrupt someone; it is also possible that your idea of what the caller is going to say is not accurate.

Go to

Audio Exercise 3.3

Listen to Audio Exercise 3.3 on the CD in the back of this book. Then, answer the questions below.
① How would the user feel following this interaction?
② What would have made the interaction more positive for the user?

78 Introduction to Help Desk Concepts and Skills

▲ MAKES LEARNING FUN!
Rich, colorful text and varied pedagogy brings technical subjects to life.

▲ OFFERS PRACTICAL EXPERIENCE
Feature sidebars and hands-on assignments develop essential skills and put concepts in real-world contexts.

Proven Learning Method Keeps You on Track

The Mike Meyers' Computer Skills series is structured to give you a practical working knowledge of baseline IT skills and technologies. The series' active learning methodology guides you beyond mere recall and, through thought-provoking activities, examples, and sidebars, helps you develop critical thinking, diagnostic, and communication skills.

Effective Learning Tools

This pedagogically rich book is designed to make learning easy and enjoyable and to help you develop the skills and critical thinking abilities that will enable you to adapt to different job situations and troubleshoot problems.

Susan Sanderson's proven ability to explain concepts in a clear, direct way makes these books interesting, motivational, and fun.

Chapter Review sections provide concept summaries, key terms lists, and lots of questions and projects.

Did You Know boxes tie information to the real world.

Reading Check questions reinforce comprehension and promote critical thinking.

ENGAGING AND MOTIVATIONAL

Using a conversational style and proven instructional approach, the author explains technical concepts in a clear, interesting way using real-world examples.

ROBUST LEARNING TOOLS

Summaries, key term lists, quizzes, critical thinking questions, hands-on projects, and case studies help you practice skills and measure progress.

Each chapter includes:

Learning Objectives that set measurable goals for chapter-by-chapter progress

Two-Color Illustrations that give you a clear picture of the concepts

Step-by-Step Tutorials that teach you to perform essential tasks and procedures hands-on

Feature Sidebars that encourage you to practice and apply concepts in real-world settings

Example scripts and rephrases that guide you through difficult areas

Chapter Summaries and **Key Terms Lists** that provide you with an easy way to review important concepts and vocabulary

Challenging End-of-Chapter Tests that include vocabulary-building exercises, essay questions, hands-on projects, and case studies

Contents

Foreword from Mike Meyers

This book, like the other books in this series, is designed for exactly one function: to give you a broad introduction and overview of various aspects of the information technologies (IT) world. If you're new to computers, then welcome! This book is for you. If you're trying to decide where you want to go within the big world of IT, then again welcome—this book will help you sort out the many options and figure out where your interests may or may not lie. Do you want to become a Microsoft Windows expert? Do you want to get into troubleshooting and repair of PCs? What about becoming a network administrator? These books will help you understand the many aspects of IT and the many jobs within the IT world that are available.

So how will this book help you understand what IT is all about? Well, let's start by exploring the text in front of you right now. Like all of the books in this series, it is written in a very relaxed, conversational style that's a pleasure to read. We've tossed the staid, boring technical writing style out the window and instead write as though we're speaking directly to you—because as far as we're concerned, we are. In this and the other books in this series, we aren't afraid of the occasional contraction, nor do we worry about staying in third person. We've pretty much dumped all those other dry, pedantic rules that most technical writing embraces. I've suffered reading those books, and I swore when it came time to put together this series that we were going to break that mold—and we have! With over a million copies now in print using this series' conversational style, we think a lot of folks agree with what we're doing.

Keep your finger on this page and leaf through this book for a moment. Isn't it beautiful? Sure, there are plenty of exercises and questions for you to use to practice your skills, but let the left side of your brain take a nap and let the right side appreciate just how attractive a book this is. The two-color printing and all of the interesting elements give the book what I describe very scientifically as a *happy feeling*—akin to walking the aisle at a grocery store.

Last—and this is very important—you'll never find yourself lost in any of these books. You'll never get blindsided by a term that hasn't been defined earlier. You won't find yourself reading one topic and suddenly finding yourself grinding gears as new, totally unrelated topics smack you in the face. Every topic leads from simple to complex, from broad to detailed, and from old to new, building concept upon concept while you read, making the book hard to put down. This is what I call *flow*, and it's the most important aspect of these books.

So enjoy your reading. If you have any questions, feel free to contact me at michaelm@totalsem.com.

Mike Meyers
Series Editor

Introduction

What Will You Learn?

In this book, you'll learn about help desks—what they are, what the people who work at one do, and why they are an essential part of every organization. You'll learn about how help desks are structured, and what kind of support they provide. You'll learn what skills are required for success on the help desk, and you'll gain hands-on practice developing some of these skills. You'll discover the problem-solving process used to tackle challenging computer problems, as well as the tools and technologies that are used to determine the causes of problems. Finally, you'll learn how to manage stress and thrive in the fast-paced, exciting world of the modern help desk. This book is organized into ten chapters:

- Chapter 1, "Introduction to the Help Desk," will give you an overview of the help desk and will introduce you to the basic components and processes that make up today's help desk. You'll also discover the most common problems computer users experience, and read about the basic tools used by help desk personnel to solve problems.
- Chapter 2, "Organization and People," provides you with an understanding of the different ways in which help desks are structured to provide support. In this chapter, you'll also learn about the professional certifications available to help desk workers, the stages of a help desk career, and the career paths open to help desk personnel.
- Chapter 3, "Receiving the Incident," will introduce you to the first step in the process of solving technology problems. You'll learn how to handle incoming calls and how to determine the priority of a problem. You'll also see why communication skills are just as important as technical skills for individuals working in a help desk environment.
- Chapter 4, "Processing and Resolving the Incident," details the next steps in the process of solving computer problems. In this chapter, you'll become familiar with the techniques used in the problem-solving process, from gathering data about the hardware and software involved, to the use of creative techniques such as brainstorming. You'll also realize why documenting problems and their solutions is such an important part of the process.
- The title of Chapter 5, "Computer Telephony Integration," is a term that refers to the coming together of telephone systems and computer technology. Advances in the integration of these two fields makes it possible to know who is calling, what hardware and software they are using, the last time they called the help desk, and other important pieces of information—before the call is answered. You'll also learn

about the latest developments in speech recognition technology and the impact it is having on help desk procedures.

- Chapter 6, "Web-Based Support," introduces you to the ways in which help desks are using websites to provide support to users. One of the functions of a support website is to offer tools that enable users to solve their own problems, without calling the help desk. You'll learn about the advantages of providing support via the Web, and also some of its shortcomings.

- Chapter 7, "Performance Management," covers the topic of tracking and measuring help desk performance. How many seconds passed before the average call was answered? How long did it take on average to find a solution to a problem? These are just some of the statistics that are captured and evaluated on a regular basis to determine whether the help desk is functioning effectively.

- Chapter 8, "Knowledge Management," will provide you with an understanding of the ways in which help desks share what is already known to solve technology problems. You'll learn how knowledge differs from information, and how information becomes knowledge. You'll also discover some of the barriers to implementing a successful knowledge management system.

- Chapter 9, "Asset and Security Management," presents an overview of the role of the help desk in tracking technology assets—such as PCs, laptops, software, and wireless devices. You'll learn about the major threats to computer security—including viruses, power outages, hackers, and terrorist attacks—and the role of the help desk in preventing and responding to security violations.

- Chapter 10, "Help Desk Survival Guide," teaches you how to survive in the fast-paced, always changing world of computer support. You'll master techniques for managing stress and learn how to keep up with—and not be overwhelmed by—the amount of information in the field.

You Will Learn to...

We don't want to simply give you an encyclopedia of information—we don't want you to feel like you're standing in front of an information fire hose! Rather, we're going to present just the key points about help desks and guide you in your own exploration of the topics presented. This book is designed to teach you skills that you'll need to be successful on the job.

Walk and Talk Like a Pro

Each chapter starts with a list of learning objectives followed by lucid explanations of each topic, supported by real-world, on-the-job scenarios. To give you hands-on experience and to help you "walk the walk," you'll be given the opportunity to practice the skills you learn through computer and audio exercises. To help you "talk the talk," each chapter contains definitions of computer terms, summarized in a Key Terms list and compiled into a Glossary at the end of the book. Be ready for a Key Term Quiz at the end of each chapter!

Think Like a Pro

We've also included special full-page features in each chapter, which provide insight into some of the subtleties and realities of life on a help desk. These include Help Desk Concepts, Help Desk Trends, Help Desk Careers, and Help Desk In Action. Reading Checks appear throughout each chapter to help you solidify your understanding of key concepts and technologies.

At the end of each chapter, you can measure what you've learned through written activities including Reviewing Key Terms, Reviewing Key Facts, and Understanding Key Concepts. Critical Thinking activities require that you use what you have learned to respond to thought-provoking questions, while Help Desk Strategies exercises ask you to apply the knowledge and skills to respond to challenging scenarios. Help Desk Projects are activities that are performed alone or in pairs or groups that explore topics presented in the chapter in greater detail.

Resources for Teachers

Resources for teachers are provided via an Instructor's Manual that maps to the organization of the textbook. This manual includes:

- Answer keys to the end-of-chapter activities in the textbook
- ExamView® Pro testbank software that generates a wide array of paper or network-based tests, and features automatic grading
- Hundreds of questions, written by experienced IT instructors
- Wide variety of question types and difficulty levels, allowing teachers to customize each test to maximize student progress
- Engaging PowerPoint slides on the lecture topics

About the HelpSTAR Help Desk Software

The purpose of help desk software is to *automate* and *optimize* the process of providing service to end users.

The term "help desk" has been around for years. It became popular with the proliferation of personal computers and PC networks in the business environment. The help desk gradually supplanted the Data Center, which had become associated with a monolithic, often unresponsive ivory tower of corporate data keepers. The new generation of computer types was comprised of young tinkerers who didn't wear blue suits and spoke a completely different language from upper management and even MIS management.

This young generation of computer types facilitated an information power shift from the data center to the people who actually did the work—the knowledge workers. Almost overnight, knowledge workers were no longer reliant on writing memos and requesting reports from the data center. Instead, they typed a few commands on their keyboards and got the reports and analysis they needed to do their jobs.

With all the euphoria arising from the empowerment of knowledge workers, little notice was taken of the fact that the new paradigm was rapidly leading to a chaotic workplace. True enough, the old way (centralized computing) was cumbersome, unwieldy, and controlled by a small group of oracles who didn't always understand the needs of knowledge workers. But the new paradigm lacked standards, was fraught with trial and error, and required an ever-increasing level of support. This support came not only from the computer types, but often from peers.

By the early 1990s, studies were being published by well-respected consulting groups stating that organizations were spending a shocking amount of money on peer and informal technical support. These studies all pointed to the fact that organizations were spending about *three* times the amount on support (both formal and peer) as they did on hardware and software. The figures were almost unbelievable. Clearly, something had to be done.

For many organizations, the answer was to be found in standardizing and automating the processes for resolving issues that arose from the new way of deploying computing resources.

It is against this backdrop that HelpSTAR (**Help**desk **S**ervice **T**racking **A**nd **R**eview) was developed in 1989 by Igal Hauer.

HelpSTAR V1.0 ran on the VAX series of mini computers. The objective was to automate the process of reporting problems, prioritizing and routing these problems to skill-based queues, and ensuring they were resolved. From its origins HelpSTAR was a workflow-based help desk program, the focus of which was reliable administration of end users' requests.

In 1991, HelpSTAR was ported to PC-based networks such as Novell. Additional functionality such as the ability to conduct text searches on historical problems was incorporated. This new functionality gave support reps instant access to prior problems and their solutions.

In 1993, HelpSTAR was ported to Windows-based platforms. Enhancements included enabling end users to log their own requests, to monitor the progress, and to rate the resolutions with respect to quality and timeliness. HelpSTAR now included dynamic priority management, and enhanced reporting and management of level-of-service, resource constraints, and resources consumed.

As Technology has evolved, HelpSTAR has evolved in tandem—from mini computers to full functionality over the web. HelpSTAR has been installed in thousands of sites worldwide, including most Fortune 500 companies, universities, hospitals, financial institutions, governments, and the armed forces.

The MS Access version of HelpSTAR, provided on the CD-ROM that accompanies this book, offers all of the functionality required to manage a mid-sized help desk.

HelpSTAR's functional areas are comprised of:

- Problem Management and Workflow
- Knowledge Management
- Asset Management
- Data Analysis and Reporting

Problem Management

- *Call tracking:* HelpSTAR's call logging, routing, scheduling, and event-monitoring features ensure that calls are effectively tracked from creation to resolution.
- Service requests (calls) logged via email and the Windows and Web interfaces are automatically authenticated against users in the system to ensure that support is targeted to the correct individual and call costs and charges accumulate accordingly.
- *Event Notification:* HelpSTAR generates alarms when new requests arrive, when they are forwarded to queues, when they are escalated, and in response to various system events. Support reps can choose to receive alarms through the HelpSTAR interface, or to be paged.
- *Problem History:* HelpSTAR enables support reps to view both the history of the problem that they are working on as well as the history for the requester and company/department, directly from the service request. This facilitates full understanding of the problem and the discovery of problem trends.

Knowledgebase/Knowledge Management

- *Standard Solutions:* Standard solutions to known/common problems are available for both internal and external use. Technical staff can create standard solutions detailing both the symptom/problem and the corresponding resolution. Solutions published for external use are available to end users via the Web interface as a self-help resource.
- *Historical Searches:* Every service request that has been created in the system (even closed requests) is available as part of the knowledgebase. Each time a request is created the symptom/problem is documented and the request is updated with the resolution by the support rep. This information is invaluable as a knowledgebase, not only allowing support reps to be trained quickly by using the experience of more senior reps but also as a method of retaining corporate knowledge when reps are transferred.

Asset Management: Hardware and Software Auto Discovery

- *Hardware Audit:* HelpSTAR provides the capability for the user's machine to be scanned at predetermined intervals set by the network manager. The information gathered is then imported into the system and can be viewed by the support reps when diagnosing a problem with the user's machine. Machines can also be scanned via the Web interface to allow technicians to gather information from remote machines.

- *Software Audit:* The software audit provides the capability to selectively scan machines for a particular collection of software programs or to scan for all of the software installed on that machine. This will allow the support reps to check for license compliancy or problems caused by a particular combination of files.

Internal/External HelpDesk

HelpSTAR supports both internal users (organized by departments) and external users who are associated with clients or prospects.

Metrics: Data Analysis and Reporting

- *Charts:* These allow you to quickly examine help desk performance and output this information in an easy-to-view, graphical format.
- *Queries:* HelpSTAR allows you run pre-defined queries or design your own queries to customize the information that you view for your help desk.
- *Reports:* HelpSTAR provides the ability to run standard (pre-defined) reports that allow you to select the criteria you wish to view.

Chapter 1

Introduction to the Help Desk

Objectives

After reading this chapter, you will be able to:

1. Discuss the reasons technical support has become more important in organizations.
2. Describe the role of a help desk.
3. List the three types of technology used in organizations.
4. Discuss how users differ from one another.
5. List the five major problems that users experience.
6. Describe the components of a successful help desk.
7. Identify five important skills of support specialists.
8. Discuss the most common help desk processes.
9. Describe the types of tools used by the help desk professional.
10. Discuss how help desk performance is measured.

Chapter Overview

The computer monitor freezes. Your proposal is due by 3:00. You have tried shutting down the computer and restarting it, but the problem persists. What do you do now? In most organizations, the answer is "call the help desk."

In the twenty-first century, organizations rely on technology to achieve business goals. In many cases, the technology must be up and running 24 hours a day, 7 days a week. However, despite everyone's best efforts, today's computers systems are so complex that technical problems occur frequently. Some of these problems are relatively simple and can be solved without help. Other problems are more complex. Organizations need a central location at which individuals can get help with technology. Enter the modern help desk.

This chapter introduces the concept of the help desk, and describes characteristics of computer users as well as the common technology problems they experience. The chapter also explores the people, processes, and tools that contribute to a successful help desk. Finally, the chapter discusses common methods of measuring and evaluating help desk performance.

1.1 Origins of the Help Desk

Today's help desk has it origins in the early 1980s, when employees of corporations first began using personal computers. Before that, computer hardware and software were primarily used in the Information Technology (IT) department. Data were stored and processed on large mainframe computers within the IT department. Workers outside the IT department had little or no contact with computer technology.

The introduction of the personal computer (PC) in the early 1980s greatly increased the need for **technical support**—services that enable individuals and businesses to effectively use technology. For the first time, individuals with little or no technical background were using computers on the job. As they began working with the new technology, they had questions—and nowhere to go for answers. To get help, they would often ask a coworker in their department. Eventually, some people in the department became known as "experts" and were sought out by colleagues who had questions or problems.

When problems arose, organizations dispatched technicians to users' workstations. As requests for support increased, technicians were no longer able to respond in a timely manner. This led to the creation of telephone centers, called hotlines or helplines, staffed by support personnel responsible for responding to employees' questions and problems. Because these support services were provided at no charge, many users took advantage of them. Organizations hired and trained additional staff to handle the volume of requests. Formal procedures for tracking incoming calls were developed. These early tracking systems were the forerunners of today's sophisticated help desk processes.

In the late 1990s organizations began using new technologies to sell products and services on the Internet. Previously, computers had primarily been used to support business processes, not to bring in revenue. As computer technology became more closely linked to profits, technical support assumed a much more significant role. Table 1.1 illustrates the major changes in the nature of support over the past two decades.

Technology is largely responsible for dramatic increases in worker productivity over the last decade. Companies invested heavily in computer equipment, software, and services. Using new technologies, factories could

TABLE 1.1

The Changing Nature of Support

Support in the 1990s	Support in the Twenty-First Century
Reactive (waits for phone calls from users)	Proactive (notifies users of system problems before the user calls)
Technical skills most important	Interpersonal and customer service skills most important
Support specialists isolated from users	Support specialists involved with users
Support specialists not required to understand business	Support specialists must understand business as well as technology
Small number of applications supported	Large number of applications supported
Narrow scope (technical support)	Broad scope (technical support, knowledge management, change management, asset management)
Support provided during business hours	Support provided 24 hours a day, 7 days a week
Users lack experience with technology	Users have experience with technology
Users rely solely on help desk for support	Users rely on help desk and use self-help tools

produce more goods in less time. They could also manage their inventories more effectively. By 2000 the effect of technology on productivity was measurable. Nonfarm labor productivity grew at a rate of 2.5 percent per year between 1996 and 2000, according to the U.S. Bureau of Labor Statistics. By comparison, between 1991 and 1995 the increase was just 1.5 percent per year.

✓ **READING CHECK**

1. **READING REVIEW** What development in the early 1980s increased the need for technical support to aid computer users? Why?

2. **CRITICAL THINKING** In what general ways does technical support today differ from technical support in the 1980s?

1.2 What Is a Help Desk?

A **help desk** is a single point-of-contact in an organization that provides support to individuals who use technology to perform their jobs. Without a help desk, employees would not know where to take their technology-related questions and problems. They might, for example, ask a coworker in their department. If that person did not know the answer, a second call might be made. With a help desk in place, only one contact is required, and a person experiencing a problem knows exactly where to go for help.

A company's internal help desk may take several forms. It may be a physical location with help desk support specialists, desks, and equipment. It may be a telephone number that users can call to report a problem. It may also be a Web site designed to provide users with a variety of help options. Whatever the form of contact, the goal is the same: to increase the productivity of people who rely on technology to do their jobs.

There are two primary types of help desks. An **internal help desk** supports individuals within the organization. While an **external help desk** may also support individuals within the company, its main purpose is to support external clients. This book focuses on internal help desks, but most of the concepts apply to external help desks as well.

Support for Users

Whether internal or external, a help desk is a service organization. It provides services to its customers, commonly referred to as **users**—people who perform tasks with the aid of technology. For example, we are all telephone users. We use a device (the telephone) to perform a task (contact a person or business). At a more complex level, we use computer hardware (personal computer, modem, telephone line) and a Web browser (software) to make airline reservations on the Internet.

Within a corporation, most (if not all) departments use technology to accomplish their goals. The accounting department uses spreadsheets to analyze accounts. The human resources department maintains an employee database. The sales department relies on a software contact program to manage information about existing and potential customers. The marketing department uses graphics software and a color printer to produce product brochures. Figure 1.1 illustrates the average number of employees supported by help desks, as reported in the Help Desk Institute's 2002 Best Practices Survey.

Technologies in Use

The types of technology used in business can be categorized as hardware, communication devices, and software. Hardware includes computers, printers, cables, and modems. Communication devices enable two or more computers to exchange data, instructions, and information with each other. Software refers to operating systems and applications software.

Organizations use many types of applications software. The major categories of applications software include

- *Word processing:* Word processing software allows users to enter and edit text. It can be used to write letters and memos, to create reports, and to create other documents. Almost all departments use word processing software.

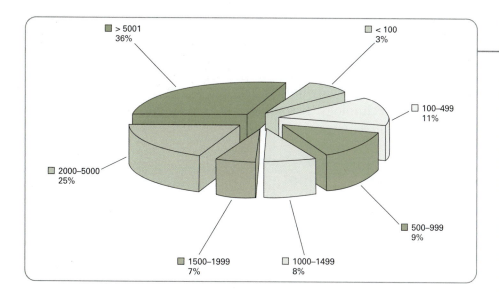

FIGURE 1.1

Number of Customers
Supported by Help Desk
(Source: 2002 Best
Practices Survey, Help
Desk Institute)

- *Spreadsheet:* Spreadsheets are programs used to manipulate numeric data. They are commonly used to prepare budgets, to produce monthly sales reports, to forecast future performance, and to compile financial statements.
- *Database:* Database software stores information in an organized way. For example, an employee might call the Human Resources department to find the names and phone numbers of physicians who are close to home and in the company's health insurance plan. Using a database, the Benefits person is able to search by zip code for physicians within ten miles of the employee's home. Databases are used by most departments in an organization, from facilities management to accounting and legal.
- *Web browser:* A Web browser is a software application that retrieves and displays information from the Internet.
- *Graphics:* Graphics programs are used to create and manipulate images, such as charts, graphs, and pictures. These images can then be printed, placed on the Internet, or used in a presentation that is created with a graphics program such as Microsoft PowerPoint.
- *Scheduling and planning:* Scheduling programs allow users to find meeting times that are convenient to all attendees. The programs search each person's electronic calendar for an open time slot of the required length. Planning software packages are used to plan, schedule, and track projects.
- *E-mail:* E-mail, or electronic mail, involves the transmission of messages from one computer to another.

✓ READING CHECK

1. **READING REVIEW** Why does a company need a help desk to be the single source of technical support for employees?

2. **CRITICAL THINKING** How is an internal help desk different from an external help desk? How are they the same?

1.3 Characteristics of Users

The users served by the help desk vary greatly in knowledge, skills, and how they use technology. It is important to recognize these differences when interacting with users.

Experience with Technology

Some users have little or no experience using computers on the job. As more and more individuals with computer experience enter the workforce, there are fewer people in this category. At the other end of the spectrum are individuals—sometimes referred to as "power users"—who possess a high level of skill in the use of computer technology.

Exposure to Technology

Users also differ in their exposure to different types of technology. An accounting manager may be an expert spreadsheet user, but may not know how to export that data in a form that a marketing manager can use in a presentation. Similarly, an employee in the marketing department may be very skilled at creating graphics for presentations, but may be unable to use a planning program to plan an upcoming project. As businesses begin to use information in new ways, employees are often asked to be proficient in a number of software programs.

Reliance on Technology

Users vary in the extent to which they use and rely on technology to do their jobs. Some jobs require the regular use of technology, while others demand less frequent use. An administrative assistant, for example, uses word processing, e-mail, and scheduling software on an hourly basis. A sales representative uses a database before and after a sales call to keep track of customers. A manager in the facilities department relies on a Web browser to order supplies on a monthly basis.

Another factor to consider is the importance of the technology to the business. For example, if a catalog company's Web site fails to function, the company loses money every second the site is unavailable to customers. On the other hand, if a user is unable to print a report that is due at the end of the week, the business operations are not adversely affected. When there are multiple requests for support at one time, support specialists must determine which problems take priority. For this reason, the help desk follows a set of predefined rules to determine the order in which requests are handled.

1. **READING REVIEW** Is the number of users who have no prior experience with computers growing or shrinking?

2. **CRITICAL THINKING** Suppose a help desk gets three problems at once: the Web site on which the company takes sales orders is not working; a vice president cannot print a report that he must distribute in three days; and several employees are unable to send e-mail. What priority would you give to each of these problems, and why?

1.4   Common User Problems

Most problems that users experience with technology are in one of these five categories:

- Hardware problems
- Software problems
- Network problems
- Security problems
- Operating system problems

Hardware Problems

Hardware problems usually occur when a change is made to the current configuration by adding new hardware or upgrading existing equipment. A typical hardware setup consists of products from different manufacturers. When new hardware is added, it may not be compatible with the system that is already in place. For example, a user may request and receive a scanner designed to be used with a Universal Serial Bus (USB) port. However, the user's computer is several years old and does not have any USB ports. The new hardware is incompatible with the existing hardware.

Software Problems

The majority of software problems are related to installation, compatibility, and performance. Most of today's software includes an automatic installation program. The user starts the installation program, and the program writes the necessary files to the user's hard drive. In addition to installing the actual program file, the installation makes changes to the operating system so that it will recognize the new software. This may create conflicts between the new software and the programs already installed.

For example, a user responsible for creating the company newsletter requested a sophisticated photo-editing program. The request was approved, and the new software was installed. The user calls the Help Desk and states that the computer crashes every time the new software is opened. This is most likely caused by a software conflict between an existing file on the user's PC and a file that was installed as part of the new photo-editing program.

Software performance is also the reason behind many requests for help. Software programs do not always run at the same speed. Depending on a number of factors, such as how full the user's hard drive is and how many programs are running at the same time, performance can vary widely.

Network Problems

In most companies, applications software is located on a central computer, and individuals access these programs through a network. A network is a group of two or more computers linked together by a communications device. A communications device is a modem, a cable, a satellite, or any other device that enables a computer to send and receive data from another computer. The Internet is an example of a computer network involving thousands of computers linked together that can share data. Because of the complexity of network communications, errors may originate from a variety of sources, making network problems difficult to diagnose.

Suppose a user preparing a report in Microsoft Excel needs to access data stored on another computer in the network. The user is unable to connect to the database and receives a message "Unable to connect to destination." This message indicates that the connection to the server failed and the database could not be contacted. The support specialist must determine why the connection did not go through—perhaps because the server was down.

Security Problems

One of the most common forms of computer security is limiting access to the company's network. Companies do this by creating user accounts. User accounts contain a variety of information about the user, and include a user ID and password for signing on to the network. Without an account, a user is unable to log in and use the network. User accounts also limit users' access to certain areas of the network. For example, a user in the marketing department may be able to access sales and marketing data, but not data from the accounting department.

Problems can also occur when users try to access network data from a different location. For example, an associate working in the legal department goes to the desk of an employee in the sales department to follow up on a contract review. When the employee from the legal department tries to log on to the network from the salesperson's desk to make changes to the contract, an error message is displayed on the screen. The user calls the help desk to find out why the network cannot be accessed. In this case, the user's account allows access to the network from a single workstation at a time, and the user did not log out at his desk in the legal department.

Operating System Problems

Operating system errors can manifest themselves in many different ways, including

- A frozen cursor or screen
- A blank or flickering dialog box
- An error message on the screen
- A terminated application

There can be many different causes of operating system errors, including conflicts among software and hardware, computer viruses, and corrupt files. Operating system errors can vary in severity. Major problems prevent the user from accessing any application, while less severe problems may occur only when a certain application is used, such as a memory-intensive graphics program.

While most user problems fall into one of the previous five categories, some problems are the direct result of doing something incorrectly, such as hitting the wrong key, which can cause the text to disappear from the screen. Problems can also occur when users have not been adequately trained on the software they are using. For example, a user reports that when editing text in a word processing program, each keystroke replaces a character that already exists. This is not a problem with the software; it is a user training problem. The user is unfamiliar with the editing features of the program, which provide the option of typing over existing text. Occasionally there are mistakes (bugs) in the software itself, but this occurs less frequently than user errors.

> ✔ **READING CHECK**
>
> 1. **READING REVIEW** Problems that users experience with technology generally fall into which six categories?
>
> 2. **CRITICAL THINKING** If a user calls the help desk because of inability to connect with the company's network, which categories are most likely to be sources of the problem?

The Help Desk Personality

Some personalities are more suited than others to careers in technical support. Most successful help desk analysts find satisfaction in meeting intellectual challenges and finding solutions that help users. Still, technical support work can be stressful. A help desk analyst, who is often under pressure to resolve problems quickly, must provide courteous service to all kinds of people, many of whom are tense or angry. One way to explore whether you have the temperament to succeed as a help desk analyst is to take a personality test.

The Myers-Briggs Type Indicator (MBTI) is among the personality tests most commonly used by corporations, employment agencies, and career counselors. The MBTI is a questionnaire based on the teachings of Carl Jung, a Swiss psychiatrist who was a pioneer of modern psychoanalysis.

The MBTI uses four scales to rate preferences and determine personality types. The scales measure

- **Introversion versus extraversion**
An introvert prefers to focus on the inner world of ideas, while an extravert is more inclined to focus on people and things in the outside world.

- **How you acquire information**
Some people generally acquire information through their five senses, while others tend to use intuition.

- **How you make decisions**
While some people usually base their decisions on thought and logic, others base them on feelings.

- **Your attitude toward the outer world**
You judge the outer world based on your thoughts and feelings, or you might be more inclined to perceive the world based on your senses and intuition.

Each scale has four possible rankings, and each combination of rankings supposedly represents one of sixteen distinct personality types. For example, a person whose rankings on the four scales are introverted (I), sensate (S), feeling (F), and judging (J) would be described as an ISFJ personality.

According to Consulting Psychologists Press, Inc., which owns the rights to the MBTI, more than 2 million people take the test each year. Corporations sometimes use the MBTI to assess whether applicants are temperamentally suited to the jobs they are seeking. Many companies use the MBTI in leadership training and other programs involving people who already work for them. By using the test to help people understand themselves and their coworkers, they hope to build stronger and more productive teams and organizations.

REVIEWING CONCEPTS

1. What do the MBTI's four scales measure?

2. Do you think employers should use personality tests to decide which candidates are best suited to technical support careers? Why?

1.5 Components of a Successful Help Desk

The size and scope of help desks vary greatly from one organization to another. The ingredients for success do not vary. Whether located in a large, global organization or in a small, local one, all help desks have one thing in common: they require people, processes, and tools to be effective. The following sections examine these three key areas.

People Skills

Effective support people are good listeners, good communicators, customer-service oriented, expert at gaining knowledge by asking questions, and excellent problem-solvers. This is according to the Help Desk Institute's 2001 Best Practices Survey. The Help Desk Institute conducts a survey on an annual basis to identify the activities and practices of help desks. The survey indicates that the most important competencies are in the areas of communication skills and interpersonal relations.

The skills necessary for success as a support specialist can be grouped into five categories:

- Communication skills
- Problem-solving skills
- Customer-service skills
- Technical skills
- Business skills

Communication Skills

The communication skills that are most important for a help desk position are listening, questioning, and communicating.

- *Listening:* To help a user, support specialists must first listen to the user's description of the problem. While gathering information from the description, the support person must also let users know that they are being heard. Good listening is not passive; it is an interactive process of hearing and responding.
- *Questioning:* Closely linked with listening, questioning is the process of extracting information from the user that will help resolve the problem as quickly as possible. If the information obtained is not accurate, the support specialist has little chance of resolving the problem.
- *Communicating:* Once the initial information is presented by the user, the support specialist must actively participate in the interaction by communicating with the user. Communication with the user can be verbal (in person or on the telephone) or written (via e-mail).

Problem-Solving Skills

Once enough information about the problem has been obtained from the user, the support specialist begins the problem-solving process. The goal of the help desk is to identify and solve complex problems quickly and effectively.

The basic steps in the problem-solving process are to

- Define the problem
- Analyze the facts to determine the underlying cause
- Generate possible solutions
- Evaluate solutions and decide which is most viable
- Develop a plan to implement the solution

To solve problems, the support specialist uses a variety of skills, including critical-thinking skills and decision-making skills. Critical thinking is the process of analyzing a situation using a variety of cognitive skills to determine the possible causes of the problem. Decision making is evaluating several options according to criteria and deciding which is best.

Customer-Service Skills

Customer service is the process of satisfying customers. Customer satisfaction is based on the actual service delivered and on the customer's expectations of the service. Most users who call the help desk are experiencing problems that prevent them from performing some aspect of their jobs. They expect the problems to be resolved as quickly as possible. They also expect to be treated in a courteous, professional manner. Some callers, such as those trying to meet deadlines, may be frustrated or angry. Callers experiencing problems that are less critical from a business priority point-of-view may demand immediate attention. The support specialist must be able to respond to all types of callers in a calm manner and with a positive attitude.

Customer satisfaction depends on how well the support specialist meets the customer's expectations. If a customer has high expectations, such as an immediate solution to a problem, anything less will result in dissatisfaction. Some help desks have developed Service Level Agreements to help manage customer expectations. A **Service Level Agreement (SLA)** is a formal, quantitative statement of the scope and level of services provided by a help desk. An SLA plays an important role in setting user expectations of help desk services. For example, if the SLA states that incoming calls will be answered within one minute, users will expect their calls to be answered within that time frame. If it takes longer, they will likely be dissatisfied with the level of service provided.

Technical Skills

Help desk personnel are required to have technical skills that support the technologies used in the business. When entry-level support specialists are hired, they are expected to know how to use a PC and to be familiar with major operating systems, software packages, and basic networking. Several organizations offer professional certifications in the help desk field. These are discussed in Chapter 2.

Once on the job, support specialists learn about the specific software used by the company. A company may use applications purchased from outside vendors, such as Microsoft Office. Companies often develop their own programs to perform certain tasks. The exact configuration of technology varies widely from one company to the next. Thus, the ability to learn technical information quickly and accurately is more important than the knowledge possessed at the time of hiring.

Help desk personnel and managers must always remember that no amount of technical mastery can overcome a deficiency in communication or interpersonal skills. If the knowledge cannot be delivered to users in a manner they can understand, it is of little value to the company.

Business Skills

Help desk personnel are also required to learn about the industry they support, whether financial, retail, manufacturing, or other. Callers expect the support person to understand what they are trying to accomplish with the technology, not just how the technology works. Once support specialists understand what users are trying to do, they can communicate more effectively about the problem. Without this understanding, the support person may be unable to identify the nature of the user's problem and, as a result, will fail to meet the customer's expectations.

In most companies, help desk personnel are encouraged to interact with their customers—the company's employees. It is as important to understand how the technology fits into the larger business context as it is to know how to solve a particular technical problem.

Process Management

In addition to people, the help desk must have processes to be successful. A process is a set of activities performed in a specific order that results in a desired end. In the context of a help desk, processes can be thought of as the major tasks for which the help desk is responsible. The following processes are common to most help desks:

- Problem management
- Request/change management
- Knowledge management
- Asset management
- Network management
- Security management

Problem Management

Problem management is the process of receiving, monitoring, and resolving problems that are reported to the help desk. Most people think of this aspect of the help desk's work when they hear the term help desk. When a user reports a problem, the help desk is responsible for resolving the problem and enabling the user to return to work as quickly as possible.

Users report problems to the help desk via phone or e-mail, or in person. According to the Help Desk Institute's 2001 Best Practices Survey, the top five problems are with applications/software, hardware, data communications/network, security/passwords, and operating systems. Figure 1.2 shows the average number of service requests responded to in a one-month period.

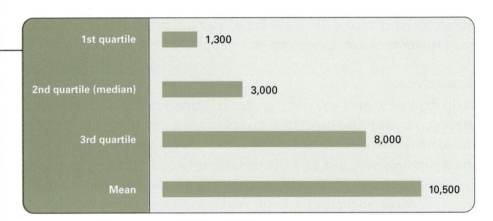

FIGURE 1.2

Number of Service Requests Per Month (Source: 2002 Best Practices Survey, Help Desk Institute)

1st quartile	1,300
2nd quartile (median)	3,000
3rd quartile	8,000
Mean	10,500

Request/Change Management

Request/change management is the process of responding to user requests for hardware, software, or services. These requests may come from an individual, a department, or an entire organization. For example, a user may call the help desk to inquire about upgrading a PC, obtaining a new program, or receiving training. A department may contact the help desk when new printers are being installed. Sometimes a change may involve an entire organization, such as when a company decides to upgrade to a newer version of an operating system.

In all of these cases, the help desk works with the user(s) to ensure that the transition to the new technology results in as little disruption in the work flow as possible. The support specialist gathers information about the user, determines what is needed to complete the request, schedules the change, and tracks the request until it is filled.

When a software upgrade is implemented, the help desk notifies users about the change in advance and informs them of the need for and benefits of the change. When a major hardware or software change is being planned, support specialists may conduct training sessions for end users. By anticipating the change, informing users in advance, and providing education, the help desk ensures that the transition to new technology will result in fewer problems. Any change will result in a short-term drop in

Introduction to Help Desk Concepts and Skills

productivity; it is the help desk's responsibility to see that the productivity loss is as brief as possible.

Knowledge Management

Knowledge management is the process of collecting, organizing, analyzing, and distributing information. Help desks often collect and manage the knowledge they gather in responding to users' problems and requests. These data can be used to create a **knowledge base**, which is a database of related information used as a resource by help desk personnel and end users.

To provide easy access to the information, knowledge bases are usually made available online. Help desks continually add information to the knowledgebase. As more solutions are documented by the help desk and added, more and more users are able to find answers on their own without needing to call the help desk.

Asset Management

Asset management is the process of collecting and maintaining data about a company's technology assets. A typical asset management program tracks all of the hardware that is currently used in the organization, including serial numbers, installation dates, and maintenance histories. Important information about software, including licensing and version update histories, is also part of an asset management program. When employees move to different departments, the asset management database must be updated to record the transfer of the hardware to the new location. When new employees are hired, information about the hardware and software assigned to them must be recorded.

The information stored in an asset management program is usually accessible to support specialists. When users contact the help desk with problem or change requests, the support specialist accesses the asset management program to identify the user's exact hardware and software configuration. Similarly, when users request additional memory for their computers, help desk staff members use the asset management program to determine the amount of memory currently installed and the maximum amount of memory the machine can use.

Network Management

Network management is the process of managing and controlling the network configurations within the organization. With employees located on different floors of a building or in different parts of the world, networks allow workers to use their computers to exchange information efficiently. Network management software monitors the amount of traffic (the number of transactions) on the network and the level at which the network is performing. The organization must know how well the network is performing at all times; a problem has the potential to affect hundreds or thousands of workers.

Some help desk software programs are integrated with network management software and automatically notify support specialists if there is a network problem. In some cases, the help desk is responsible for letting users know when a network is experiencing problems that could affect them, such as slow response time. Not only does this alert users to a potential problem, it also prevents many users from calling the help desk at the same time to report the same problem.

Security Management

Security management is the process of providing and maintaining security for the organization's assets—in this case, information. Most commonly, security involves preventing unauthorized users from gaining access to the data.

Help desk personnel receive many calls from users who want their passwords reset. Most programs that require passwords have built-in security features that limit the number of times a user can try to log in with an incorrect password. After a set number of attempts (usually three to five), the program will no longer allow a login attempt. At this time, the user must contact the help desk to have the password reset.

The same security is in effect at most bank ATM machines. After a certain number of login attempts, the machine will either display a message telling the customer to contact the branch, or, in some cases, the machine will not return the ATM card to the customer.

Help Desk Tools

Just as technology has dramatically changed business processes, it has also changed the ways in which help desks provide support. Today, a large number of programs can be used to increase help desk efficiency and improve service delivery. There are programs for managing incoming calls, diagnosing problems, sharing solutions with users, measuring performance, and creating reports. Commonly used programs include FrontRange Solutions' Heat, Help Desk Technology's HelpSTAR, and BMC Software's Remedy.

More and more help desks are using software that integrates a number of these features. These programs, for example, can integrate a sophisticated management program (such as a program that is able to log, track, and route calls) with an asset management program (that is able to display information about the user's hardware and software configuration) and a diagnostic program (that is able to take control of the user's computer to diagnose problems). Figure 1.3 shows a sample computer screen from an integrated help desk program. The majority of these products can be grouped into two categories: problem management tools and problem resolution tools.

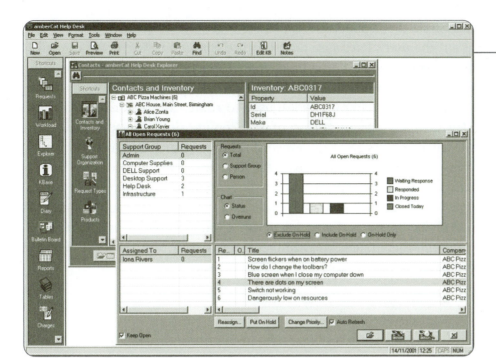

FIGURE 1.3

A sample screen from an integrated help desk software program.

Problem Management Tools

Problem management tools log, track, route, and record information about problems reported to the help desk. Most problem management tools perform the following tasks:

- Authenticate calls (Is this a known user?)
- Prioritize calls (What priority should be assigned to the call?)
- Route calls to support specialist (Who is qualified and available to receive the call?)
- Display information about the caller (name, title, department)
- Display information about the user's technology (hardware and software configuration)
- Display caller problem history (previous contacts with the help desk)
- Track calls (follow the problem until it is resolved)
- Provide notification of outstanding calls and, if necessary, refer these calls to a more experienced support specialist (problems not resolved in specified time frame)
- Produce reports (number of calls received, length of time until call answered)

A major component of a problem management system is computer telephony. The term **computer telephony** describes tools that combine telephone and computer technology into one system. This technology makes it possible to access information about the user who has called that is stored in a computer database. For example, when a user phones the help desk, the support specialist's computer screen displays information about the user's hardware and software configuration, recent upgrades, and prior problems. This is much more efficient than asking the user questions to elicit the same information.

Telephone technologies are used to route calls, prioritize calls, and play recorded messages. Most of us encounter similar systems every time we call a business and hear a recorded message such as "Press 1 for sales; press 2 for customer service; press 3 for warranty questions." The system uses the information that has been input via the telephone keypad to route the call to a particular department. A help desk application works much the same way. Some telephone systems allow users to enter data using the telephone keypad and receive a prerecorded response based on the input.

Problem Resolution Tools

Problem resolution tools are used to determine the causes of users' problems and develop effective solutions. Problem resolution tools perform the following tasks:

- Diagnose problems
- Generate solutions
- Enable users to solve some of their own problems

Support specialists use **diagnostic tools** to identify the source of a user's problem. One popular diagnostic tool allows support specialists to gain access to a computer that is at a remote location. Without ever going to the user's desk, a support specialist can view the desktop and control the activity of the user's PC. Commands entered via the support specialist's mouse and keyboard are implemented on the remote PC.

Knowledge bases can be used to generate solutions to user problems. Support specialists search a knowledge base for problems similar to the one reported by the user. If a similar problem has been reported in the past, its solution will be stored in the knowledgebase. When users experience problems, a knowledge base is one of the first places to look for a solution.

A knowledge base is an example of self-help technology. **Self-help technology** provides users with the resources to solve their own problems. The Web is emerging as a significant means of providing self-help tools to users. On internal Web sites, users can submit problems to the help desk, track help requests, send e-mail messages to the help desk, or engage in live chat with a support specialist (see Figure 1-4). They can also view a list of current system problems and outages and discover information about upcoming system changes.

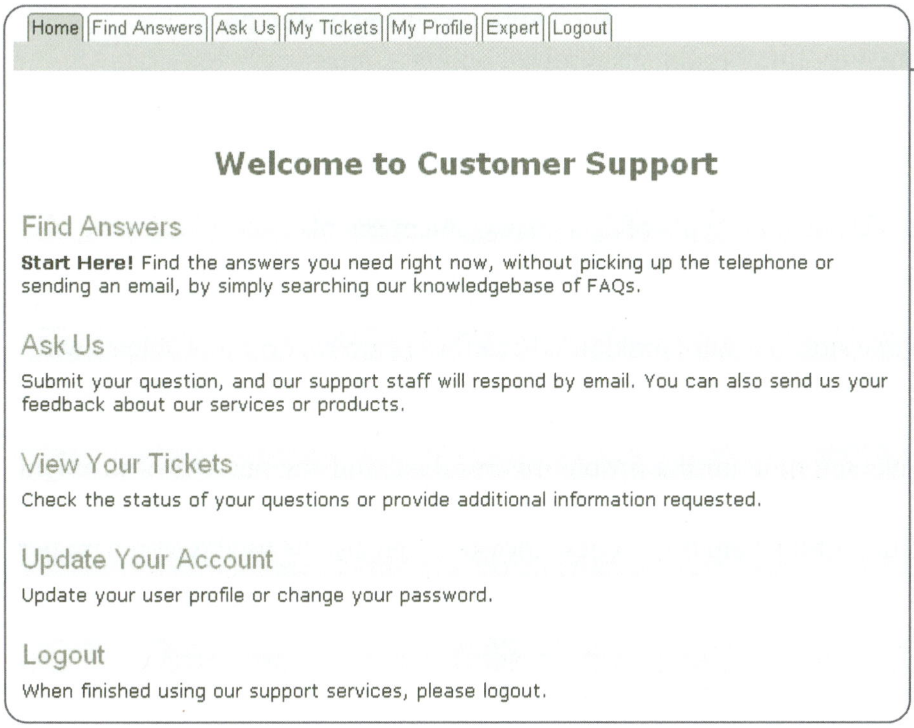
Home
Find Answers
Ask Us
My Tickets
My Profile
Expert
Logout
Welcome to Customer Support
Find Answers
Start Here! Find the answers you need right now, without picking up the telephone or sending an email, by simply searching our knowledgebase of FAQs.
Ask Us
Submit your question, and our support staff will respond by email. You can also send us your feedback about our services or products.
View Your Tickets
Check the status of your questions or provide additional information requested.
Update Your Account
Update your user profile or change your password.
Logout
When finished using our support services, please logout.

FIGURE 1.4

A sample screen from a support Web site.

READING CHECK

1. **READING REVIEW** What three elements do all effective help desks have in common, regardless of their size?

2. **CRITICAL THINKING** Which of the three elements is most important? Explain your answer.

1.6 Measuring Help Desk Performance

The performance of the help desk is measured and evaluated on a regular basis. To determine the effectiveness of the help desk, management analyzes the efficiency of the help desk itself and the satisfaction levels of customers.

Objective Measures

Raw data obtained from problem management programs are used to provide an objective snapshot of help desk performance. **Metrics** are quantitative measures of the efficiency of the help desk. Examples of commonly used metrics include

- Average length of an incoming call
- Average time a call is in the queue before it is picked up

- Number of calls abandoned before being picked up
- Percent of problems resolved on first contact
- Average time until problem is resolved
- Percent of cases still open beyond a set period of time

Using these types of data, management can plan and allocate help desk resources. For example, if reports indicate that the highest volume of calls are received between 7 and 9 A.M., additional staff can be assigned to that time slot. If a substantial number of users are reporting problems with a particular program, management can assign help desk personnel to investigate and correct the source of the problems. Key measures such as the average time until a problem is resolved and the percent of problems resolved on the first contact are very useful in evaluating the current operation of the help desk. These measures can also be used to compare performance to other help desks, or to industry best practices.

Customer Satisfaction

Metrics alone provide an incomplete picture of the effectiveness of the help desk, since they do not take customer satisfaction into account. Customer satisfaction ratings indicate end users' perception of the help desk's value. This satisfaction cannot be fully measured by analyzing statistics from a call management database. To gain an understanding of the customer's perception of service quality, companies may need to use customer satisfaction surveys or focus groups.

Today, when computer problems occur, the effect is felt throughout the organization. Both productivity and profits are at risk. Most companies acknowledge their dependence on technology and the resulting surge in the demand for technical support. The pressure to resolve problems quickly has dramatically increased. System problems are no longer an inconvenience to a few; they are now a costly time-out from conducting business. More than ever before, this is an exciting time to be pursuing a technical support career.

 READING CHECK

1. **READING REVIEW** What metrics are commonly used to gauge help desk efficiency?

2. **CRITICAL THINKING** A report from a problem management program shows that nearly half of the calls to the help desk at Zebulon Communications are abandoned before they are picked up. The abandoned calls occur mostly between 2 and 4 p.m., which is the help desk's busiest time. Overall, the average time calls are in the queue before being picked up is less than 1 minute. Based on the metrics, what might the manager do to reduce the number of abandoned calls?

Software Support at a Price

For many years, users of PC hardware and software could generally obtain free technical support by means of e-mail or calls to help desks. Increasingly, though, companies are charging customers fees for helping them when they have problems using products.

One such company is Dantz, which produces backup software. Dantz once offered unlimited technical support, but in 2002 the company began offering free technical support for only 30 days after initial purchase. To get help from support specialists after the first month, customers pay $40 to $70 per incident, depending on which product they have purchased. No free support is available to people who buy upgrades of Dantz products they already own.

Dantz acknowledges that the support fees have displeased some customers, but contends that the company needed to institute them to stay competitive. According to metrics Dantz has collected, the average number of calls to the help desk to resolve a single user's problem is 2.8, and each call lasts an average of 18 minutes. With help desk salaries and other expenses, says Dantz, handling each service request costs the company about the same amount that it now charges users for telephone and e-mail support. Like many other software companies, Dantz encourages users to obtain free self-service help from its Web site, using knowledge bases, troubleshooting tips, and other resources posted there.

Other software companies that charge customers for help desk support include some of the largest in the industry: Microsoft, Intuit (which produces Quicken accounting software), and Symantec (which produces Norton antivirus software and other utility programs). According to the Gartner Group, customer support fees barely cover the cost of the service and do not produce profits for most companies that charge them.

A 2002 poll by Consumer Reports found that customer satisfaction was declining among subscribers who had obtained support from some of the largest PC manufacturers. The Gardner Group said its research of customer satisfaction with software support produced similar results.

Many technology companies still offer free product support. One such company is Sophos, which makes antivirus software. Sophos management views its free 24-hour-a-day telephone support as a public relations tool. Sophos says the free support builds customer loyalty and enhances the company's reputation.

LOOKING AHEAD

1. Do technology users generally have alternatives to paying for customer support? If so, what are they?

2. Do you think users should have to pay for help with software they have purchased? Why? Write an essay that presents your opinion.

Chapter (1) Review

>> Summary

The following points were covered in this chapter.

1. Technical support has become more important in organizations because of the increased use of technology not just to support business processes, but also to contribute to a company's profits.

2. The role of the help desk is to provide support services to users of technology, so that technological problems have minimal effect on worker productivity.

3. The three types of technology used in organizations are hardware, communications, and software. Hardware refers to PCs, printers, modems, and other equipment. Communications includes devices that enable computers to send data to and receive data from other computers. Software refers to operating systems and application programs.

4. Users differ in their technical knowledge and skills, in the range of exposure to different technologies, and in the extent to which they use technology to do their jobs.

5. The most common problems experienced by users involve the hardware, software, network, security, and operating system.

6. A successful help desk is composed of the people who provide support, the processes used to provide support, and tools used to track and solve problems.

7. Support specialists should possess communication skills, problem-solving skills, customer service skills, technical skills, and business skills.

8. Common help desk processes include problem management, request/change management, knowledge management, asset management, network management, and security management

9. Support specialists use problem management tools and problem resolution tools to solve users' problems. Problem management tools log, track, route, and record information about problems reported to the help desk. Problem resolution tools are used to determine the causes of users' problems and develop effective solutions.

10. Help desk performance is measured in two ways. First, reports are created using quantitative data from a problem management program. Second, feedback is solicited from customers to evaluate customer satisfaction.

>> Key Terms

The following terms were defined in this chapter:

a asset management		**k** network management	
b computer telephony		**l** problem management	
c customer service		**m** problem management tools	
d diagnostic tools		**n** problem resolution tools	
e external help desk		**o** request/change management	
f help desk		**p** security management	
g internal help desk		**q** self-help technology	
h knowledge base		**r** Service Level Agreement (SLA)	
i knowledge management		**s** technical support	
j metrics		**t** users	

>> Reviewing Key Terms

Write the letter(s) of the key term that matches each definition below:

____ **1** Quantitative measures of the efficiency of the help desk.

____ **2** The process of providing and maintaining security for the organization's information assets.

____ **3** A single point-of-contact in an organization that provides support to individuals who use technology to perform their jobs.

____ **4** The process of tracking and resolving problems that are reported to the help desk.

____ **5** Tools that combine telephone and computer technology into one system.

____ **6** The process of responding to user requests for hardware, software, or services.

____ **7** Tools, such as knowledge bases, that provide users with the resources to solve their own problems.

____ **8** A database of related information used as a resource to provide information.

____ **9** A formal, quantitative statement of the scope and level of services provided by a help desk.

____ **10** Tools that log, track, route, and record information about problems reported to the help desk.

Chapter 1 Review

>> Reviewing Key Facts

True/False

Identify whether each statement is True (T) or False (F). Rewrite the false statements so that they are true.

____ **1** Technical skills are the most important qualifications for the job of support specialist.

____ **2** All requests for support should be given equal priority.

____ **3** Problem management is the process of tracking incidents that are reported to the help desk until they are resolved.

____ **4** Metrics are the best indicator of help desk performance.

____ **5** Service Level Agreements (SLAs) play an important role in setting user expectations of the help desk.

Completion

Write the answer that best completes the question:

1 The five most important skills of support specialists are communication skills, problem-solving skills, customer-service skills, technical skills, and _____.

2 Request management is the process of responding to requests for hardware, software, or _____.

3 The introduction of the _____ in the early 1980s greatly increased the need for technical support.

4 An internal help desk can take a variety of forms; it can be a physical location with equipment and people, a telephone number, or a _____.

5 Network problems can be difficult to diagnose because of the _____ of most network configurations.

>> Understanding Key Concepts

Provide brief answers to the following questions:

1 How does a help desk contribute to a company's success?

2 What is the level of technical knowledge and skills of users who call help desks?

3 How are metrics useful to help desk managers?

>> Critical Thinking

As directed by your instructor, write a brief essay or discuss the following issues in groups:

1. Why are technical skills and knowledge not the most important requirements for a support specialist?

2. In the next decade, do you think the role of the help desk is more likely to increase or decrease?

3. What are the benefits of integrated help desk tools? For example, why would a company want to link its asset management program with its problem management program?

>> Help Desk Projects

Complete the projects listed below:

1. **Conduct a Web search for companies that provide outsourcing of help desk services.** What do these companies list as the benefits of outsourcing? Do you agree? Do you see any drawbacks to outsourcing?

2. **Research the history of your school's help desk.** When was it created? How much has its staff size increased since then? How many applications did it support then, and how many does it support now? How is its work different now than when it began? Write a report on your findings.

3. **Form a group with several classmates to research the computer technology your school uses, including hardware, software, and communications technology.** Each member of the group can focus on a different group of users; for example, one group can focus on students, another on the school's administration, and the remainder on other departments. Report to the class on your findings. [Group]

4. **Interview someone you know who uses computers but is not very experienced with them.** Ask what kinds of problems this person most often encounters when using a computer. Does he or she usually call a help desk, ask a friend or coworker, or solve the problems independently, and why? Then interview another person who is a power user of computers and ask the same questions. Write a report that compares their problems and their efforts to resolve them.

5. **Interview a member of your school's technical support staff about its network management.** How many people use the school's network? What tools and methods does the school use to prevent unauthorized people from using the network? How does it control access to confidential information that is stored on the network? Report to the class on your findings.

6. **Using the Occupational Outlook Handbook, employment advertisements, and any other resources available to you, research two kinds of jobs in technical support.** Find out the requirements and responsibilities of each position, the salary ranges, and what opportunities the jobs offer for advancement. Report to the class about the jobs.

>> Help Desk Projects *(continued)*

7 **Team up with a classmate and use the skills discussed in this chapter to gather information about a problem the classmate has had with technology.** Then switch roles and tell your classmate about a problem you have had using technology. Write a report describing your experiences in both roles. For example, how did you indicate to your classmate that you were listening? Did you notice anything about your classmate's behavior as a listener that will help you listen better yourself?

8 **Compare the features offered by integrated help desk software packages.** Using the Internet, locate information about the following products: Magic Solutions' Service Desk and BMC Software's Remedy Help Desk.

9 **Visit the Web site at http://www.internettrafficreport.com.** This site monitors the flow of information on networks around the world. Explore the site. Discover which country currently has the fastest network. Which is currently the slowest? Try to explain the results.

10 **Pick a program you already use, and try to locate a help desk or customer support center on the company's Web site.** What services are provided? Are there any self-support tools such as frequently asked questions (FAQs) or a knowledgebase? Think of a question, and search for an answer on the Web site. Was it difficult to find the answer? Why?

>> Help Desk Strategies

Review the following case studies and respond to the questions:

1 Rogers Electric Supply now uses an integrated voice response (IVR) system with an automated call director (ACD) for customer support. Customers have complained that they often have to wait too long for help. The company's management is considering a switch to a Web-based system.
- What are the advantages of Web-based support over telephone support for the company and its customers?
- Can you think of any disadvantages?

2 Vladimir Karpov, a technical support specialist at Continental University, receives several help requests at the same time. One is from a user whose monitor is blank. The others are from users who cannot connect with the school's network.
- Which problem should Vladimir address first? Explain why.

3 Fargo Manufacturing is considering using an asset management system throughout the company. Jordan Williams, a support specialist, has been asked to prepare a brief report listing the potential benefits of an asset management system to the help desk.
- What benefits should she list?
- Which benefit would be most appealing to management? Why?

2

Organization and People

Objectives

After reading this chapter, you will be able to:

1. Describe the differences between a centralized and decentralized help desk.
2. List the five primary help desk structures.
3. Discuss the advantages and disadvantages of dispatch and tiered structures.
4. Explain the difference between a product model and the business model of specialized help desk support.
5. List three reasons for outsourcing the help desk support function.
6. Describe the two categories of certification available to help desk personnel.
7. Discuss the three stages of a help desk career.
8. List seven career paths for help desk employees.

Chapter Overview

How should a help desk be organized? What structure should it have? The best approach depends on the answers to such questions as: How many users will the help desk support? Are the users in one location or in many locations? What is the typical user's level of computer experience? How many hardware and software products must be supported?

This chapter examines the different ways help desks are organized and structured. In recent years, more organizations have been hiring outside companies to provide support to users. This chapter explores the reasons for this trend as well as the advantages and disadvantages of using outside firms. One factor common to all support environments is the constant need for qualified personnel. The chapter describes the stages of a help desk career, the advantages of certification, and the career paths open to help desk specialists.

The first consideration when planning a help desk is whether there should be one central support location or several locations throughout the organization. Each approach has advantages and disadvantages.

Centralized

A **centralized help desk** is a single physical location within an organization that provides support to all users. A centralized help desk provides users with one place to go for answers; there is no confusion about where to get assistance when a problem occurs. Most centralized help desks are located within the information technology (IT) department, for logical reasons. If a user problem is about software, the help desk specialist can ask a program development staff member who was involved in writing the program or an IT staff member who was trained in that specific program. If a call comes in about a network error, it is easy to ask a network specialist for input. Locating these specialists in close proximity maximizes the efficiency of the help desk.

The information coming in to a centralized help desk all goes to the same location. Within a short time, support personnel are exposed to a wide range of problems because they are the only source of technical support in the corporation. This enables specialists to build upon their own knowledge, and it is especially helpful to new employees who are trying to become familiar with all the technology in use. Members of a centralized help desk also share information with each other, increasing their knowledge of problems and solutions. A more knowledgeable staff results in faster problem resolution.

Another advantage of a centralized location is that when the frequency of questions increases, support specialists know right away when a problem is affecting a large number of users. Once aware of the problem, help desk personnel can alert the appropriate IT group to ensure that the problem is addressed before even more users are affected.

In a centralized help desk, requests are tracked and resolutions are recorded in one location. Not only is the information accessible to all support personnel, but the support personnel can also more easily standardize responses to problems. Users experiencing the same problem should receive the same solution.

Centralized help desks have a number of limitations. Divisions in other locations may need on-site support, which cannot be provided. If they are in different time zones, they may also require support during different times of the day. In addition, it is not always feasible for staff members of a centralized help desk to understand the unique needs of each business unit.

Did You Know?

In its 2002 Best Practices Survey, the Help Desk Institute found that 35% of all help desks provide support for users in more than one country.

Decentralized

A **decentralized help desk** consists of multiple support sites located throughout an organization. Multiple sites are necessary for a number of reasons. Companies with offices in different geographic locations want to provide on-site support to field offices. Offices may be located in several different time zones, creating a need for support during hours when a centralized site might be closed. For example, corporate offices in the United States and in Japan require support at very different times of the day.

Multiple support sites also provide an opportunity for specialization. Some companies have entire business divisions in locations far from the central office. These divisions perform specific business functions, such as research and development, operations, or manufacturing. In a decentralized help desk structure, each division can have its own help desk, staffed with specialists. Technology varies from one business unit to another; the technology used by the research division differs greatly from the systems used in human resources. A dedicated help desk has specialists who not only know the technology used by the division, but also understand the unique business challenges facing the unit.

One challenge for decentralized help desks is to provide standardized information to all users. If support sites do not provide the same solutions, employees in different divisions may not be using the technology as the organization would desire. Another potential concern for decentralized help desks is the need for a common mission and set of goal statements. Measuring the performance of various help desk sites is also difficult if a common method for tracking and recording data is not used. Table 2.1 lists the advantages and disadvantages of decentralized and centralized help desks.

Advantages of Centralized Help Desks	Disadvantages of Centralized Help Desks	Advantages of Deentralized Help Desks	Disadvantages of Decentralized Help Desks
Easy for users to locate	Inability to provide on-site support to remote locations	Ability to address local site needs (time zone, language, products)	Difficulty of providing standardized information
Better communication among specialists	Difficulty of understanding business needs	Availability of on-site services	Need for common mission and goals
Easier to enforce standards	Challenge of providing support in multiple time zones		Challenge of measuring performance
Better use of resources			
Exposure of specialists to a broad range of issues			

TABLE 2.1

Advantages and Disadvantages of Centralized and Decentralized Help Desks

1. **READING REVIEW** How many locations does a centralized help desk have?

2. **CRITICAL THINKING** Would a company with divisions in many countries be most likely to have a centralized help desk or a decentralized help desk? Why?

2.2 Help Desk Structure

Whether centralized or decentralized, help desks must have an underlying organizational structure. They can be organized in a number of ways, depending on the needs of the organization. The five primary structures are pool, dispatch, tiered, specialized, and method. Most help desks use mainly one structure, although several structures may be combined.

Pool

The simplest help desk structure is a pool structure. In a **pool structure**, all support staff members support the same technology, serve the same customers, and perform the same job duties. Staff members are generalists; they are required to have knowledge of a broad range of products and services. In all likelihood, the person who takes a call will be familiar with the user's problem or a similar problem. However, the staff member may not have the in-depth knowledge required to solve more complex problems.

Dispatch

The **dispatch structure** is aptly named because the first-line personnel act as dispatchers, taking just enough information to refer the question to the appropriate group. In a dispatch structure, the first-level personnel receive requests from users and refer the requests on to the appropriate groups without trying to solve the problems themselves.

The primary advantage of a dispatch structure is that there is little or no phone queue; the customer gets to talk to someone, usually within a relatively short time. However, once the call has been answered and passed on to the relevant support group, it may end up in a queue. This type of structure does not eliminate waiting. Rather, the wait occurs at the second level of contact instead of the first. Despite this, many problems are solved at the second level, since they have already been screened and assigned to a support person who specializes in the particular type of problem.

Another advantage of the dispatch structure is that first-level personnel require limited training. Individuals with a computer background and an introduction to the company's use of technology can begin taking calls. However, this can also be a drawback when it comes to staffing and employee turnover. First-level staff members are not provided with the opportunity to resolve problems. They have little opportunity to learn, which can limit their career advancement options. This can create a problem in retaining personnel; turnover may be especially high in a dispatch help desk.

In a dispatch help desk, callers may have to give the same information to several people. The caller explains the problem to the first-level staff member who receives the call. The staff member then describes the problem to the specialist who receives the referred call. At this point, the only information the specialist has about the situation has come from the first-level staff member, not from the user. What happens if the first-level worker did not fully understand the caller or did not effectively describe the problem to the specialist? Once the caller gets through to a specialist, information may need to be repeated. This usually annoys the caller and also results in lost productivity due to the wasted time.

Problems can also occur when users try to work around the first-level by contacting a specialist directly. For example, if users have called before and have been referred to a specialist, the next time they have a problem they may call the specialist directly. By eliminating contact with the first-level dispatchers, users may eliminate having to wait in a queue. Unfortunately, one or two specialists may receive the bulk of the calls while others sit idle.

Tiered

In a **tiered structure**, the help desk is divided into several groups, commonly referred to as levels (see Figure 2.1). Each level provides a different degree of support. The first-level personnel receive problems and requests from users via phone, fax, or e-mail. First-level specialists are the first points of contact with users. Incoming requests span a wide range of products and services. For this reason, first-level personnel must be familiar with many varieties of hardware and software. At the same time, they are not required to have the depth of knowledge that a higher-level support specialist would possess.

Ideally, the first-line specialist resolves the problem, and there is no need to escalate the request to the second level. In fact, over 80 percent of all incoming problems are resolved at the first level. Whether the problem is solved at the first level depends on the expertise of first-level staff members. In some companies, these analysts are trained to handle only the most basic problems. In other organizations, first-level analysts are able to handle more complex problems.

In either case, the first-level staff member usually takes ownership of a problem. **Ownership** refers to taking responsibility for a problem and seeing it through until it is resolved. This includes maintaining regular contact with the user from problem inception until problem resolution—and beyond. Ownership does not end until a follow-up contact is made to ensure that the resolution has been successful. Help desks that promote first-level ownership usually report high customer satisfaction, since users know that someone is in charge of handling their problem.

FIGURE 2.1

Help desk tiered structure

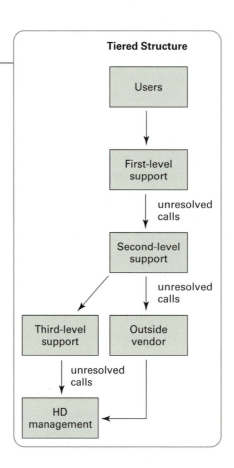

In many companies, there is a predetermined period of time for the first level to resolve the issue. This time varies from organization to organization. In general, it may be as short as fifteen minutes or as long as 24 hours. If a problem is not resolved within that time frame, the call is escalated to the next level.

Members of the second-level support team are specialists. Second-tier staff usually do not take incoming requests directly from users. They are required to have in-depth knowledge in a limited number of areas. They are not expected to answer questions that are not in their areas of expertise. However, they are expected to solve complex problems in their areas of expertise.

One problem that occurs with a tiered structure is that some first-level staff members may refer calls to the second level without making much of an effort to solve them. Sometimes this happens because the organization bases its performance rewards on the number of calls answered, not the number of problems actually resolved.

For a tiered structure to work effectively, a company must invest in its personnel. Either highly skilled analysts must be hired, or less experienced analysts must be hired and trained. In either case, the costs may be high.

When they work as intended, tiered structures tend to produce high customer satisfaction, since most calls are resolved by the first person with whom users speak. Users do not get the feeling that they are being passed from one person to the next. Instead, they feel as if one person is in charge of solving their problem.

Another advantage of tiered help desks is employee satisfaction. Analysts have the opportunity to learn and develop additional skills, while also getting the satisfaction of solving user problems.

In some organizations, problems occur when higher-level help desk staff members look down on lower-level staff members. In reality, first-level analysts are dealing with less complex problems, but at the same time they must possess very good interpersonal skills, since they are always the user's first contact with the help desk. Often the first impression created during this initial contact has a great effect on user's reports of customer satisfaction with help desk services.

Response Time versus Time to Resolution

In a tiered structure, the user may wait in a queue before speaking to a staff member. This results in a significantly longer response time than with a dispatch structure. In a dispatch structure, the time it takes to respond to a caller is minimal. Someone typically answers the call within a very short time period, usually less than thirty seconds—this is known as response time. **Response time** is the amount of time that passes until a call is answered. This statistic indicates nothing about how much time passes before the problem is resolved—time to resolution. **Time to resolution** is the amount of time that passes until a problem is resolved. In some cases the time to resolution in a dispatch structure is longer than in a tiered structure because all calls have to go through dispatch before actual problem solving begins.

Specialized Structure

In a **specialized structure**, there are two types of support models: product and business. When a call comes in to the help desk, it is routed to a support group based on either the product the problem pertains to or the business unit that is making the request. One other type of specialized help desk structure provides support based on the method of the request.

Product Model

In a **product model**, the help desk is divided into a number of groups, each responsible for supporting a specific product group (see Figure 2.2 on page 34). A very basic product structure might be composed of one support group for hardware and another support group for software. In a slightly more complex structure, this is further broken down into types of hardware and software. Within the hardware support group, for example, there may be a group specializing in printer support, another in laptop support, and so on. A similar delineation can exist within software support. For example, the help desk may include groups that specialize in support for database applications, spreadsheet applications, and presentation applications, among others.

FIGURE 2.2

Specialized
product model

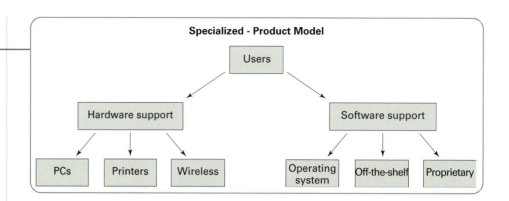

Each group handles only those problems related to its area of expertise. Within each product group, the support staff may be also broken down into levels as in a tiered structure. Within a network group, for example, there may be first-level, second-level, and third-level specialists, with specialists at each level possessing greater expertise. If a specialist at the first level is unable to resolve the problem, it is referred to the second level, and then if necessary to the third level.

Product-based support provides help desk personnel with the opportunity to become experts in a particular area. With their extensive knowledge, specialists are more likely to be able to solve problems quickly, even when complex issues are involved.

If an organization has too many product specialty groups, it may be difficult to determine which group should handle a problem. On the other hand, with too few product groups, support staff members are required to know a lot about a broad range of issues and may not have the in-depth knowledge to resolve calls. This can result in longer time to resolution.

In some cases, at the beginning of a call it is not always clear what is causing a problem. If a user is unable to print to a network printer, there could be a network problem, a printer problem, or a software problem. Support staff must be flexible so that if a problem they are working on turns out to be outside their product group, they are willing to pass it on to the appropriate group.

Business Model

Another way of organizing a help desk is into groups based on the business units they support. This is known as a **business model** (see Figure 2.3). One group supports the sales staff, another product development, another human resources, and so on. Dividing the support staff into groups based on business units allows them to gain a better understanding of users' needs.

This approach offers a significant advantage over the product method: help desk support staff understand what users are trying to accomplish with the technology from a business standpoint. Each time users call with a request, someone in the dedicated group assigned to support that business unit responds. Since the same analysts and users work together over time, a relationship can be established. This leads not only to faster resolution times, but to greater user satisfaction as well.

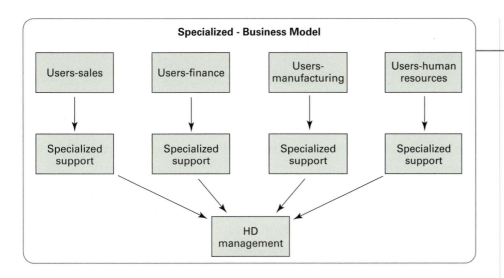

FIGURE 2.3

Specialized business model

One disadvantage of this model is that support staff are exposed to a limited range of technology, depending on what the division or department is using. This may negatively affect an analyst's career advancement. On the other hand, there may be opportunities for the analyst to advance into a position within the department, as the analyst has become well-versed in the business.

Method Structure

In a **method structure**, help desks are organized by the manner in which support is provided. One group handles all incoming telephone requests; another group responds to e-mail and Web site inquiries. In this arrangement, support personnel must be generalists, since they receive requests about all types of hardware and software.

The method structure assigns staff based on specific skills. Individuals who respond only to e-mail requests need good writing skills. Interpersonal skills are somewhat less important, since there is no phone or face-to-face contact with customers. Specialists possessing strong interpersonal skills provide desk-side support and respond to phone calls. In this position, writing skills are secondary.

This structure works best when requests are evenly distributed across several inquiry methods. It may not be effective for help desks that receive one form of inquiry much more frequently than any other. For example, a help desk that receives 90 percent of its requests via telephone would not use this structure. One group would be overloaded while the other groups were idle.

✓ READING CHECK

1. **READING REVIEW** What are the five primary structures help desks can have?

2. **CRITICAL THINKING** Which kind of help desk structure offers the best career opportunities for a help desk analyst? Why?

2.3 Outsourcing

Outsourcing is the process of using an external company to provide support services for internal employees. When organizations invest heavily in new technologies, there is a large increase in their need for user training and support. Rather than develop these capabilities internally, some companies select an outside firm to provide support services.

Outsourcing is on the rise because of a number of factors, including

- Increased use of technology in business
- Increased workload for existing support centers
- Increased need for around-the-clock support
- Increased cost of hiring and training an internal staff
- Increased number of products to support

Some companies outsource the entire support function; others choose to keep some areas of support in-house. For example, some businesses use an outside firm for hardware support. If a printer or monitor ceases to function, the outside firm is notified and is responsible for repairing or replacing the equipment within a predetermined time frame. Other organizations outsource support for popular off-the-shelf software programs such as *Microsoft Office* and *Lotus Notes*. Since these programs are used by thousands of companies, support services are widely available.

Reasons for Outsourcing

Specific reasons that a company may choose to outsource all or part if its support function are

- *Lack of resource:* Some companies outsource because they lack the resources—for example, knowledge, personnel, and space—to develop an internal support structure.
- *Global business:* Outsourcing is popular in companies that maintain offices around the world. Supporting offices in different countries requires a help desk to expand its hours of service to coincide with office hours in different geographic regions. Outsourcing can also be used to fill in gaps when internal staff members are not available. For example, suppose a company's internal help desk is staffed from 9 A.M. until 6 P.M. EST. The company has offices on the East and West Coasts of the United States. To meet the needs of its West Coast offices, the company hires an outsourcing firm that provides support from 6 P.M. until 12 P.M. EST.
- *Language differences:* Many companies with offices around the world find outsourcing beneficial not just for time zone differences, but for language differences as well. Imagine the challenge of trying to assemble a staff with technical knowledge, interpersonal skills, and the ability to

speak several languages. Large outsourcing firms can provide support in any number of languages 24 hours a day, 7 days a week.

- *Core competence:* Organizations may also work with outsourcing vendors because they want to concentrate their resources in other areas. For example, a pharmaceutical company may prefer to focus its efforts on one of its core competencies, such as researching new products, rather than on developing an internal support function. The company still requires support for its computer technology, and hiring an outside firm to provide support is a viable option.

Advantages and Disadvantages of Outsourcing

Outsourcing the support function offers a number of advantages for companies of all sizes, including

- *Reduced support costs*: The organization does not need to provide payroll or benefits to an internal support staff. In addition, outside vendors may be located in areas of the country in which the cost of living and wages are lower.
- *Access to latest tools and technology*: Outsourcing firms make a significant investment in the latest tools and technology so that they can perform support tasks with great efficiency.
- *Flexible staff size*: Without going through the process of hiring and terminating employees, organizations are able to expand or reduce the size of the support staff according to business needs. This also helps keep costs down.
- *Highly qualified support staff*: Individuals working for outsourcing firms receive ongoing training in the latest technology. They also have experience diagnosing and solving a wide variety of technical problems.

There are also disadvantages to outsourcing help desk functions, including

- Lack of familiarity with how the business operates
- Lack of control over the quality of technical support and customer service

Outsourcing and Job Opportunities

The growth of outsourcing has resulted in an increase in the number and type of jobs available to support specialists. In contrast to in-house support jobs, working for an outsourcing firm provides analysts with the opportunity to interact with a variety of clients in different industries. Some individuals prefer working in a support role that offers contact with a variety of businesses. For example, suppose an analyst is employed by a support firm that specializes in providing support for wireless modems. During a typical day, the analyst may assist traveling corporate executives, real estate salespeople, and hospital emergency room personnel.

A Staff Job versus a Contract

Paula Goodman has been in her first IT job, on the help desk at Rasmussen & Co., for nearly three years. She started as a level-one analyst, obtained HDA (Help Desk Analyst) certification, and was promoted to level two a year ago.

Paula handles all kinds of calls, but the majority are from people whose PCs have crashed or frozen because of conflicts between the company's operating system and the applications the users are running. She is more interested in network support than in PC hardware or software. She plans to take a course next fall to become a Microsoft Certified Systems Engineer. Although Paula enjoys working in technical support, she would like to eventually become a systems administrator.

Paula's employer has recently been acquired by The Thompson Corporation, which has its headquarters—and its help desk—in a city more than 1,000 miles away. Paula has been offered a transfer to the new headquarters. Although she has not turned down the transfer, Paula does not want to move, so she sent her resume to a number of companies within commuting distance.

The response to Paula's resumes was encouraging. She accepted several invitations for interviews and has been offered three jobs. She has already turned down one offer because it involved working only with software and would also have required her to work every weekend. She is still considering the other two jobs:

An outsourcing company has offered her a job as a senior help desk analyst. This company provides technical support for several large international companies. The job would pay $3,000 per year more than she makes at her present job, with similar insurance and other benefits.

A local company with a pooled help desk has offered Paula a supervisory job and a $12,000 salary increase, better health insurance, and an additional week of vacation.

Meanwhile, a colleague who is now managing a help desk in another company has offered her a six-month contract as a senior analyst at an hourly rate that is nearly twice what she now earns and much more than any of the other employers would pay her on an hourly basis. She is also considering this option.

EXPLORING CAREERS

1. **What are the advantages and disadvantages for Paula of each of the career moves she is considering?**

2. **Suppose you were considering the same three employment possibilities as Paula and had the same amount of experience and education. Which one would you choose? Why?**

Other people in the support industry choose to work for outsourcing firms because of the flexibility offered by contract work. Contract work is work performed by an individual who is not an employee of a company, but instead has signed a contract to perform a specific job for a certain amount of time. A company might hire help desk personnel for additional support during the implementation of a merger, for example. When the contract ends, the position ends, unless the company offers to renew the contract. A contract assignment may last several weeks, months, or even years.

READING CHECK

1. **READING REVIEW** Briefly, what four advantages does outsourcing offer to companies?

2. **CRITICAL THINKING** Has the growth of outsourcing increased or decreased career opportunities for support specialists? How?

2.4 Help Desk Careers

A job on the help desk is one of the best ways to break into the information technology industry and gain valuable experience. The support field is growing, offering opportunities for individuals with all levels of skill and experience. New help desk employees are able to use their existing technical knowledge and rapidly develop new competencies. The exposure to a wide range of technical products and services is one of the major benefits of a help desk job. Once on the job, a new support specialist rapidly learns about the company's hardware, software, and network configurations.

Career Stages

Like other professionals, individuals who work in a help desk environment go through a series of stages during their career. The three primary stages are accelerated learning, competence, and reevaluation.

1. *Stage One: Accelerated Learning.* When first joining a help desk, an individual learns at an accelerated pace. Even experienced support specialists have a lot to learn. Companies use many different types of hardware and software. Industries require different technologies. The computers and software used in a bank are not the same as those used in a manufacturing plant; the challenges faced by the help desk vary as well. Even when some of the same technology is used, chances are that it is used differently.

2. *Stage Two: Competence.* After completing the initial learning period, the help desk analyst is able to solve most day-to-day problems and

requests. Occasionally a problem will need to be referred to a higher level. During this career stage, the analyst continues to learn about the technology. In addition to new technologies, there are regular upgrades to existing products. The analyst also continues to learn about the different areas of the business.

3. *Stage Three: Reevaluation.* Once an analyst has spent some time at stage two, a period of reevaluation occurs. The analyst considers whether the job is still satisfying and whether to pursue another position. If the job is still appealing, an upper-level help desk position may be appropriate. If the job is no longer satisfying, the analyst must decide whether to look for another position within or outside the IT area.

Did You Know?

The length of time first-level staff members stay in one support organization is

- **< 1 yr 2%**
- **1yr 12%**
- **2 yr 39%**
- **3 yr 22%**
- **4 yr 6%**
- **5 yr 4%**
- **5+yrs 15%**

Source: Help Desk Institute, 2002 Best Practices Survey

Position Requirements

The types of positions available to individuals beginning careers as help desk analysts are varied. The required skills and abilities also vary from company to company. Figures 2.4, 2.5, and 2.6 are examples of actual advertisements for help desk positions.

FIGURE 2.4

Sample job descriptions for help desk personnel—entry-level help desk analyst

Entry Level Help Desk Analyst

Position Description:

*100% phone support
*Provide technical support, this position is the first point of contact for the end users
*Support 50,000 end users
*Responsible for entering detailed information into the tracking system
*Responsible for routing the ticket if resolution cannot be reached
*Types of calls: password resets, printer resets, Internet defaults, etc.

Requirements:

*Solid PC skills, A+ and MOUS certification desired
*Work experience in a Windows environment
*Must be flexible with the work schedule and able to do overtime
*Must be able to work holidays if needed
*Must have excellent communication skills, verbal and written
*Must have proven customer services skills

FIGURE 2.5

Sample job descriptions for help desk personnel—help desk support analyst

Help Desk Support Analyst

Job Responsibilities: support technical staff that is currently at 80 and growing rapidly. Support Users in 2 remote offices and traveling users. Troubleshoot software and hardware issues. Configure and setup new computers. Daily maintenance on servers (check backup, investigate event errors, etc.) Help with various other IT projects. Customer service knowledge, skills, and abilities include trustworthiness and honesty. Problem Solving and analytical. Possess a positive team player attitude. Excellent communication skills. Ability to multi-task in a fast-paced environment.

Required Skills: Perform PC hardware and software installations and configurations. Understanding of Microsoft Windows XP and NT operating systems. Understanding of Microsoft Office Suites. Familiarity with TCP/IP Network. Microsoft Access programming a plus. MCSE certification a plus.

Computer Services Support Specialist Level 1

The ideal candidate for this position must have a good working knowledge of different workstation hardware, peripheral devices, networks, and system software. This position will be responsible for supporting desktop configurations, Windows XP and NT, Office 2002, general network connectivity issues and Outlook 2002. Advanced knowledge of PC troubleshooting is required as well. The candidate will assist other IT employees as needed. Some evening shift work may be required.

The ability to diagnose and resolve various computing problems in a short timeframe and under stressful circumstances is a must. Providing in-depth technical PC support and analysis for multiple products or one or more complex products / services is also important. Identifying and implementing process improvements as well as providing some project assistance in support of IT and Computing Services will be necessary, but not as high priority.

Technical Skills: Candidate must have a working knowledge of Novell NetWare, Windows XP and NT, MS Office, GroupWise and general understanding of LAN/WAN networking, virus protection product and communication protocols. Novell CNA/CNE or A+ certification preferred.

Other Skills: Candidate must have exceptional customer service and communication skills as well as strong verbal and written skills. Candidate must be a successful team player in a multi vendor-working environment. Candidate must be assertive in a tactful manner and maintain service levels to the highest standards.

✔ READING CHECK

1. **READING REVIEW** What makes support work a good way to begin a career in information technology?

2. **CRITICAL THINKING** In your opinion, what are the most likely reasons that most first-level support workers stay in one organization for three years or less?

Did you Know?

The average annual salary for entry-level help desk jobs in 2002 was $32,678. Second-level support specialists earned an average of $41,322, while help desk managers averaged $62,739.

(Source: Help Desk Institute, 2002 Salary Survey)

2.5 Certification

The employment ads in Figures 2.4, 2.5, and 2.6 have one word in common: *certification*. **Certification** is the process of measuring and evaluating an individual's knowledge and skills in a particular area. Within the IT field, certification is a popular way to demonstrate competency to prospective employers.

Certification provides a number of benefits to corporations and to individuals. Corporations find it easier to identify and hire qualified support personnel since certification indicates a certain level of competence. Individuals who obtain certification find themselves differentiated from the competition when looking for a new position. Positions for certified support specialists often have higher starting salaries as well.

Some individuals study and become certified before a company hires them. Others obtain certification once on the job. In some cases companies pay for training and certification. In return, employees are usually required to sign a contract stating that they will not leave the company for a certain period of time. If they do choose to leave before this time period has ended, they are required to pay back a portion of the costs associated with their certification.

Help desk professionals can obtain several different types of certification. The two primary types are position certification and product certification.

Position Certification

Position certification suggests than an individual has the skills and abilities to perform the duties associated with a specific position. The following are considered position certifications.

Certified Help Desk Analyst (CHDA)

The Help Desk Institute's Help Desk Analyst certification recognizes an individual's knowledge of the terminology, concepts, processes, and technology needed to perform the duties of a help desk analyst.

Certified Help Desk Professional (CHDP)

STI Knowledge offers a Certified Help Desk Professional credential intended for frontline support staff. This certification emphasizes customer service and problem solving as well the fundamentals of help desk structure and procedures.

Product Certifications

Product certification represents a person's competencies in a particular product area. Examples of product certifications are listed below.

IC^3

IC^3 stands for Internet and Computing Core Certification. It consists of three separate general tests covering computing fundamentals, key applications (*Word* and *Excel*) and living online (Internet information). The program gives individuals sufficient Internet and computing literacy skills to enter current job markets or begin higher education programs.

A+

The A+ certification program is designed to ensure that individuals can assess and diagnose PC hardware and operating system problems. The program was developed by the Computer Technology Industry Association (CompTIA), and covers a broad range of technologies from a number of different vendors. To obtain A+ certification, a candidate must pass the Hardware Service Technician and Operating System Technologies examinations.

Network+

CompTIA also offers Network+ certification. This certification attests to the individual's knowledge of network components and ability to install, configure, and troubleshoot basic networking hardware peripherals and protocols. Most candidates for Network+ certification already have A+ certification or equivalent on-the-job experience. As with the A+ certification, Network+ is not specific to one vendor's product.

Microsoft Certified Systems Administrator (MCSA)

The Microsoft Certified Systems Administrator (MCSA) is a vendor-specific certification. It measures technical and administrative expertise in various areas relating to Microsoft software, including designing, installing, supporting, and troubleshooting information systems that run on *Windows 2000*, *Windows XP*, and other Microsoft software.

Microsoft Certified Systems Engineer (MCSE)

The Microsoft Certified Systems Engineer (MCSE) is a vendor-specific certification that builds on the MCSA certification with more technical detail.

Microsoft Office User Specialist (MOUS)

Microsoft also offers the Microsoft Office User Specialist (MOUS) certification. Certified individuals possess expertise in one or more software programs in the *Microsoft Office* suite. A person with expertise in *Word*, *Excel*, *PowerPoint*, *Access*, and *Outlook* is awarded the status of Master MOUS.

Certified Novell Engineer (CNE) and Certified Novell Administrator (CNA)

The Certified Novell Engineer (CNE) certification provides evidence of an individual's ability to plan, install, configure, troubleshoot, and upgrade Novell's network products and services. Individuals with CNE certification possess the knowledge and skills to solve complex network problems. The Certified Novell Administrator (CNA) certification is designed for individuals who are responsible for the day-to-day administration of a Novell networking system.

> ## Did You Know?
>
> More than 500,000 IT workers have MOUS certification. Approximately 150,000 workers have MCSE or CNE certification.

✔ **READING CHECK**

1. **READING REVIEW** Why is certification popular among people who work in support?

2. **CRITICAL THINKING** If you were a manager who was trying to raise the support staff's level of interpersonal and customer service skills, which kind of certification would you most likely require? Why?

2.6 Information Technology Career Paths

Several years' experience in a help desk environment can lead to many other career possibilities within the IT department, such as network and systems administration, applications development, database administration, project management, and help desk management. In fact, many information technology professionals began their careers working in a help desk environment. Working on a help desk offers the opportunity to learn about the different job functions in the IT organization. This perspective is very helpful when considering possible career moves. Figure 2.7 lists the common stages of a help desk career.

FIGURE 2.7

Stages of a help desk career

Career Stages

Like other professionals, individuals who work in a help desk environment go through a series of stages during their career. The three primary stages are Accelerated Learning, Competence, and Re-evaluation.

Stage One: Accelerated Learning
When first joining a help desk, learning occurs at an accelerated pace. Even for experienced support specialists, there is a lot to learn. Companies use many different types of hardware and software. Industries require different technologies. The computers and software used in a bank are not the same as those used in a manufacturing plant; the challenges faced by the help desk vary as well. Even in situations in which some of the same technology is used, chances are it is used in a different way.

Stage Two: Competence
After the initial learning period is over, the help desk analyst is able to solve most day-to-day problems and requests. Occasionally a problem will need to be referred to a higher level. During this career stage, the analyst continues to learn. In addition to new technologies, there are regular upgrades to existing products. At this stage the analyst also continues to learn about the different areas of the business.

Stage Three: Re-evaluation
Once an analyst has spent some time at stage two, a period of re-evaluation occurs. The analyst considers whether the job is still satisfying, and whether to pursue another position. If the job is still appealing, an upper level job with the help desk may be appropriate. If the job is no longer satisfying, the analyst must decide whether to look for another position, either within or outside the IT area.

In some companies, help desk personnel are required to perform other IT duties, such as configuring workstations for a network. This knowledge and experience can make it possible for help desk employees to advance into other positions in the company.

Help Desk Management

A logical career step for a support specialist who wants to remain at the help desk is a management position. Again, project management and leadership experience is invaluable. Help desk managers perform a variety of

Did You Know?

If you enter the term *help desk* in the job search box at Monster.com (http://www.monster.com), your search will probably result in more than 1,000 positions.

tasks, including monitoring service levels, planning staff schedules, measuring help desk performance and customer satisfaction, and determining the appropriate use of technology.

Network Engineering

One logical career move for a help desk analyst is to a network engineering or systems administration position. While working on the help desk, most analysts become familiar with the network configuration and common network problems.

Network engineering involves building and maintaining the technology that supports user applications. Network engineers implement local area networks (LANs) for intraoffice communication and wide area networks (WANs) to support an Internet connection. It is the job of the network engineer to see that all aspects of the network are functioning optimally.

Network administrators and systems administration staff help improve a company's efficiency and productivity by installing and upgrading computers, installing software, backing up data, setting up e-mail accounts, and resetting passwords, among other activities. They also respond to emergencies such as computer viruses or breaches of security.

Support specialists interested in network or systems administration should work toward relevant certification while still on the help desk. For network engineering or administration jobs, MCSA, MSCE, or Network+ would be appropriate. Individuals interested in systems administration positions should pursue training in different operating systems, such as *Unix* and *Linux*.

Quality Assurance

The **quality assurance (QA)** area of the IT department is responsible for ensuring that a company's technology products are free of errors before they are released and marketed. For example, in a company with a Web presence, quality assurance personnel check that the site is fully functional before it is activated. In all cases, a QA technician locates the sources of problems so developers can remedy them before distribution.

Software Engineering

The **software engineering** group designs, develops, and revises the software used by the company and/or its external customers. In a small company, a software engineer might work on more than one program. In a very large corporation, an engineer might work on only one aspect of a software application. Individuals interested in a software engineering career should take courses in popular languages and tools, such as Visual Basic, C++, Java, and SQL Server, among others.

Finding the Best Support Specialists

A typical help desk analyst is expected to play all of the following roles:

- **Team member**
Cooperating with other support staff members to ensure that the help desk meets its goals

- **Problem-solver**
Not only solving problems but also eliminating their root causes and preventing their recurrence

- **Communicator**
Exchanging information with users and with others on the help desk

- **Marketer**
Encouraging users with technical problems to turn to the help desk as a first resort

- **Researcher**
Gathering data from users and consulting reference materials and other sources about problems and how to solve and prevent them

- **Expert**
Possessing a depth of knowledge and instinct about how to solve and prevent problems

- **Customer service representative**
Providing prompt, professional, and courteous help to customers and internal users

To ensure that the people they hire can fill those roles, managers look for these qualities:

- Focus on the help desk's goals
- Problem-solving skills
- Initiative
- Communication skills
- Technical aptitude and skills
- Customer relations skills

In addition to information from resumes, job applications, school transcripts, tests, and reference checks, hiring managers rely on interviews to determine whether candidates have the necessary skills and traits. Managers often invite other members of the help desk staff to participate in interviews of candidates, and sometimes they invite users. The screening process often includes a series of interviews, one of which may be conducted by telephone so the manager can check the candidate's telephone manner.

APPLYING SKILLS

1. Explain why each of the traits managers look for in technical support candidates is important for a help desk worker to have.

2. Write a one-page assessment of how well your own skills and personality traits match the requirements for working on a help desk. Indicate which of the required traits and skills are your strongest and which you feel you need to develop further.

Database Administration

The **database administration** area of IT develops, implements, updates, tests, and repairs a company's server database. Help desk positions offer the opportunity to develop many of the skills required to be an effective database administrator, especially problem-solving skills. Database administrators work primarily with applications development professionals and other IT personnel rather than with end-users.

Company databases typically store huge amounts of information, and the database administration group is responsible for maintaining those data. For example, mail-order companies maintain extensive databases that include customers' preferences, order histories, and demographics. A database administrator is responsible for monitoring performance, backing up data, and ensuring the security of the information stored in the database program.

Support workers interested in database administration should become familiar with relational databases, SQL, and Oracle, among others.

Project Management

While working on a help desk, support workers usually have an opportunity to work on special projects, such as updating the help desk's knowledgebase or working as part of a team to gather feedback from users. This type of project experience, especially if it involves a leadership role, is particularly valuable when trying to move into a project management position within the IT organization.

Web Production and Development

Every company that maintains a Web presence has a group responsible for creating, maintaining, and revising the Web site. Web designers transform the company's Web site needs and requirements into a Web site design. Web developers transform that design into a finished product, including coding and the creation of graphics.

Guidelines for Career Advancement

To prepare for a career move from a help desk position into other IT areas, the support worker may find the following guidelines helpful:

- *Seize opportunities for learning*: While working on a help desk, there are always opportunities for learning. Mastering different applications and environments can only enhance a help desk analyst's attractiveness to a prospective employer.
- *Obtain a certification*: More and more help desk workers are becoming certified, either within the profession or in a specific product or group

Did You Know?

Twelve to eighteen months is the average tenure of a help desk employee. This rapid turnover is usually attributed to burnout because of the stressful nature of the position. Could it also be that help desk workers are leveraging their experience to move into different positions in the company?

of products. Not only does certification make it easier to obtain a help desk position; it also helps a worker move up the career ladder.

- *Network*: Many help desk positions demand constant contact with people. This is why interpersonal skills rank so high on help desk employers' lists of desirable traits. Take advantage of the opportunity to develop a network of people throughout the company. Later, when the help desk analyst is seeking an internal career move, these relationships are invaluable.

✓ **READING CHECK**

1. **READING REVIEW** What are some jobs within the IT department that might be available to an individual who has help desk experience?

2. **CRITICAL THINKING** In your opinion, should companies require help desk employees to perform other kinds of work, such as configuring workstations for a network? Why?

>> Summary

The following points were covered in this chapter.

1 A centralized help desk provides support to all users in the company, regardless of department or location. With a decentralized help desk, there are a number of support sites within an organization.

2 The five primary help desk structures are pool, dispatch, tiered, specialized, and method.

3 Advantages of a dispatch structure:

  a Minimal wait before calls are answered at the first level

  b High level of problem resolution

  c Little training required for first-level personnel

  d Disadvantages of a dispatch structure:

  e Lost productivity because callers must describe problems more than once

  f Limited career advancement for first-level personnel

4 Advantages of a tiered structure:

  a High rate of resolution at the first level

  b High level of customer satisfaction

  c High level of employee satisfaction

5 Disadvantages of a tiered structure:

  a Lack of attempt to solve problems before referring calls

  b Costs of highly skilled personnel

  c Internal friction between higher and lower levels

6 In a product model of support, help desk personnel are divided into groups that provide support to users of a specific product or products. In a business model, support is provided by help desk personnel dedicated to a specific business unit or department.

7 Companies outsource support services for several reasons, including a lack of internal resources, the need for support at different times and in different languages, and a desire to concentrate resources on areas of competitive strength rather than on a support function.

8 Certification is available in product knowledge and position knowledge.

9 The three stages of a help desk career are accelerated learning, competence, and reevaluation. The accelerated learning stage occurs when a support specialist begins a new position. Once the initial learning period is over, specialists can handle most user problems without consulting other resources. Finally, a stage of reevaluation occurs. At this time the specialist decides whether to pursue advancement within the help desk or move to another position outside of support.

10 The opportunities for career advancement within the information technology department are numerous. Support specialists often move into positions in network engineering, quality assurance (QA), software engineering, database administration, project management, help desk management, and Web production and development.

Chapter 2 Review

>> Key Terms

The following terms were defined in this chapter:

a business mode		**k** pool structure	
b centralized help desk		**l** position certification	
c certification		**m** product certification	
d database administration		**n** product model	
e decentralized help desk		**o** quality assurance (QA)	
f dispatch structure		**p** response time	
g method structure		**q** software engineering	
h network engineering		**r** specialized structure	
i outsourcing		**s** tiered structure	
j ownership		**t** time to resolution	

>> Reviewing Key Terms

Write the letter of the key term that matches each definition below:

_____ **1** The process of measuring and evaluating an individual's knowledge and skills in a particular area.

_____ **2** Help desk structure in which first-line personnel take just enough information to refer the call to the appropriate group.

_____ **3** Help desk structure in which help desks are organized by the manner in which support is provided (telephone requests, e-mail).

_____ **4** The process of using an external company to provide support services for internal employees.

_____ **5** Help desk structure in which support is provided based on the product or business unit requiring support.

_____ **6** Help desk structure in which specialists at different levels have different levels of expertise.

_____ **7** A kind of specialized structure in which a help desk is organized into groups based on the business units the groups support.

_____ **8** Taking responsibility for a problem and seeing it through until it is resolved.

_____ **9** A structure in which all help desk staff members support the same technology, serve the same customers, and perform the same job duties.

_____ **10** Work that involves the design and development of software used by the company and/or its external customers.

>> Reviewing Key Facts

True/False

Identify whether each statement is True (T) of False (F). Rewrite the false statements so that they are true.

_____ **1** Compared to a dispatch structure, a tiered help desk structure provides the fastest response time.

_____ **2** It is more difficult to enforce standards in a decentralized help desk than in a centralized help desk.

_____ **3** Certified Help Desk Analyst (CHDA) is an example of position certification.

_____ **4** One advantage of outsourcing is access to the latest support tools and technologies.

_____ **5** In a dispatch-structured help desk, it is not uncommon for calls to be answered within 30 seconds.

Completion

Write the answer that best completes the following statements:

1 Product and _____ are examples of specialized help desk structures.

2 The _____ area of IT develops, implements, updates, tests, and repairs a company's server database.

3 Microsoft Certified Systems Engineer (MCSE) is an example of a _____ certification.

4 _____ provides organizations with the ability to expand or reduce the size of the support staff according to business needs.

5 The amount of time that passes until a call is resolved is known as _____.

>> Understanding Key Concepts

Provide brief answers to the following questions:

1 How is a decentralized help desk different from a centralized help desk?

2 What are the three stages of a typical help desk career?

3 What three guidelines should help desk analysts follow to advance their careers in IT?

>> Critical Thinking

As directed by your instructor, write a brief essay or discuss the following issues in groups:

1 You are the head of IT in a medium-sized company with approximately 1,000 employees that manufactures rock-climbing equipment. You have facilities in Texas and South Korea. The company recently invested heavily in new technology for inventory and distribution. You are writing a proposal suggesting that support services be outsourced. List your reasons for the recommendation.

Chapter 2 Review

>> Critical Thinking (continued)

2. Which of the five primary help desk structures provides the most challenging environment for first-level workers? Which would be least challenging? Explain your answers.

3. List three scenarios in which a centralized help desk may not be appropriate.

4. Why are help desk jobs often the starting points for many successful IT careers?

>> Help Desk Projects

Complete the projects listed below:

1. **Form a team with several classmates.** Select a help desk structure, and imagine that you are working as a support team within it. Select one person to play the role of a user who is calling for assistance, and assign support roles to each of the other members. Enact a scenario for the rest of the class showing what would happen when the help desk receives the user's call and how the call would be handled within the structure you have chosen.

2. **Imagine that you took a call from a user who could not connect with the company's network, that you passed the call to a second-level analyst because you could not solve the problem within the allotted time, and that you have retained ownership of the problem.** Write a description of your responsibilities as the owner of this problem and explain how you would carry them out.

3. **Use the Internet to research two different certifications—one product-based and the other position-based.** How many examinations are required? What content is covered? What does the certification cost?

4. **Using classified ads from the newspaper or from an Internet job site, locate job ads for each of the IT areas listed as career advancement possibilities for help desk personnel.** What are the job requirements? Are any certifications required? If listed, what are the salaries?

5. **Find an advertisement for a help desk job, and imagine that you have applied for the job and that you are qualified for it.** Team up with a classmate who will play the role of a help desk manager who is interviewing you. Respond to the interviewer's questions in a way that will demonstrate your qualifications. Then switch roles with and interview your classmate for the job he or she has selected.

6. **If your school has a help desk, find out how it is structured.** If there are multiple levels, determine the responsibilities of support specialists at each different level.

7. **Go to the IBM and EDS Web sites, and read about the user support outsourcing services that are offered.** Make a list of the benefits listed by each company.

>> Help Desk Projects *(continued)*

8 **Familiarize yourself with two major help desk certification organizations: the Help Desk Institute and STI Knowledge.** Are the certifications the same, or do they cover different subjects? Is more than one help desk certification offered?

9 **Imagine you are a veteran IT manager and that a young person has asked you for career advice.** Compose a letter in which you offer advice on how to start and advance a career in IT.

10 **Think about how you would like your own career in IT to progress over the course of your working life.** Create a chart or an outline that represents the different positions you envision, and list the steps that you would take to advance from each position to the next.

>> Help Desk Strategies

Review the following case studies and respond to the questions:

1 Airflow Industries has just expanded its operation to include sites in Oregon, Illinois, and Arkansas in addition to its original site in New Jersey. Airflow has a centralized help desk with a pool structure. Because of the company's expansion, the technical support manager needs to add more help desk analysts and reorganize and restructure the help desk.

- What options does the manager have for reorganizing and restructuring the help desk?
- If you were the manager, how would you reorganize Airflow's help desk? Explain your reasons.

2 You are the manager of a help desk with a tiered structure. Your job performance ratings for help desk analysts are based primarily on the number of calls they handle. The first-level analysts who answer all calls have 15 minutes to resolve problems before passing them on to second-level analysts. The first-level help desk analyst with the highest rating does not solve as many problems as most of the other first-level analysts.

- What might explain why this analyst solves fewer problems than others at the same level?
- Would you want this analyst to solve more problems? Why? What steps could you take to encourage the analyst to solve more problems?

3 Omega Productions has busy seasons and slow seasons. During the busy seasons, Omega's centralized help desk takes as many as 50 calls a day, but during slow seasons the volume of calls is much lower. Consequently, the response and resolution times are very fast during slow seasons and very slow during busy seasons.

- What options could Omega consider that might enable its help desk to provide more efficient service to users?
- If you were Omega's technical support manager, which option would you choose? Why?

Chapter

3

Receiving the Incident

KEY TERMS

Look for the following key terms as you read this chapter:

- **Active communication style**
- **Attentive communication style**
- **Authentication**
- **Communication style**
- **Competitive communication style**
- **Incident management**
- **Logging**
- **Prioritizing**
- **Screening**
- **Verification**

Objectives

After reading this chapter, you will be able to:

1. List the six steps required to process a call.
2. Describe the three categories used to classify calls.
3. Explain the difference between logging and screening.
4. Discuss several issues that must be taken into account when prioritizing an incident.
5. List the four steps in the listening process.
6. Discuss the challenges of listening in a help desk environment.
7. Discuss the guidelines for effective communication and the behaviors that interfere with communication.

Chapter Overview

The process of receiving, processing, and resolving user problems at a help desk is known as the **incident management** process. This chapter focuses on the initial stages of this process—stages that are critical to the entire help desk experience. The first few minutes of any encounter directly affect every event that follows, including problem diagnosis, problem solving, and user satisfaction. This chapter describes the practical steps used by help desk analysts when an incident is received.

The ability to take practical steps, however, is not the only skill needed to process most incidents. Help desk personnel must also possess specific interpersonal skills to manage and resolve problems successfully. Thus, this chapter also emphasizes communication skills, paying particular attention to the skills associated with good listening. Some help desk managers think that listening—not technical knowledge—is the most important skill required of a help desk analyst. As you read this chapter, ask yourself why these managers may value a help desk worker's ability to listen over all other traits.

3.1 Receiving the Incident

Incident management is the process of receiving, processing, and resolving user problems. The first step in incident management is receiving the incident (see Figure 3.1). The second step is processing the incident, and the third step involves resolving the incident. This chapter will discuss the first step; the second and third steps are discussed in Chapter 4.

When a call comes in to the help desk, the support specialist performs a number of tasks designed to determine the type of problem and its severity (see Figure 3.2). These tasks are described in the following section.

FIGURE **3.1**

The incident management process

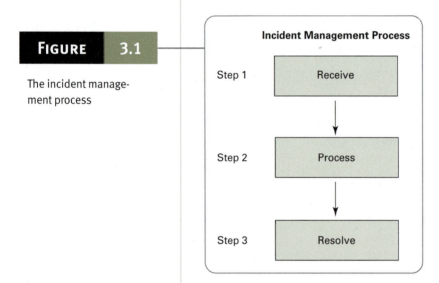

Step 1: Becoming Aware of the Problem

A contact with the help desk begins when a user becomes aware of a problem, question, or need. Most users do not contact the help desk every time they have a technology-related question or problem. They usually try to solve the problem themselves, or they ask a coworker for help. Sometimes the problem remedies itself within a short time.

Most computer users contact the help desk when they cannot easily solve a problem. In fact, a company encourages users to call for help rather than spending a lot of time trying to resolve problems themselves. In terms of productivity, the user is much more likely to be back to full speed if the help desk is contacted, since the help desk specializes in solving user problems.

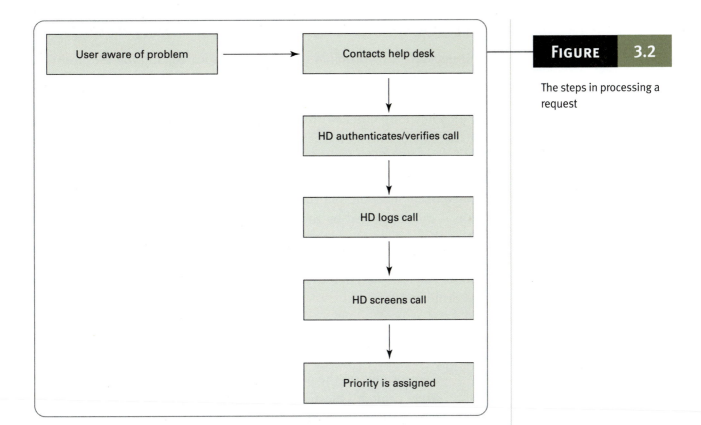

FIGURE 3.2

The steps in processing a request

Step 2: Contacting the Help Desk

When a user first contacts the help desk, two critical events take place: information is gathered about the user and the nature of the problem, and a positive relationship is established with the user. Users make contact with the help desk through a variety of methods including e-mail, fax, and telephone. This chapter focuses on problems communicated via the telephone. As discussed in Chapter 2, calls may be handled by a dispatcher and then routed to an analyst, or they may come in directly to the analyst. This chapter focuses on calls that come directly to the analyst.

Most help desks have developed scripts for answering calls. The use of scripts is one way of ensuring that users receive the same treatment regardless of which analyst receives the call. When users call the help desk, they have no idea with whom they will be speaking—or the type of response they will receive. Call-handling scripts provide a level of consistency from one call to the next.

Here are two examples of scripts used for incoming calls.

EXAMPLE 1: "Thank you for calling the XYZ Help Desk. This is Brenda. How may I help you?"

EXAMPLE 2: "Help Desk. This is Brenda. May I please have your user ID?"

Did you Know?

In 2002, 69% of requests to help desks came in the form of telephone, while 17% arrived via email and 14% were submitted via a support website. (Source: Help Desk Institute, 2002 Best Practices Survey)

Step 3: Authenticating the Problem and Verifying the User

During step 3, the problem must be authenticated, and the user must be verified. The goal of the **authentication** step is to gather enough information from the user to establish whether the issue falls within the help desk's domain. In other words, is it a problem that the help desk is authorized to handle? Not all technology problems are handled by the help desk. If a product is covered by a warranty or service contract, services are provided by outside vendors. If a user calls the help desk complaining about a software application that runs slowly, the user may be told that the program is not supported by the help desk. Help desks are responsible for supporting only applications that are approved by the organization.

Some help desks prescreen calls at this stage to determine the type of call. In general, calls fall into three primary categories: questions, requests, and problems.

1. Questions are attempts by a user to find out something he or she does not know. For example, a user calls and asks how to print to a color printer on the network rather than to the default black-and-white printer. Questions are not necessarily problems. For example, equipment may be functioning as desired, but the user does not know how to use it to perform the required task. Help desks respond to questions in different ways, depending upon the scope of their responsibilities. If user training and education is a duty of a help desk, the analyst will try to answer the user's question in an appropriate manner. If the help desk is not responsible for user education, the analyst may simply route the call to the appropriate group, such as the training and development department.

2. Requests are often for new hardware or for new or upgraded software. Most help desks are not responsible for responding to user requests for enhancements to hardware and software.

3. Problems occur when a user is unable to perform a task because of a technology issue. Problems make up the majority of help desk calls.

During the authentication step, the analyst obtains basic information from the caller, such as

- A brief description of the problem
- The hardware in use (model, serial number)
- The software in use (program, version number, license number)

If the company has an asset management program, the analyst may be able to discover the user's hardware and software configuration by entering the user's ID in the system. An asset management program tells the analyst what equipment is registered to the user and whether it is still under warranty or a service contract.

Focus on Fingerprinting

In the futuristic film *Minority Report*, retinal scanners are located at the entrances to all buildings and offices. Before individuals can enter, they look at the scanner, which takes a retinal reading. If the scan matches one on file in the system, the person is permitted access.

Retinal scanning is one example of biometrics, the study of discerning an individual's identity through the use of physiological or behavioral characteristics. For security purposes, biometric techniques are superior to other methods of identification because they are nearly impossible to forge or imitate. The most familiar example of biometric identification is the fingerprint. Judicial institutions such as police departments and the FBI have been using fingerprints as a form of identification for almost 100 years. Fingerprinting became a standard form of identification because of its relatively low cost and easy implementation. It is also very accurate, with an error rate of less than one in a million.

Biometric user authentication techniques can be used to protect PCs and networks from unauthorized access. Authentication is based on a physical feature such as a fingerprint, retina, or face. In a help desk environment, biometric identification systems can also be used to verify or authenticate callers. Many users contact the help desk because they have forgotten their passwords. A biometric identification system could verify a user's identity and assign him or her a new password without help desk intervention. This system would eliminate the need to call the help desk for a password reset, resulting in significant cost savings to the company.

New technologies being developed in the field of biometrics include

- **Electronic fingerprinting**

To implement electronic fingerprinting, a small fingerprint scanner is added to each PC system. The scanner either connects to a port on the PC or is integrated directly into the keyboard. Fingerprint authentication is the easiest and most economical biometric PC user authentication technique to implement.

- **Retinal scanning**

Retinal scan technology employs optical technology to create an image of the capillary pattern of the retina of the eye, an image similar to a fingerprint. Retinal scans have a 100 percent accuracy rate, but the technique will probably not find universal acceptance because it requires individuals to look directly into an infrared light. The equipment required to implement retinal scanning is also quite expensive.

- **Facial feature recognition**

Developments in multimedia technology have produced facial feature recognition systems. In these systems, photographs of faces are stored in a database. When an individual tries, for example, to enter a building, a security camera compares the live image of the individual's face with the facial images on file. Since many offices already have security cameras in use, these systems are less costly than retinal scans.

LOOKING AHEAD

1. As a computer user, identify which biometric technique you would be most comfortable with and explain why.

2. Do you have any privacy concerns about biometric data being stored by an organization? Write a brief essay describing your concerns and suggesting ways to prevent organizations from invading the privacy of others while still maintaining their security.

In addition to determining whether the issues are within the help desk's domain, this step also involves **verification**—determining whether the user is eligible for support. In some companies, support is not provided free of charge to all departments. It is important to confirm the user's eligibility to receive support before proceeding further. Typically the user's eligibility is determined by entering his or her user ID into a database.

Step 4: Logging the Call

After the problem is authenticated and the user is verified, the analyst performs the fourth step by logging the call. **Logging** is the process of recording basic information about the call. In most companies, the information is entered in a software program, but some small companies may still fill out pencil-and-paper log sheets. A sample problem log screen from a help desk software program is displayed in Figure 3.3.

FIGURE 3.3

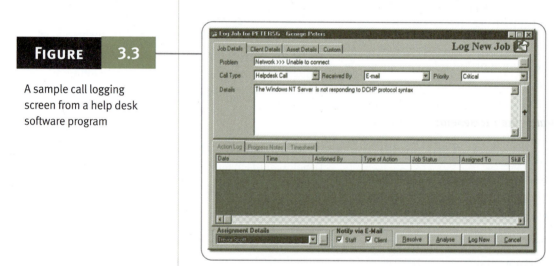

A sample call logging screen from a help desk software program

The analyst may need to enter a lot of information or only a brief description of the problem. This process depends on what type of software the help desk uses. Some programs store detailed information about a user and the technology in use, including a history of prior problems and their resolutions. When this type of program is in place, the rest of the information may automatically appear on the screen once the analyst has entered the user's ID. Other programs may not contain much more than the user's name and ID.

Certain essential information must be logged, including

- The user's name and ID
- The time and date of first contact
- A brief description of the problem

Once the call has been logged (entered into the system), it is assigned an incident number. This number may be referred to as a tracking number or a ticket number. It is a unique identification number associated with the particular call, and it will be in use until the problem is resolved. At any time, this number can be entered into the help desk program to review the history and current status of the problem.

Computer Practice 3.1 | Add a New Service Request

Complete the following exercise using the HelpSTAR software that is located on the CD in the back of the book. Note: *The password for all of the sample users in these exercises is 'helpstar'.*

1. Start HelpSTAR.
2. Login to HelpSTAR as Beth Markham.
3. Click OK to close the 'Tips' window that is displayed.
4. Select *File > New > Service Request* from the main menu.
5. The 'New Request Wizard' appears along with the 'New Request' window.
6. Using the information listed below, follow the Wizard instructions to enter the new request. Use the 'Next' and 'Back' buttons to move through the Wizard screens. Click the 'Next' button to get started.

   Wizard - Step 1: General

   Requester: Renya Torres (double-click on the user name to select it)

   Title: "Shortcut Not Working"

   Problem Type: Software – Sales Application

   Email: Accept the default option.

   Wizard - Step 2: Specifying Workflow Part 1

   Forward to: Dispatch

   Urgency: Medium

   Wizard - Step 3: Specifying Workflow Part 2

   Due By: ASAP

   Wizard - Step 4: Memo Part 1

   Time Worked: Accept default entries

   Time Code: Accept default entries

   Wizard - Step 5: Memo Part 2

   Memo: "When sales application desktop shortcut is double-clicked, program does not launch."

   Private Memo: Accept default.
7. The information entered in the Wizard fields will simultaneously appear in the 'New Request' window.
8. When finished entering the request, a message appears stating that the request has been logged and assigned a reference number. Click OK.
9. Verify that the request has been added. Select *Service Requests > My Workspace > In Dispatch* from the main menu. The 'All Requests – In Dispatch' window will be displayed.
10. Confirm that the new request appears in the list.
11. Close any open windows.

Step 5: Screening the Call

After the call has been logged, the analyst screens it to determine the next step in the process. **Screening** is the process of gathering information about the problem so that problem solving can begin. In a help desk structure in which first-level analysts are generalists, the analyst may begin gathering additional information to begin solving the user's problem. In a dispatch structure, the analyst must obtain enough information about the problem to determine to which group of specialists the call should be routed.

To begin, the analyst must establish the nature of the call. If pre-screening was not performed in step 3 (authentication and verification), it must be done now. The analyst must determine whether the call is a

- Question
- Request
- Problem

Once the call has been placed into one of these categories, additional information is obtained from the user about the exact nature of the problem. Using this information, the analyst writes a brief description of the problem and enters it into the system.

The description must be brief, but not so brief that it does not provide the essential facts. Descriptions of user problems recorded by help desk analysts might include the following:

- *Microsoft Word 2002* does not load when the desktop shortcut icon is clicked.
- *Windows 2000 Professional* boots into SafeMode.
- When attempting to print, the user receives the following error message: "Error writing to LPT1 May2004.xls: The system cannot find the file specified."
- User is unable to download an attachment to an e-mail message in *Microsoft Outlook 2002*.

Problem descriptions provide essential starting-point information to the analyst who will attempt to solve the problem.

Step 6: Prioritizing the Call

After the call has been screened, it must be assigned a priority level. In a help desk, **prioritizing** is the process of determining both the timing and the level of support that will be provided. In general, the priority level is an indication of how serious the problem is. Some problems receive immediate attention; other calls are placed in a queue and will be answered when an agent becomes available.

Help desk analysts determine a call's priority based on predefined criteria. The job of the analyst is to evaluate the call and decide which priority level is appropriate. The priority level assigned to the call determines where the call will be routed. This depends on several factors, including the nature of the problem and the caller's position in the organization. Figure 3.4 displays sample priority definitions and response times for one organization.

Level	Response Time	Definition	Example
1-Emergency	15 minutes	Network outage; multiple users affected	Internet router down; Administrative system down
2-Severe	30 minutes	Major system problems, multiple users affected	Departmental printer down
3-Critical	2 hours	Critical application down, single user affected	Hardware failure; corrupt operating system
4-Routine	12 hours	Application question; work-around available	User unable to print to local printer; locked out of mail post office
5-Non-critical	24 hours	Unsupported software	How do I set up nicknames in Eudora?

FIGURE 3.4

Sample help desk priority level and response times

Companies establish a number of priority levels, typically from three to five. A four-level priority system might be set up as follows:

- *Level 1: Emergency:* A significant number of users are affected. The incident has a critical effect on the business.
- *Level 2: Serious:* Many users are affected. The incident has a serious effect on the business, but some workarounds exist.
- *Level 3: Standard:* A single user is affected and is unable to perform certain tasks.
- *Level 4: Low:* A single user is affected, but the business is not affected. The incident is not an urgent question or request.

A number of factors determine which level is appropriate, including

- Caller's position in the company
- Effect on the business
- Number of people affected
- Possibility of a workaround
- Effect on key business initiative

- Time of day, month, year
- Increase in the number of reports

What Is the Status of the Caller?

The status of the caller is usually taken into account when assigning a priority level to a call. Simply put, a request from a senior vice president frequently takes priority over a call from an administrative assistant in marketing. There are some instances in which a highly ranked individual may be assigned a lower priority. For example, if the help desk is working on another problem that is having a serious effect on the business, the caller's request may be assigned a lower priority. If this is the case, it is important to explain the circumstances to the caller as early in the call as possible.

What Is the Problem's Effect on the Business?

The extent of the problem's effect on the business is another important factor in establishing priorities. To determine the effect of the problem, an analyst must have at least a basic understanding of the business he or she is supporting. Analysts need more than just technical skills; they also need to understand the company that employs them.

How Many People Are Affected by the Problem?

Is the problem confined to one office or one department? In general, the greater the number of users affected, the higher the priority assigned. For example, if all the computers in the shipping department are unable to access the customer database to obtain the information needed to print labels for today's shipment, the problem not only affects a number of people but also affects the business. If labels cannot be printed, packages will not ship out as planned, and customer expectations will not be met. Thus, it is not enough to consider the problem or how many users are affected in isolation; a number of additional factors must be considered.

Does a Workaround Exist?

Another factor that is taken into account when evaluating a problem's seriousness is the existence of a workaround. A workaround is an alternative method of performing a function. A workaround may not be as efficient as the primary method, but it nevertheless allows the work to be performed.

Whether a workaround is acceptable to a particular individual or group is another issue. For example, if the workaround requires users to perform many more steps and takes twice as long as the other method, it may not be acceptable. Often some negotiating is required to develop a mutually agreeable solution.

Does the Problem Affect a Key Business Initiative?

Suppose a user calls to report that a color printer in the marketing department is not responding to user requests for print jobs. At first this may not seem to be an urgent request. However, if the user is printing materials for a major new product introduction scheduled for the next day, the problem is urgent. Clearly, the relationship of the problem to the overall business plan must be taken into account.

What Is the Timing of the Problem?

Many business processes operate on cycles. A simple example of a business cycle is employee payroll. Every two weeks or once a month, the payroll department uses technology to process payroll for employees. Similarly, the critical nature of the tasks performed by the accounting department increase as the end of a business quarter nears.

When evaluating a problem's severity, it is necessary to determine whether the timing of the problem is an issue for that individual or group. In some cases, timing will not be relevant; in other instances, it will be of great importance.

Are Reports of the Problem Increasing?

A problem report begins with a call from a single user to a single analyst. The call is logged and tracked. While this problem is being worked on, another caller reports the same problem. Within the hour several more calls are received. If the number of calls coming in to the help desk reporting the same problem is on the increase, this may be a reason to assign a higher priority level than usual. By addressing the problem sooner rather than later, the number of users affected and the potential effect on the business can be limited.

Is the Problem Important or Time-Critical?

In some companies, priority level definitions are included in a service level agreement. This approach minimizes conflict between the user and the help desk when assigning a priority level to a problem, since the user is already aware of the categories of severity. Even so, some callers will disagree about the urgency of their requests. It can be helpful to distinguish between the importance of a problem and the urgency of a problem.

Some requests are time-critical—these are considered urgent. In such cases, a problem will worsen the longer it goes unresolved. For example, with only three days left in the quarter, a benefits specialist in human resources may be unable to post the quarterly update to the online employee benefits guide. This is urgent—the update is posted before each new quarter begins and there are only three days remaining. However, it may not be important. This is not to say it is unimportant, just that it is just lower on the importance scale than other problems.

Important requests are critical to the success of the business. Importance is often determined on the basis of where the request is coming from and on the significance of that group's contribution to the business. For example, a problem in sales is usually more important than a problem in purchasing. The sales department contributes directly to the company's quarterly profits; the purchasing department does not. Unlike urgent requests, important requests may have little to do with the timing of the problem. When a request is both important and urgent, it usually receives the highest priority.

Some systems base priority on age or history alone. In this type of system, calls are handled in the order in which they are received. One of the drawbacks of this approach is that is does not take into account other factors that may be important, such as the number of users affected, the effect on the business, and the caller's position in the organization. An analyst could be working on a single user's problem while a larger problem waits in the queue.

Overall, the process of assigning priority levels to problems coming in to the help desk is an art, not a science. Some calls do not fit neatly into any one category, and in these cases experience on the help desk is of greatest value.

Computer Practice 3.2 — Dispatch a Service Request

Complete the following exercise using the HelpSTAR software that is on the CD in the back of the book:

1. Select *Service Requests > My Workspace > In Dispatch* from the main menu.
2. Select the "Shortcut Not Working" request from Renya Torres.
3. Click the 'Update Service Request' button ( ) on the toolbar. The 'Update Request' window appears.
4. In the 'Forward to:' drop-down box, select 'Queue', and choose the 'Application Support' queue from the list that appears (by double-clicking on the required queue).
5. Assign a 'High' priority to the request.
6. Click the 'Save' button.
7. A message will appear reminding you that you have not entered a memo for the request. Click the 'Yes' button to save the request.
8. In the 'All Requests - In Dispatch' window, click the 'Refresh' button ( ). The request that was forwarded to queue will no longer be displayed in the list of requests.
9. Verify that the request is in the correct queue.
10. Select *Service Requests > All Requests > In Queue* from the main menu. The 'All Requests – In Queue – All Queues/All' window will be displayed.
11. Click the 'Find' button.
12. A list of all requests in all queues will be displayed. Verify that the request just forwarded to queue appears in the list with the correct queue information.
13. Do not exit HelpSTAR.

Computer Practice 3.3 — Accept a Service Request from Queue

Complete the following exercise using the HelpSTAR software that is on the CD in the back of the book:

1. Select *Service Requests > My Workspace > In Queue* from the main menu.
2. The 'My Workspace—In My Queues—All' window will be displayed.
3. Click the 'Find' button.
4. Select the "Shortcut Not Working" request from Renya Torres. Click the 'Accept the Request' button (☑) (on the secondary toolbar). The request will disappear from the list of requests in queue.
5. Confirm that the request is 'In Service'.
6. Select *Service Requests > My Workspace > In Service* from the main menu.
7. The 'My Workspace – In Service (I'm the Support Rep) - All' window will be displayed.
8. Click the 'Find' button.
9. The request will appear in the list of 'In Service' requests.
10. Close any open windows.

Computer Practice 3.4 — Add a New User

Complete the following exercise using the HelpSTAR software that is on the CD in the back of the book:

1. Select *Administration > User > New User* from the main menu.
2. The 'Add User Wizard' appears along with the 'New User' dialog box.
3. Follow the Wizard instructions to add the new user using the information listed below. Click Next to begin.

User Information
Name: Jane Brightman
Telephone: 408-555-1000
Extension: 65
Fax: Leave Blank
User Type: Internal
Department: Sales (double-click to select)
Location: Floor 3
Workstation ID: WKST0068
Network Address: 0060BFD70
Internet Address: 111.22.33.68
Logins: Enabled
Password: Leave this blank to use default of 'helpstar'
Email: Enabled

Email Address: jbrightman@larkspurtech.com
Post Office Path: Leave Blank
Pager Email Address: Leave Blank
Inventory Memo: Leave Blank
User Memo: Leave Blank

4 When finished, a windows appears stating that the user has been added to the database. Click OK.

5 When prompted to set the user's HelpSTAR privileges and add another user, select 'No'.

6 Select *Administration > User > List Users > All Users* from the main menu. The 'List All Users' window will be displayed.

7 Confirm that the new user appears on the list.

8 Exit HelpSTAR.

✓ READING CHECK

1. **READING REVIEW** Explain the purpose of screening calls.

2. **CRITICAL THINKING** Briefly summarize the factors that determine how incoming calls are prioritized, and evaluate why some factors are considered to be more important than others.

3.2   The Listening Process

Though often referred to as "soft skills," communication skills are critical to all business transactions. If people could not communicate, how would orders be entered and products packed and shipped? How would a company decide on a marketing strategy? How would a business interview prospective employees or communicate with customers?

In reality, all areas of a company are dependent on the ability of employees to communicate—whether face-to-face, on the telephone, or in writing. Acknowledging this dependency, training organizations offer courses on public speaking, presentation skills, and business writing, but they usually do not offer a course on listening skills.

In most interactions, listening and speaking are equally important to effective communication. If a person is unable to express ideas verbally, communication is hampered. Likewise, if a person is unable to listen closely, the message will not be received even if it is clearly delivered.

Listening and hearing are not the same thing. If you are in a crowded restaurant, you may hear the voice of the woman at the next table, but you may not be listening. We hear sirens, dogs barking, radio static, and car

Did You Know?

People speak at 100 to 175 words per minute, but they can listen intelligently to 600 to 800 words per minute.

alarms, but we rarely listen to them. Hearing is a mechanical event carried out by the ear. Listening involves much more than just hearing. While hearing is a passive event, listening requires action.

Listening is actually a four-step process that begins with receiving a message from another person and ends with responding to the message (see Figure 3.5). The four steps in the listening cycle are as follows.

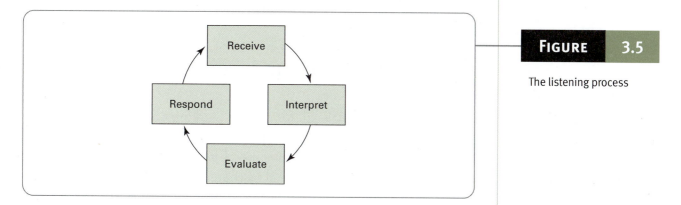

FIGURE   3.5

The listening process

Step 1: Receiving the Message

In the first stage of the process, the listener receives the communication from the other person. Using the senses, the listener attends to the speaker's tone of voice and to the words spoken.

Step 2: Interpreting the Message

During the second stage of the process, the listener interprets the information that was received in step 1. The goal of this stage is to analyze the message to determine what the speaker is saying.

Step 3: Evaluating the Message

In the third stage of the listening process, the listener evaluates the message. Often this includes determining whether the listener agrees or disagrees with what has been said. The listener's attitude, beliefs, and biases may interfere with an accurate evaluation of the message.

Step 4: Responding to the Message

The listening process does not end with the evaluation of the message. In the final stage of the process, the listener responds to the speaker. The process is not complete until the listener acknowledges what the speaker has said. Many people mistakenly assume that acknowledging what someone has said is the same as agreeing with it. Acknowledgement does not indicate agreement with, or approval of, a message. It does, however, indicate that the person was paying attention, and it provides an opportunity to check whether the listener has understood the message.

1. **READING REVIEW** Identify whether the speaking or listening process is more important to a help desk specialist, and briefly explain your choice.

2. **CRITICAL THINKING** Describe how listening is different from hearing. Analyze why listening rather than hearing is an essential skill for all help desk personnel.

3.3 Help Desk Challenges

Listening is an essential skill for anyone working on a help desk. Most of the work performed by help desk personnel would be of little value if the individuals receiving calls were not good listeners. Calls would get assigned the wrong priority levels or would be routed to the wrong specialists. Listening is particularly important when a call first comes in to the help desk and the support person must determine the nature of the problem.

Effective listening in a help desk environment presents a number of challenges. Some of the more common challenges are described below.

Handling Emotions

Users calling the help desk are experiencing problems that are interfering with their ability to perform their jobs. They may be experiencing negative emotions such as anxiety and anger. If a major problem is occurring, such as a system outage, other help desk personnel may be exhibiting signs of stress. Maintaining a calm demeanor and listening closely in this type of environment is especially difficult, but it is a requirement for any help desk position.

Ignoring Distractions

The help desk environment may also be filled with distractions, such as the sounds of ringing telephones and talking. There may be visual distractions as well, such as people walking around, computer monitors flashing, and specialized help desk tools such as electronic message boards. Distractions make it more difficult to concentrate on what the user is saying, especially on the telephone.

Dealing with Different Levels of Knowledge

Support personnel are also dealing with users who have varying levels of expertise when it comes to technology. Some have years of experience, while others are novices. Some people intuitively understand technology, while others find it difficult to grasp. Whatever the characteristics of the caller, the support person must listen closely to try to establish the user's level of expertise, and then communicate accordingly. Talking above a novice user is just as inappropriate as talking down to an experienced user.

Communicating by Telephone

Most help desks still rely on telephones to communicate with users. Listening on the telephone presents its own set of challenges. Many people find it more difficult to communicate on the telephone than face-to-face. How many times in a conversation do you take a cue from the nonverbal behavior of the person to whom you are listening? For example, a person who does not understand what you have said may raise one eyebrow. You then either ask what the person does not understand or simply restate your message is a different way. When you are on the telephone and someone does not understand, you must rely solely on the words used and the speaker's tone of voice to detect the user's lack of comprehension.

Look at the information in Table 3.1. In face-to-face interactions, we rely on three sources of information to determine the caller's mood as well as the meaning. Note that 55 percent of this information comes from nonverbal behaviors, such as gestures and facial expressions. Now look at the column for telephone communication. There are only two sources of information: tone of voice and word content. Of those two categories, tone of voice accounts for 85 percent of information. This table also points out that the way we say things (tone of voice) is much more important than the actual content of our speech (word content). Telephone communication is clearly more challenging than face-to-face encounters.

Type of Communication	Face-to-Face	Telephone
Body language, gestures, facial expressions	55%	0%
Tone of voice	38%	85%
Word content	7%	15%

TABLE 3.1

Factors That Contribute to Understanding in Face-to-Face and Telephone Communication

Despite the challenges, effective telephone communications result in more satisfied users and often lead to more rapid identification and resolution of problems. Figure 3.6 summarizes the characteristics of a successful telephone interaction.

Effective Telephone Communication Skills
- Positive, non-judgmental attitude toward the caller
- Appropriate tone of voice
- Ability to listen actively
- Empathy for the other person's situation
- Ability to question to obtain information or clarify what has been said

FIGURE 3.6

List of effective telephone communication skills

No one communication style is always appropriate; the appropriateness of a style depends on the particular issue and the personalities of the individuals. Each of us takes on a number of different roles—employee, spouse, parent—and in each role we are somewhat different listeners. For example, an individual may be a more active listener when in a parental role and a more attentive listener when in a spousal role.

In general, the competitive style is generally not effective, since most people react negatively when they are talked down to or controlled. The attentive style, while effective in some situations, can be too passive, especially if the other person also has the same style. The active style works best in most situations. Individuals with this style are confident, but also respect other people's knowledge. They do not always have to be right, and they work to arrive at compromise solutions. Persons with the active communication style are also good listeners. Figure 3.7 lists some characteristics of active listeners.

Regardless of the results of the assessment, it is possible to become a better listener by practicing some of the suggestions in this chapter. Even those with an active listening style could benefit from studying the guidelines for effective communication that follow. As you read the next section and the rest of the chapter, be aware of your own listening habits and the areas that could use improvement. Select one or two of these areas, and use the skills and techniques described in this chapter to become a more effective communicator.

FIGURE	3.7

Characteristics of an active listener

Characteristics of an Active Listener

- Focuses attention entirely on the speaker throughout the conversation.
- Does not finish the speaker's sentences for him or her.
- Aware of own attitudes or biases and does not let them influence the interaction.
- Identifies and acknowledges the caller's emotional state.
- Conveys interest in what the speaker is saying.
- Asks questions to clarify what has been said, to convey understanding, and to acknowledge the speaker.
- Lets the speaker finish talking before coming to any conclusions.
- Provides a non-judgmental environment for the conversation to take place.
- Asks questions when he or she does not understand something.
- Keeps own ego out of the communication.
- Recognizes that understanding is not equivalent to agreeing.

✓ READING CHECK

1. **READING REVIEW** Explain the term *communication style* and identify the three styles discussed in this section.

2. **CRITICAL THINKING** Describe and evaluate the different factors that make telephone communication more challenging than face-to-face communication.

HELP *desk* Concepts

Accent the Positive

Many technology companies employ people who have come to the United States from non-English-speaking countries. While most of these individuals can speak and write in English, many retain their native accents, which may be difficult for some people to understand. This situation presents a particular challenge for help desk agents who spend most of their time communicating with users over the telephone. The lack of visual cues makes telephone communication more difficult than communicating in person. A marked accent can make it even more challenging.

Researchers have discovered that it is very difficult for adults to learn to speak a language exactly like a native-born speaker. English is a complicated language to learn for a number of reasons. In the English language, the meaning of words is determined primarily by the emphasis placed on certain syllables and the timing of speech. In some languages, meaning is not determined by how certain syllables are emphasized. In addition, the English language contains some consonant sounds not found in other languages and often has a greater variety of vowel sounds.

In the workplace, strong foreign accents can lead to particular kinds of problems. For example, employees who are unsure of their English language capabilities may not call the help desk for assistance. Those who do call the help desk may have difficulty explaining the exact nature of problems.

The following techniques are helpful when communicating with people who have strong accents:

- **Be patient**

To understand what is being said, it will often be necessary to ask a caller to speak more slowly. For a help desk agent whose evaluation may be based on the time it takes to resolve a call, this is easier said than done. Keep in mind that it is more important to fix the user's problem than it is to have the fastest problem resolution time every month.

- **Paraphrase often**

Since there is an increased risk of misunderstanding, frequently paraphrase what the caller is saying. Use some of his of her own words whenever possible. Not only will paraphrasing help you confirm the nature of the problem; it will also reassure the caller that you are listening closely to what he or she is saying.

- **Speak slowly**

In some cases, the caller will appreciate it if you talk more slowly. However, try to evaluate how well the user understands you before doing so. Someone who has no difficulty understanding English may be annoyed if you speak extra slowly.

- **Pronounce each syllable**

Whether the caller has a strong accent or not, it is always good practice to speak clearly and pronounce each syllable when communicating at work.

REVIEWING CONCEPTS

1. List some reasons why it may be difficult for an adult to learn to speak English.

2. If, after using all of the methods listed above, you still could not understand a caller, what else could you do? Write a short script illustrating how you would improve communication between yourself and an individual who is not comfortable speaking English.

Communicating with the Caller

How you respond to a caller's message has a direct effect on whether your interaction will be a success or a failure.

Keep It Simple

Keep your conversation clear and direct. The less you say, the less chance of miscommunication. There is no need to launch into a long-winded explanation of why something is not working; the user is more concerned about when the problem will be fixed. Also avoid using an overly technical vocabulary. Explain things simply, always being careful not to talk down to the caller.

> **EXAMPLE:** "Have you recently changed your IP address or your subnet mask?"

> **REPHRASE:** "Is it possible that your Internet connection settings have recently been changed?"

> **EXAMPLE:** "Turn your computer off using the ShutDown command located on the Start menu. Wait 30 seconds. Now turn your computer back on by pressing the power button on the front of the computer. Describe what you see on the screen as your computer restarts."

> **REPHRASE:** "Turn your computer off; wait 30 seconds; and turn it back on. Tell me when it has finished booting and you are at the *Windows* desktop."

Allow the Caller to Speak

Wait for the caller to finish a sentence or thought before speaking; do not step in and finish the caller's sentence. Sometimes people become impatient because the other person speaks slowly or does not get to the point in a timely manner. You may think you know what the caller is going to say. Not only is it rude to interrupt someone; it is also possible that your idea of what the caller is going to say is not accurate.

Go to

Audio Exercise 3.3

Listen to Audio Exercise 3.3 on the CD in the back of this book. Then, answer the questions below.

1. How would the user feel following this interaction?
2. What would have made the interaction more positive for the user?

Suspend Judgment

When a call begins, you need to set aside any feelings you have about the caller. People calling for support should receive the same positive attitude, regardless of your personal feelings or attitudes.

Audio Exercise 3.4

Listen to Audio Exercise 3.4 on the CD in the back of this book. Then, answer the questions below.

1 Did the rep handle the situation appropriately?
2 What would you have done differently?

Clarify the Caller's Statements

If you are not sure what the caller is saying, ask questions to clarify, such as

"If I understood correctly, you said…"

"This is what I am hearing…"

"I'm not sure I follow—can you tell me more about that?"

Use a Positive Tone of Voice

When responding to a user's call, your tone of voice should be positive. A positive tone of voice is sincere, friendly, confident, and enthusiastic. Speak clearly and not too fast. Do not mumble or speak quietly. Pause at appropriate places for the caller to process the information or ask a question.

Maintain a Positive Attitude

Even though you cannot be seen by the person on the other end of the telephone, your attitude comes across to the caller. For this reason, it is important to be aware of your attitude toward the caller. If you have had prior experiences with the caller that were problematic, your feelings must be put aside. All users should have the benefit of speaking with a support professional who has a positive attitude.

Audio Exercise 3.5

Listen to Audio Exercise 3.5 on the CD in the back of this book. Then, answer the question below.

1 Was the support rep effective? How do think the user feels in this interaction?

Do Not Use Jargon

Do not use technical language that the caller may not understand.

> **EXAMPLE:** "If you will just change your frame type to 802.3 on your IPX/SPX protocol setting, you will be able to connect to the Internet."

> **REPHRASE:** "We'll change some of your computer settings and see if that will help you connect to the Internet."

Do Not Finish the Person's Sentences

It is not good practice to interrupt the caller to finish a sentence. Most people become annoyed when interrupted and would rather be able to express their ideas than have someone else guess what they were going to say.

> **EXAMPLE:**
> (Speaker) "When I turned on my PC this morning, a screen came up that I never saw before. It asked me if I wanted to..."
> (Listener) "boot into Safe Mode"

Do Not Assume

Do not provide a solution until you have gathered all the facts. In an effort to provide a quick solution, support personnel sometimes jump to conclusions before they have all the facts.

> **EXAMPLE:** "(Speaker) "When I move my mouse, it has no effect on the screen ..."
> (Listener) "It's probably a corrupt driver..."

Do Not Use Abbreviations or Acronyms

Avoid the use of abbreviations or acronyms, no matter how common they may be. Callers possess varying levels of knowledge and experience, and it is important to be sensitive to that.

> **EXAMPLE:** "How many megs of RAM do you have?"

> **REPHRASE:** "Let's check the system to see how much memory your computer has."

Do Not Use Negative Language

Avoid the use of negative language. Find a better way to deliver the message.

> **EXAMPLE:** "I can't do that."

> **REPHRASE:** "I'm sorry, I do not have authorization to do that."
>
> Or: "If I am unable to solve your problem, I will find someone who can."

Do Not Argue

It is never a good idea to get into an argument with a caller. Maintaining a calm approach when dealing with an angry user is especially challenging, but is an essential skill for help desk personnel.

> **EXAMPLE:** (Speaker) "Listen, I need this fixed now. Don't tell me it's going to be five hours; I want someone over here in five minutes."
>
> (Listener): "You listen to me. That is not how it works. Someone will be over to help within five hours, that is how it is."

> **REPHRASE:** "We will send someone over as soon as possible. As you probably know, we are serving several thousand users, and because of that we are not always to provide service as quickly as we would like."

The ability to listen to a user—to receive, interpret, evaluate, and respond to what is said—is the backbone of any successful help desk. Listening affects all major aspects of the help desk's mission: identifying problems, establishing positive relationships with users, and communicating solutions. While much of the focus of help desk training and certification is on technical knowledge and skills, listening remains the most important quality desired in new help desk employees.

✔ READING CHECK

1. **READING REVIEW** Describe one way in which communication problems can originate with a speaker.

2. **CRITICAL THINKING** Evaluate which communication problems would interfere most with a help desk interaction—problems originating with a speaker, or problems originating with a listener.

Go to

Audio Exercise 3.6

Listen to Audio Exercise 3.6 on the CD in the back of this book. Then, answer the question below.

❶ What could the rep have done differently to avoid the user's confusion?

Chapter Review

>> Summary

The following points were covered in this chapter:

1 The six steps required to receive an incident are awareness, contact, authentication and verification, logging, screening, and prioritizing.

2 Calls are classified as questions, requests, or problems.

3 Logging involves recording information about the call, such as the caller's name, the time of the call, and a brief description of the problem. Screening is the process of obtaining information to determine the nature of the problem.

4 Factors to be considered when prioritizing an incident include the status of the caller, the effect on the business, the number of people affected, whether there is a workaround, whether a key business initiative is affected, the timing of the incident, and whether reports of the problem are increasing.

5 The four steps in the listening process are receiving the message, interpreting the message, evaluating the message, and responding to the message.

6 Listening in the help desk environment presents a number of challenges. Help desk personnel must learn to cope with distractions, stress, emotions, users' varying knowledge levels, dependence on telephones, and users' varying communication styles.

7 There are a number of methods used to effectively communicate, such as empathizing, responding to check understanding, allowing the caller to speak without interruption, and listening between the lines. It is important to avoid behaviors that can interfere with communication, such as minimizing the problem, making assumptions, judging the speaker, and using negative language.

>> Key Terms

The following terms were defined in this chapter:

a active communication style

b attentive communication style

c authentication

d communication style

e competitive communication style

f incident management

g logging

h prioritizing

i screening

j verification

›› Reviewing Key Terms

Write the letter of the key term that matches each definition below:

____ **1** The process of gathering enough information from the user to establish whether the issue falls within the help desk's domain.

____ **2** A pattern of speaking and listening in which importance is placed on winning arguments, promoting one's own point of view, and feeling more knowledgeable than other people.

____ **3** A way of speaking and listening in which a person listens closely to other people, prefers others to make decisions, and believes that others are more knowledgeable.

____ **4** The process of determining both the timing and the level of support that will be provided.

____ **5** The process of determining whether the user is eligible for support.

____ **6** A style of speaking and listening, in which a person listens and asks questions to confirm understanding, conveys empathy, and negotiates with others.

____ **7** The process of receiving, processing, and resolving user problems.

____ **8** The process of gathering information about the problem so that problem solving can begin.

____ **9** The process of recording basic information about the call.

›› Reviewing Key Facts

True/False

Identify whether each statement is True (T) of False (F). Rewrite the false statements so that they are true.

____ **1** Asking questions and being present are two components of effective listening.

____ **2** During the screening process, the support specialist obtains a description of the problem.

____ **3** One of the challenges of communicating in a help desk environment is the different knowledge level of users.

____ **4** In telephone interactions, tone of voice accounts for 15 percent of the information we receive about the caller.

____ **5** The status of a caller does not influence the priority level of the call.

Completion

Write the answer that best completes the following statements:

1 Calls coming in to the help desks are classified as problems, requests, and _____.

2 During the authentication and verification step, it is important to obtain a brief description of the problem, as well as _____.

3 The _____ communication style is passive rather than active.

›› Reviewing Key Facts *(continued)*

4 The final step of the listening process is _____.

5 A problem may receive a lower priority level assignment if a _____ exists.

›› Understanding Key Concepts

Provide brief answers to the following questions:

1 What factors can influence how a call is prioritized by help desk personnel?

2 Why is responding considered part of the listening process?

3 Why is it important to pay attention to the caller's emotional state?

›› Critical Thinking

As directed by your instructor, write a brief essay or discuss the following issues in groups:

1 You are the manager of a help desk, and you are interviewing candidates for a first-level position. Your must choose between a person with five years' experience in a PC repair business and someone with five years' experience answering customer service calls for a major retail catalog operation. Which person would you hire? Explain your reasoning.

2 Callers to a help desk have different levels of knowledge and experience. How is it possible to detect the caller's background during a telephone call without directly asking the person?

3 Think of the last time you contacted a company about a problem with something you purchased, or returned goods to a retail store. How did the person representing the company treat you? As the customer, would you have preferred anything to be done differently?

›› Help Desk Projects

Complete the projects listed below:

1 **Ask a classmate to describe a project that he or she is working on in a different course.** Choose several of the techniques for effective listening discussed in the chapter, and practice using them with this classmate as he or she describes the project. Practice paraphrasing, questioning, and responding to information. Ask the other person for feedback about your listening skills.

>> **Help Desk Projects** *(continued)*

2 **Read the situations listed, and decide whether the problem is important, urgent, or both.** Rank the items in priority order from highest (1) to lowest (4). Explain your rankings.

- A vice president in the marketing department reports that her antivirus software has found a virus but is unable to remove it from her PC.
- An analyst in accounting is having difficulty accessing information on the network that he needs for the end-of-month report due in two days.
- A client has encountered a bug in a new product that is due to be released in 10 days.
- An administrative assistant reports that the printer was not working when she went to retrieve the color overheads needed for the senior vice president's presentation to the board. This presentation is scheduled to take place tomorrow.

3 **Form a group with two other classmates.**   Your task is to explain to each person how to download and install *Adobe Acrobat* from the Adobe Web site. One person takes the role of a user who is new to computing and has been on the Internet for only a week. The other person plays the role of a user with some Internet experience, but no experience downloading a program from the Web. How did your instructions differ? What assumptions did you make when giving your instructions? Ask for feedback from your classmates.

4 **Think of a problem that would require the services of a help desk.**   For example, you might have questions about computer software; you might want to know about some charges on your telephone bill; or perhaps you just need advice on how to get a stain out of your favorite shirt. Call the help desks of three different companies and compare how they listen to your problems. Make a chart like the following to analyze your results, and evaluate which company was the best and which could improve.

Listening for Information	Asking Questions to Get Information	Communication	Ranking Style
Company 1			
Company 2			
Company 3			

5 **In a group, discuss times when each of you had communication problems with a salesperson or a family member.**   Write down descriptions of the situations, and then try to isolate what went wrong in each case. Which problems originated with the speaker and which with the listener? Brainstorm ways to avoid repeating these mistakes in the future.

7 **Imagine that you have been asked to establish a help desk in a local high school.**   How would you determine the priority of calls to your help desk? Identify which callers in the school would have priority over others. Which problems would need to be addressed rapidly, and which would receive a lower priority?

Chapter 3 Review

>> Help Desk Projects *(continued)*

7 **Body language is an important aspect of communication.** Even on the telephone, our body language comes through. Observe at least five people talking on telephones. How does their body language reflect their tone of voice and the words they are saying? Try smiling next time you talk on the telephone, and see if that affects how you sound.

8 **Go to the Web and search for training courses and materials on listening skills.** Review the sites, and make a list of the topics common to most courses. Then imagine that you have been asked to develop a course that will teach listening skills for help desk personnel. Create an outline listing the topics that you would cover in your course, and explain why these topics are important. [Internet]

>> >Help Desk Strategies

Review the following case studies and respond to the questions:

1 The help desk received the following e-mail message:

Subject: E-Mail Problem
Date: 07/16/2005
From: Michael D'Amato
To: Help Desk

Two weeks ago my e-mail address would not work, and I missed an important conference call because I did not get the information. Then I was told that I had to have a new address. That address was set up, and it worked! Then it stopped working this week. I called the help desk and they reestablished the old e-mail account. They assigned me a new password that did not work. However, my old password did work. I had e-mail again. Two days later neither the old password nor the new password will work. Please get this straightened out!

- Paraphrase the user's description of the problem.
- What information do you still need to find out from Mr. D'Amato to solve his problem?
- What steps should you take before you respond to this message?

2 A customer calls to complain that she ordered a custom football jersey for her grandson and that she had to send it back twice. The first time, the company sent a jersey for the wrong team. This time, they sent the right team, but they spelled her grandson's name wrong. Now it is the day before his birthday, and she does not have the special present she had promised him. The woman's story is frequently interrupted by tears, and she calls you a few unflattering names. Even worse, she has a strong accent that is difficult to understand when she is crying.

- What techniques should you use in order to get the information you need to help this customer?
- Make a list of phrases that you can use to calm the customer down.

>> >Help Desk Strategies *(continued)*

3 It is almost the end of Marie's shift. She is hungry and thinking about the dinner she is planning tonight. About three minute before she is due to log off, she gets a new call. The caller talks on and on and will not get to the point. Marie feels herself becoming impatient.

- Identify the problems that Marie must deal with.
- What are some of the mistakes Marie might make in this situation?
- What should Marie do to avoid making inappropriate responses to the caller?

Processing and Resolving the Incident

Objectives

After reading this chapter, you will be able to:

1. List the five steps in the problem-solving process.
2. Discuss the importance of collecting appropriate data.
3. Describe the techniques used to determine the root cause of a problem.
4. Explain why creativity plays an important role in problem solving.
5. List the three methods used to evaluate and prioritize possible solutions.
6. Identify several criteria used to determine a plan of action.
7. Explain the responsibilities of a problem owner.
8. Discuss the importance of notification.
9. List five common reasons that problems are escalated.
10. Describe three types of difficult users.
11. List the three components of problem resolution.
12. Discuss the benefits of accurately documenting calls.

Chapter Overview

Chapter 3 discussed the procedures that a help desk analyst should follow when receiving an incident. Once a call has been received, the next step in the incident management process is to develop a solution to the problem. Most user problems are not difficult to resolve, mainly because in all likelihood the help desk has solved the same or a similar problem in the past. Other problems are more complicated and require problem solving. This chapter describes the problem-solving process and several of the techniques that help desk analysts use to solve problems.

4.1 Step 1: Identifying the Problem

Problem solving is a process used to arrive at a solution to a difficult or disruptive situation. There are five steps in the problem-solving process:

1. Identifying the problem
2. Determining the problem's root cause
3. Generating options
4. Evaluating and prioritizing options
5. Determining a course of action

The most common reason that a problem is not solved is misidentification of the problem itself. Many times a symptom of a problem is mistaken for the problem.

If the information collected during the first step of the problem-solving process is not complete or accurate, the solution will be ineffective. This is the meaning of the computer slogan "garbage in, garbage out." The solution to a problem is only as good as the information it is based on.

For example, suppose a user reports that a printer is not working. The help desk analyst who receives the call asks all kinds of questions about the printer, but none about the user's computer. Eventually, it is determined that the problem is a corrupt printer driver on the user's computer. The analyst mistakenly focused on the printer when the problem was in the computer itself. This scenario illustrates the idea that arriving at an effective solution is possible only when the right questions are asked to obtain all the necessary information—even information that may not seem immediately relevant to the user's problem.

In the first step of the problem-solving process, information is collected about the user and the problem.

Collect Data

User data—information about the user—can include the user's name, title, department, and hardware and software configuration. Much of this information may already be stored in a database, so gathering data may just be a matter of confirming that no information has changed since the user's last call. If user configuration data are not stored electronically, this information must be obtained from the caller over the telephone or via the computer.

Problem data—information about the problem itself—can include

1. *Component affected*: The particular piece of hardware or software that is not working as it should.

2. *Symptom*: The disturbance that causes the user to know that a problem exists.

3. *Date and time problem first occurred*: Information needed to determine whether any major changes were made to the system or component around the time the user realized that he or she had a problem.

4. *Description of problem*: A basic one or two sentence statement of the problem as well as a detailed description. An example of a basic problem description is "When user logs onto the network, error message XYZ is displayed." A detailed description of this problem states

   - What the user was doing when the problem occurred (double-clicked network shortcut icon on desktop)
   - What actually happens when the user performs this activity (error message XYZ is displayed)
   - What the user expected to happen (to successfully log onto the network)
   - When the problem happens (for example, only under certain conditions, only at certain times of the day, every time)

Rule Out the Obvious

Many computer problems are easily solved because the solution is an obvious one. Before moving on to more complex problem-solving techniques, it is important to consider the obvious by asking questions such as

- Is everything plugged in?
- Is everything turned on?
- Does rebooting solve the problem?

Once the obvious solutions have been ruled out, the next step is to determine whether a solution exists in the help desk knowledgebase. (The topic of knowledgebases is discussed in Chapter 8.) If a problem was reported to the help desk by another user in the past, a description of the problem and the steps required to solve it should be recorded. The information that is stored about problems and solutions is a great source of knowledge for help desk analysts. This is the major reason for keeping accurate, detailed call records. Call records used to be stored in paper files, but today most companies store them electronically.

✓ **READING CHECK**

1. **READING REVIEW** Identify the most common reason that problems are not solved.

2. **CRITICAL THINKING** During the first phase of problem solving, a help desk analyst collects information about what?

4.2 Step 2: Determining the Cause of the Problem

If information exists about a problem and its solution, in most cases the problem can be solved rather quickly. However, not every problem has a history. When a call comes into the help desk and the problem is a new one, the analyst must work to determine what is causing the problem, and then generate probable solutions. Strategies that can be useful in this process are

- Open-ended and closed-ended questions
- Replication
- Root cause analysis

Open-Ended and Closed-Ended Questions

Just as doctors do when examining a patient with general symptoms, analysts must learn to ask additional questions to narrow down the problem diagnosis. Effective diagnosis requires the use of open-ended and closed-ended questions.

Closed-ended questions can be answered with a simple answer or a yes or no. They are very useful when gathering the basic facts surrounding the problem. Examples of common closed-ended questions are

- Does the computer turn on?
- Is everything plugged in?
- What applications do you have running?
- Have you tried rebooting?
- Is anyone else experiencing the problem?

By using closed-ended questions, analysts gain an overall picture of the situation in a very short time. Often, however, this information is not sufficient for determining the cause of the problem. This is when open-ended questions can be used effectively. **Open-ended questions** are questions that cannot be answered with a yes or no; an explanation is required. These questions have the potential to reveal significant clues for solving the problem. Open-ended questions also provide an opportunity to assess the user's technical knowledge and comfort level by listening closely to the user's use (or lack of use) of technical terms or computer jargon.

In a help desk environment, the following open-ended questions are useful in diagnosing user problems.

1. *Who?* Who is affected? Who is not affected?
2. *What?* It is also helpful to find out what the user was doing when he or she first became aware of the problem. With this information,

the help desk analyst may be able to recreate the steps leading up to the problem, which may provide some clues.

3. *What?* Finding out what the user was doing before the problem occurred can sometimes aid in solving the problem. In some cases, the user may have noticed something different before the problem started. On the other hand, the problem may have come about because of an action the user took, such as deleting files.

Some questions that may help an analyst learn what the user was doing include

- What error message did you receive?
- What is on the screen right now?
- What program were you using?
- What programs do you currently have running?
- What were you doing when the error occurred?
- What (if any) changes were made to your computer recently?

4. *When?* Time and date are important because the user may be unaware of other things occurring at the time of the problem, such as network maintenance and system patches. If the analyst is able to determine that the problem began when the network software was updated, it will be easier to track down the cause of the problem.

To help pinpoint the time of the incident, an analyst can ask the following questions.

- When did the problem begin?
- How often does it occur?
- When does it occur most often? Least often?
- Has it ever happened before?

5. *Why?* Once the who, what, where, and when information is collected, the job of the help desk analyst is to find the answer to the question

- Why is this happening?

Go to

Audio Exercise 4.1

Listen to Audio Exercise 4.1 on the CD in the back of this book. Then, answer the questions below.

1. Has the rep been effective?
2. What kinds of questions could the rep have asked to obtain more information?

Computer Practice 4.1 — Add a New Problem Type

Complete the following exercise using the HelpSTAR software that is on the CD in the back of the book. *Note: The password for all of the sample users in these exercises is 'helpstar'.*

1. Start HelpSTAR.
2. Login as Beth Markham.
3. Select *Administration > Problem Type > New Problem Type* from the main menu. The 'New Problem Type' dialog box will appear.
4. Enter **Software – Accounting** in the 'New' field.
5. Click the 'Save' button. A message will be displayed to indicate that the problem type has been added.
6. Click the 'No' button when prompted to add another problem type.
7. Confirm that the new problem type has been added.
8. Select *Administration > Problem Type > List Problem Types* from the main menu. The 'List All Problem Types' window will be displayed.
9. Locate the newly added problem type in the list.
10. Do not exit HelpSTAR.

Computer Practice 4.2 — Create a New Queue

Complete the following exercise using the HelpSTAR software that is on the CD in the back of the book. *Note: The password for all of the sample users in these exercises is 'helpstar.'*

1. Select *Administration > Queue > New Queue* from the main menu.
2. Enter **Wireless Networking** in the 'New' field.
3. Click the 'Save' button.
4. A message will appear to indicate that the queue has been added.
5. Click the 'OK' button.
6. When prompted to add another queue, click the 'No' button.
7. Confirm that the queue has been added.
8. Select *Administration > Queue > List Queues* from the main menu. The 'List All Queues' window will be displayed.
9. Ensure that the newly added queue is displayed in the list.
10. Close any open windows.

Computer Practice 4.3 — Assign a Queue to Support Reps

Complete the following exercise using the HelpSTAR software that is on the CD in the back of the book.

1. Start HelpSTAR.
2. Login as Beth Markham.
3. Select *Administration > Queue Assignment > Queue to Rep* from the main menu.
4. The 'Assign Queues to Support Rep' dialog box will be displayed.
5. Select 'Wireless Networking' from the drop-down list of queues.
6. Select "John Keyser" from the list of support reps and click the 'Assign' button. His name will be removed from the 'Available' list and appear on the 'Assigned' list.
7. Select "Sandra Liu" from the list of reps and click the 'Assign' button.
8. Click the 'Save' button. A message will appear stating that the queue assignments have been updated and the dialog box will close.
9. Close any open windows.

Replication

If a problem can be replicated, it is easier to identify the cause. **Replication** refers to the process of deliberately taking steps to recreate a problem. For example, suppose a user states that her computer froze when she tried to start *Microsoft Excel* this morning. A help desk analyst may ask how she was trying to start *Excel*, and then may ask her to follow the exact same procedure. Sometimes an analyst will attempt to replicate a problem on a different computer to try to isolate possible causes. If the problem occurs on one computer and not the other, the analyst can examine the configurations of the two computers to determine what is different. Most likely one of the differences is the cause of the user's problem.

Many help desks use remote access software programs that allow them to "see" what is happening on the user's computer while the user tries to replicate the problem. These programs will be described in more detail in Chapter 6.

Some problems cannot be replicated. Most people have had this experience when taking a car in for repair. The owner reports that the car hesitates at speeds over 50 miles per hour. When the mechanic takes the car out for a test drive, there is no hesitation. The problem is more difficult to solve because the mechanic is unable to observe it directly. The same is true for the help desk. If a user cannot duplicate the problem, it will be harder for the analyst to pinpoint the source of the problem. Problems that occur sometimes but not all the time are referred to as **intermittent problems**. Intermittent problems are usually more difficult to eliminate than problems that occur every time an action is performed.

Root Cause Analysis

In an effort to solve user problems as rapidly as possible, some help desk analysts eliminate the symptoms of a problem but not the underlying cause. However, unless the root cause is identified and eliminated, the problem will recur. A familiar example is the case of a tire that has a slow air leak. Stopping by the service station to add air every few days takes away the symptom—low air pressure in the tire. However, adding air does nothing to eliminate the problem. To stop the problem from happening in the first place, it is necessary to determine its root cause—in this case, the reason the tire is losing air.

Root cause analysis is a process that can be used to identify the underlying factors that are causing a problem. The root cause is the source of the problem at its most basic level. If the root cause is eliminated, the problem will not recur.

In root cause analysis, there are three steps of information processing.

1. Identify cause areas.
2. Identify underlying causes.
3. Identify root causes.

To get to the root cause of a problem, you must keep asking the question "why." When there are no more "why" questions to be asked, you have arrived at the root cause. The following example illustrates the process as it is used to determine why a neighbor's home computer will not turn on.

1. Identify cause areas.

Problem: Why will the computer not turn on?

Possible causes: no electricity, unplugged cord, wall switch is not turned on

If the problem is that the cord is unplugged or the wall switch is not turned on, the solution is obvious. However, if the problem is lack of electricity, then additional levels of analysis are required to determine the root cause—why there is no electricity. Identifying the cause of the problem as a lack of power suggests nothing about the root cause of the problem.

2. Identify underlying causes.

Problem: Is the power outage isolated to this house, or is power out in the whole neighborhood?

Possible causes: If the power outage is in the entire neighborhood, the solution is to call the utility company and report the outage. If the problem is that this house has no power, but the rest of the houses in the neighborhood have power, additional analysis must take place to determine the root cause.

3. Identify root causes.

Problem: Why is power out in this house?

Possible causes: outside line to house is down or damaged, circuit breaker is switched off, utility bill is not paid

Fishbone Diagrams

A **fishbone diagram** is a graphic representation used to identify all possible causes of a situation. It shows the relationships between processes and solutions. A fishbone diagram is also a useful tool for identifying root causes (see Figure 4.1).

You create a fishbone diagram by following these steps:

1. Draw a straight line on a blank piece of paper. This line is the "bone."

2. Write a problem statement at the end of the "bone."

3. List potential causes along the top and bottom of the "bone" by drawing lines at a 45 degree angle above and below the straight line. Generate as many alternatives as possible.

4. If a cause has subcauses, draw branches off the cause line to represent them.

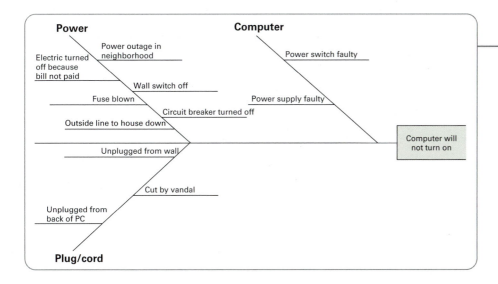

FIGURE **4.1**

A sample fishbone diagram

Once all the causes and subcauses have been listed, each one is examined closely as a possible root cause. They can be ranked from most probable to least probable. The top two or three causes are then pursued.

✔ **READING CHECK**

1. **READING REVIEW** Explain the difference between an open-ended question and a closed-ended question.

2. **CRITICAL THINKING** Explain why is it important to identify the root cause of a problem. Summarize the process of identifying a problem's root cause.

4.3 | Step 3: Generating Options

Effective problem solving requires the use of the left and right sides of the brain. The **left brain** excels at rational and analytical thinking; it also processes language. When following a set of logical steps to solve a problem, the left side of the brain is being used.

When this technique is applied and no satisfactory solution is identified, a right-brain approach may be needed. The **right brain** processes incoming colors, sounds, and patterns; it processes incoming information in a holistic manner. Using the imagination and daydreaming are right-brain activities. It follows, then, that the right brain would be the source of creativity.

To process incoming information and solve problems, both parts of the brain must be used. During the information gathering and diagnosis steps, the left brain plays a dominant role. When it is time to generate solutions, the right brain is at work. See Figure 4.2 for a list of left-brain and right-brain activities.

FIGURE 4.2

Right-brain and left-brain activities

Left Brain Activities	Right Brain Activities
Sequential Thinking	Insight
Sees Details	Imagination
Logical: Cause & Effect	Face Recognition
Language Functions/	Spatial Orientation
Grammar Rules	Drama
Uses Facts	Metaphor/Poetry
Speaks Well	Music
Good With Numbers	Meditation/Prayer
Word Puzzles	Rap/Rhyme
Analyzes	Art/Colors
Names Things	

Sometimes solving a problem requires creative thinking. Approaching the same situation from a different viewpoint can lead to new insights. Creativity requires the suppression of rigid ideas about what might and might not work in a given situation. When thinking creatively, there are no right and wrong answers. The idea is to move outside the usual routines so that fresh ideas can enter in. Brainstorming and thinking outside the box are two creative approaches that can be applied to problem solving in a help desk environment.

Brainstorming

Brainstorming is a group technique that results in creative solutions to a problem. In brainstorming, the idea is to develop as many solutions as possible without judging them. During the process, group members are encouraged to think of unusual ideas and approaches to the problem. When a person is trying to come up with new ideas by brainstorming, the right brain is being used.

When brainstorming, a group states possible solutions to a problem as quickly as possible, without stopping to analyze each idea. A member who has been appointed leader records each suggestion on a large flipchart or blackboard. All suggestions are listed, no matter how far-fetched they might seem. For brainstorming to be effective, all judgment must be withheld. Once no more ideas are generated, the group reviews the ideas and selects those that seem most appropriate.

In a brainstorming session about the problem with the neighbor's computer, possible solutions listed could be

- Blown fuse
- Computer not plugged in
- Wall jack not functioning
- Thunderstorm knocked out power
- Mice chewed through power cord
- Power lines to house were cut

As this list illustrates, the first several ideas generated in a brainstorming session are usually the more obvious possibilities. As the brainstorming session continues, the suggestions become more creative.

Some guidelines for effective brainstorming include the following:

1. Work within a preset time limit.
2. Limit the size of the group to eight or fewer.
3. Include people with varying background and experience in the group.
4. Encourage unusual and improbable ideas.
5. Do not allow criticism or judgment of ideas.
6. Write down all ideas so others can see them and build on them.
7. Maintain a rapid pace.

Thinking Outside the Box

Most people attempt to solve problems by relying on their accumulated knowledge and experiences. Such tools are quite valuable during the problem-solving process. However, sometimes these past experiences limit a person's ability to see alternate solutions.

One example of thinking outside the box is the common nine-dot puzzle. Look at Figure 4.3. Can you connect all the dots by making only four straight lines and without lifting your pen from the paper?

FIGURE 4.3

The Nine Dot Puzzle

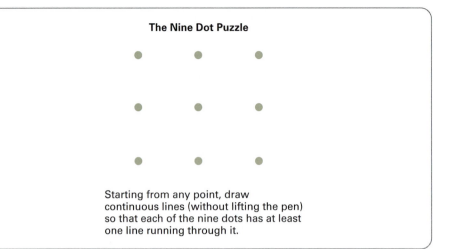

The Nine Dot Puzzle

Starting from any point, draw
continuous lines (without lifting the pen)
so that each of the nine dots has at least
one line running through it.

The solution is illustrated in Figure 4.4 on page 104.

Practice the list of suggestions below to develop creative outside-the-box thinking skills.

- Once you have an answer in mind, come up with a second answer that is also correct.
- Stimulate the right side of the brain by listening to music, working with colored pens and paper, or using another method of your choosing.
- Take on the perspective of a child. As adults, we sometimes overcomplicate situations and miss the obvious.
- Look for relationships among things that seem unrelated.

Computer Practice 4.4 — Search for a Standard Solution

Complete the following exercise using the HelpSTAR software that is on the CD in the back of the book.

1. Select *Search › Standard Solutions* from the main menu.
2. The 'Text Search – Standard Solution' dialog box will be displayed.
3. Enter **desktop and shortcut** in the 'Search Phrase' field.
4. Accept the default entries in the other fields.
5. Click the 'Find' button.
6. The 'Search Results – Standard Solutions' window will list all solutions containing the search phrase. Note the reference number assigned to the Standard Solution.
7. Click the 'View Standard Solution' button (⬚).
8. The Standard Solution Detail window will open.
9. View the details of the solution.
10. Close any open windows.

- Deliberately come up with answers that seem far-fetched.
- Once you have an answer in mind, consider the opposite as a possible solution.
- Revisit ideas that have already been rejected.
- Explain the problem to a five-year-old child.

✓ **READING CHECK**

1. **READING REVIEW** In what part of the problem-solving process is the role of the left brain dominant? When is the right brain more important?

2. **CRITICAL THINKING** Briefly describe the brainstorming process and explain why it is effective for producing solutions to problems.

4.4 Step 4: Evaluating and Prioritizing Options

In the help desk environment, three primary approaches are used to evaluate possible solutions to a problem.

- Module replacement
- Hypothesis testing
- Configuration management

Module Replacement

When a problem is hardware-related, replacing components that might be causing the problem can often solve it. This approach is known as **module replacement**. Components can be removed one at a time and replaced with a module that is known to function. If the problem is eliminated after swapping out a component, the problem is likely a defective component. If the problem is not solved after replacing the part, the original part is reinstalled and another part is removed for module replacement. Similarly, software-related problems can often be remedied by uninstalling and reinstalling the program.

Hypothesis Testing

Hypothesis testing is the process of evaluating each possible solution through testing. The following example illustrates the hypothesis-testing approach in action:

PROBLEM: The neighbor's computer does not turn on.

HYPOTHESIS 1: Power is out to the entire house.
After turning on a light in the kitchen successfully, the next hypothesis is tested.

HYPOTHESIS 2: A fuse has blown.
After checking for a blown fuse and not finding one, the next hypothesis is tested.

HYPOTHESIS 3: The cord has come unplugged from the wall socket.
After checking and finding that the computer is plugged into the wall socket, the next hypothesis is tested, and so on until the problem is solved.

FIGURE **4.4**

Solution to the Nine Dot Puzzle

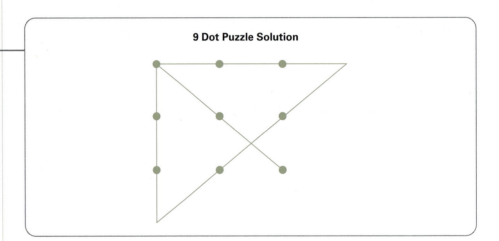

Configuration Management

Sometimes it is difficult to determine whether a problem lies within a particular piece of hardware or software, or whether the problem is the result of its interaction with other devices or programs. For example, in corporate settings, computers are usually hooked up to a network that consists of many wires, switches, and hubs. A software program may also crash only when running at the same time another program is launched.

To solve these types of problems, help desk analysts often revert to a basic configuration. This reversion may include disconnecting the computer from a network, a printer, or other peripheral devices. If the problem seems to be software-related, the user's computer may be rebooted with only those programs running that are necessary to start the computer. Once the computer has been restarted, programs are added back to the configuration one at a time until the culprit is found. While somewhat labor intensive and time consuming, this method can be used to determine the cause of a problem if other methods have failed.

4.5 Step 5: Determining a Course of Action

After identifying the most likely cause of the problem and its solution, an action plan is developed. An **action plan** lists the steps required to solve the problem as well as a timetable for implementation. In a help desk setting, a primary action plan is developed for the most probable solution. One or two alternative action plans are created in the event that the primary solution does not eliminate the problem.

Decision Making

To determine which action plan is primary, an analyst must make a decision about which solution has the greatest likelihood of being successful. **Decision making** is the process of choosing among a number of alternatives. It is a necessary step in the problem-solving process and is used to select the best option once a number of solutions have been generated. Without decision-making skills, a help desk analyst would not be able to solve problems, since it would not be possible to determine which solution should be implemented.

Help desk decisions are based on a set of criteria. The criteria vary according to a particular situation. However, some of the issues considered when solving user problems are

- How quickly a solution can be implemented
- Resources available to implement the solution
- Cost of proposed solution
- Likelihood of eliminating the root cause of the problem

Problem solving requires more than just knowing the techniques; it also requires certain personal qualities. The act of solving a problem can be frustrating when more and more time is devoted to the problem and no solution becomes evident. Hours can be spent trying to correct a situation that, as it turns out, is not the cause of the problem. At this point, an analyst may need to start the process all over. The analyst must find effective methods of handling frustration. This is discussed in more detail in Chapter 10.

Stressful Situations

The problem-solving process can also be stressful. For example, consider a situation in which a senior executive is unable to finalize a report due by the end of the day because he needs sales figures from all regions, and the network link to Asia is down. Stress is, unfortunately, a recurring problem for help desk personnel. Chapter 10 explores ways of minimizing stress in the help desk environment.

Diverse User Base

Finally, problem solving involves the challenge of interacting with a variety of people, each with his or her own personality and communication style. Some users will be courteous, while others may be anxious or angry. To be an effective problem-solver, an analyst must be patient both with the user and with himself or herself. Some users may seem to take forever to answer a question. Others may not be familiar with technical terms that seem very basic to an experienced analyst. Still others may not be skilled in communicating the nature of the problem. Despite the particular qualities of the user, the analyst must always be patient and calm. There is no room in the analyst-user interaction for impatience or annoyance on the part of the problem-solver.

Effective problem solving is partly a science and partly an art. While a logical series of steps must be followed to define the problem and determine the cause, creativity is required to generate and implement solutions.

✓ **READING CHECK**

1. **READING REVIEW** Identify two personal characteristics needed by help desk analysts.

2. **CRITICAL THINKING** Give an example of a frustrating situation that a help desk analyst might encounter.

A University's Help Desk

The University of Tennessee at Chattanooga (UTC) has a help desk that assists members of the faculty and staff by

- Installing and supporting software

- Troubleshooting computing problems

- Upgrading and performing minor repairs on computers and related hardware

- Providing information that helps people at the university use technology and solve problems on their own

In addition to fielding telephone calls from users, UTC help desk analysts make "house calls," or visits to users' offices, when needed. All help desk personnel are expected to write down every action they take in dealing with users' problems and requests. This process aids the UTC technical support group's effort to collect information it needs to keep abreast of computing trends and challenges as they develop.

Like most help desks, the one at UTC receives a heavier volume of calls at some times than at others. Have you ever wondered what desk analysts do when they have no calls to handle? UTC has suggestions for how its help desk analysts can use their time productively when calls are light and they are not working on user problems. Among the suggestions are the following.

- Check the help desk's e-mail account, and enter any e-mailed service requests into the help desk's database.

- Check the service kits that help desk personnel use on "house calls," and organize and restock them as needed. These kits include standard tools and supplies such as Ethernet cables, boot disks, and software setup CDs.

- Check the laptop computers that the help desk lends to users to ensure that they are all accounted for and stored properly, that they have all their accessories, and that they contain only the software and files they are supposed to contain.

- Help keep the help desk's workspace clean and orderly.

- Learn new applications and skills by taking computer-based tutorials, studying books or manuals, and doing research on the Internet.

- Practice installing software and repairing hardware on surplus computers that the help desk keeps for this purpose.

- Reformat and organize blank diskettes for use by the help desk.

Although UTC encourages its help desk analysts to practice and improve their technical skills, it maintains that the best analysts are not necessarily those with the best technical skills. The most important attributes of a help desk analyst are a willingness to take the initiative and keep learning, a friendly attitude toward users, and a mature and professional outlook.

Go to the UTC Web site (www.utc.edu) and locate information on the help desk. Review the information provided.

EXPLORING CAREERS

1. List four tasks that UTC help desk analysts are encouraged to perform when calls are light.

2. In your opinion, is it fair to expect help desk analysts to perform tasks other than helping users, such as cleaning the workspace and reformatting blank diskettes? Write a paragraph explaining your point of view.

4.7 Problem Ownership

Throughout the problem-solving process, a help desk employee must retain ownership of a problem. The idea behind ownership is that one person takes responsibility for seeing the problem through from beginning to end. A major part of owning a problem is providing the user with regular status updates. Some users are more patient than others. However, all users want to know that someone is working on their problem every minute. Without knowing that a person is responsible, a user may feel that the problem has been lost or, worse, that the problem is being ignored.

Obviously some problems take more time to solve. The key to handling these problems effectively is to communicate regularly with the user regarding the status of the problem. The more users are kept informed, the less likely they are to become dissatisfied and complain.

Responsibilities

In most companies, the person with ownership is responsible for communicating regular updates to the user, even if the problem has been escalated or referred to another person. In other companies, ownership changes when a problem is escalated to another person on the help desk.

The problem owner does more than track the progress of the incident and report back to the user. The owner is an advocate for the customer. Part of owning a problem involves working to get it solved on behalf of the user. Once the user places the initial call, he or she should not find it necessary to call the help desk a second time about the same problem. It is up to the problem owner to see the problem through to a satisfactory resolution.

Responsibilities of a problem owner include the following.

- Regular communication with the user regarding problem status
- Continual tracking of the problem, including who is working on it and what progress has been made
- Ensuring that the problem does not get lost or neglected
- Ensuring that the problem has been resolved to the user's satisfaction
- Entering resolution information in the database
- Closing the ticket

Successful problem solving depends on active problem ownership. If each problem does not have an analyst in charge, the problem may not be resolved in a timely manner.

Notification

In addition to updating a user about a problem's status, the problem owner is also responsible for notifying other relevant parties. **Notification** is the process of informing others about a problem. Information must be shared with other help desk personnel for a number of reasons. Another analyst may be on the phone with a user who is experiencing the same problem. If all analysts are aware of problems currently being worked on, joint problem solving is possible. This may result in quicker resolution. If a number of users call in with the same problem at the same time, notification alerts the help desk staff that they are dealing with a more widespread problem than one affecting a single user. Many times, problems affecting multiple users receive higher priority than a problem that is disturbing only a single user. If help desk analysts do not notify each other of the problems they are working on, it would be impossible to know whether the problem was confined or widespread.

Some problems must be reported to help desk management. Companies have different policies about when problems should be reported to management. In some instances, all problems that are not resolved within a specific time (such as 8 hours) must be reported. Most organizations require notifying management immediately when a significant problem, such as a system outage, is affecting a large number of users. If managers are aware of the problem, they have the option of assigning additional staff members to it. Management should also be notified when a user is not satisfied with the service provided by the help desk. This will be discussed later in the chapter.

Notification takes place by phone, e-mail, paging, or other methods as dictated by the personnel involved and the severity of the problem. Critical problems (those affecting many users and/or a key business area) should be reported by the most efficient method. In most cases this is in person or by telephone. E-mail is not appropriate for urgent problem notification; it is commonly used to notify the appropriate parties when a problem is assigned a lower priority.

✓ **READING CHECK**

1. **READING REVIEW** Explain the idea behind ownership of a problem.

2. **CRITICAL THINKING** List the responsibilities of the help desk analyst who owns a problem, and explain why it is critical for an analyst to fulfill these responsibilities.

4.8 Escalating Problems

All help desk analysts, regardless of their level of experience, encounter some problems that they cannot solve. While the optimal choice is to solve all problems at the first level, the reality is that some problems must be transferred before a solution can be found. Problems may be transferred to someone at a higher level within the help desk or in a specialty area such as network support, or even to an outside vendor. Escalation is the transfer of a problem to a higher level of support.

While to some it seems like admitting defeat to hand off a problem, it is actually in the best interests of the user and the help desk to do everything necessary to see that the problem is resolved in a timely manner. It is counterproductive for an analyst to spend too long on any one problem, and it is also counterproductive for a user to wait too long for an answer. For this reason, help desks establish policies about how long a problem can stay with an analyst before it must be transferred. These policies are designed to ensure that problems are handled efficiently.

For example, a company may have a policy that if the first level cannot solve a problem in 20 minutes, it must be escalated to the second level. This works to prevent a first-level analyst from spending too much time on a problem that he or she is unable to resolve quickly. There are exceptions, of course. If, after working on a problem for 20 minutes, an analyst believes that a solution is just a few minutes away, he or she may use discretion and decide to work past the 20 minute time limit. This should be exercised with caution. Management reviews reports on a regular basis. If they notice that an analyst is holding a number of problems beyond 20 minutes and then escalating them anyway, management may review policies with the analyst. Some common reasons for escalation are shown in Table 4.1.

Problem has not been solved within the preset time frame
User reported problem and has not heard back from the help desk
Problem is serious and time critical
Problem is worsening—more than one user is affected
User has a high-level position in the corporation
User feels analyst is talking down to him or her
User cannot understand analyst (e.g., analyst uses technical jargon, has accent)

TABLE   4.1

Common Reasons for Escalation

Escalation Policies

There are typically a number of issues regarding problem escalation that are spelled out in a formal policy, including

1. *Who can decide to transfer a problem?* In addition to the analyst who is working on the problem, most help desks also allow a call to be forcefully taken away from an analyst who is not willing to turn over the problem.

2. *When does escalation occur?* When escalation occurs depends on the nature of the problem and the priority of the call. For example, the policy may state that standard calls are escalated after a given time period, such as 20 minutes, while priority calls must be transferred immediately.

3. *How are problems escalated?* Specific procedures are established that specify the manner in which calls are transferred—by telephone, via e-mail—as well as the information that must be passed on. Enough information must be collected to provide the next level with ample background information on the call. This information should include

   - A clear description of the problem
   - Detailed information about the user and his or her computer configuration
   - The possible cause or causes of the problem
   - A list of causes that have been considered and ruled out
   - Actions taken thus far to diagnose and resolve the problem
   - The severity and priority level assigned to the call

4. *Who has ownership of a transferred problem?* Once a problem has been escalated, the first-level analyst may retain ownership of the

problem. If this is the case, the problem owner is responsible for obtaining regular updates from the second level and communicating this information to the user. In other instances, the new owner may be responsible for tracking the problem and communicating with the user. When a problem is referred to an outside department or vendor, the original analyst almost always maintains ownership of the problem.

Nontechnical Escalation

While most calls are escalated because the current problem owner cannot resolve them, some calls are escalated for nontechnical reasons. Most of these escalations are the result of customer dissatisfaction with the help desk. For example, a user might call to express frustration after a problem has gone unresolved for more than 24 hours. These calls are usually routed to management or to a special group within the help desk that responds to user complaints.

While many technical escalations cannot be avoided, the majority of nontechnical escalations can be prevented, since they are the result of poor customer service. Some analysts are so interested in pursuing a solution that they fail to acknowledge the human side of the situation. At the other end of the phone is a person who is unable to continue working as usual because of a problem. What is it like to be that person?

Many factors influence the customer's current feelings, including work and nonwork issues. Some of these factors may include the following:

- Is this the first problem the customer has had this week, or is it the latest in a string of computer problems?
- Is the problem interfering with a critical deadline?
- Was traffic particularly bad on the way to work?
- Did the customer get a good night's sleep?

Service complaints can also occur due to customer expectations. Users may expect the help desk analyst to do more than offer a solution. They may think that the support person is supposed to come to their desks and fix the problem. This is the reason help desks create Service Level Agreements (SLAs) that specify the details of services that the help desk provides. Even with an SLA in place, nontechnical escalations will occur.

 READING CHECK

1. **READING REVIEW** Explain why help desks limit the amount of time a problem can be assigned to one analyst.

2. **CRITICAL THINKING** Identify the cause of most nontechnical escalations, and analyze why nontechnical escalations occur.

Computer Practice 4.6 — Escalating a Service Request

Complete the following exercise using the HelpSTAR software that is on the CD in the back of the book.

1. Select *Service Requests > My Workspace > In Service* from the main menu.

2. The 'My Workspace – In Service (I'm the Support Rep) – All' window will be displayed.

3. Click the 'Find' button.

4. Select the "Shortcut not Working" request and click the 'Update Service Request' button (🖊). The 'Update Request' window will be displayed.

5. In the 'Forward to:' drop-down box, select 'Another Rep' and choose "John Keyser" from the list that appears.

6. Enter the following text in the memo field: ***Solution # 5 did not work. Appears to be drive mapping issue, escalating to JK*** .

   As the problem seems to have changed from a software issue to a network issue, change the 'Problem Type' from 'Software—Sales Application' to 'Networking' to ensure that the request is properly categorized.

7. Click the 'Save' button.

8. Click the 'Refresh' button (🔄) on the toolbar to refresh the window. The "Shortcut not Working" request should no longer be visible in your service as the request has been escalated to John Keyser.

9. Exit HelpSTAR.

4.9 Dealing with Difficult Users

The majority of help desk calls begin and end without incident. Most people who call are pleasant and eager to receive help. Likewise, most help desk staff members are capable and respectful when they try to troubleshoot problems. Occasionally a user will present a challenge to the analyst. Several types of difficult users are described in the following section, along with tips for handling the interactions.

The Angry Caller

Occasionally, calls are received from users who are angry—not necessarily at the help desk, but angry nevertheless. What is the best way to deal with an angry caller? Be prepared. Before a call comes in, there should be a plan in place for dealing with difficult users. This may be a formal procedure listed in a policy manual or handbook, or it may be something new employees learn during orientation to the help desk.

One of the best ways of handling the caller's anger is to be silent. In other words, listen but do not respond except for an occasional comment that indicates that you are listening. For example, use phrases such as "I see" and "That must be very frustrating." Angry users want a response; they want to know that their anger is having an effect. If they get no response from the other person, most angry callers will run out of steam rather quickly, since they have no one to whom they can direct their anger. Think of the last time that you were very angry. Without someone else around, it is not likely that you ranted and raved for too long.

It is very difficult to stand by and remain silent when the person on the other end of the phone is angry. On the other hand, if the help desk analyst tries to defend himself or herself, or tries to argue with the caller, the anger could become worse. This outcome is an example of the saying, "don't add fuel to a burning fire." Even an attempt to reason with an angry user is not effective.

The best strategy is to remain quiet, listen, and give the person the opportunity to vent the anger. Once the person has finished speaking, it may be appropriate to empathize with the caller by saying something to indicate that you understand how he or she feels. For example, if a user is angry that the problem interfered with meeting an important deadline, you might say, "I can understand how angry that must have made you." Whatever you say, say it slowly and in a calm tone of voice. Speaking slowly also helps to turn down the pace of the conversation, as angry callers tend to speak rapidly.

Guidelines for dealing with angry users include the following:

- Let the caller speak; do not interrupt.
- Acknowledge the user's anger, do not ignore it.
- Remind yourself that you have done nothing to cause the person's anger, even though you may receive the brunt of it.
- Maintain a neutral, calm demeanor.
- Offer to help with the problem, just as you would with any other user.

Go to

Audio Exercise 4.2

Listen to Audio Exercise 4.2 on the CD in the back of this book. Then, answer the questions below.

1. Why was Bob so angry?
2. Was Bob's anger justified?
3. How could the rep have handled the interaction more effectively?

Introduction to Help Desk Concepts and Skills

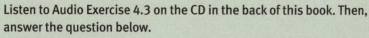

Audio Exercise 4.3

Listen to Audio Exercise 4.3 on the CD in the back of this book. Then, answer the question below.

1 How could the rep have handled this situation more effectively?

The Abusive Caller

If an angry caller should become abusive, steps must be taken right away to eliminate the abuse or terminate the call. The same goes for a caller who is not angry but who is verbally abusive.

What constitutes abuse in a help desk environment? Abuse can be derogatory remarks directed toward the analyst, or other remarks that make the analyst feel uncomfortable. The use of profanity that is directed toward a help desk employee is considered inappropriate in a professional environment. Negative comments about the analyst's color, race, age, or gender are always inappropriate and usually abusive. In addition, negative statements that reflect on the analyst's knowledge or ability may be abusive. For example, an abusive caller might say, "You have no idea what you are talking about. You don't have a brain in your head. And you think you can help me? Forget it. Let me talk to someone else." Other examples of abuse include harassment (frequent phone calls or e-mail messages from a user who is dissatisfied with the outcome of a problem) and threats (such as "I'm going to do everything to see that you are fired if you don't fix this computer now").

What should be done when a call becomes abusive? There is no need to continue trying to help a user who is abusive. Calmly tell the user that if the conversation continues in this tone, the call will be terminated. For example, you might say, "If you are going to continue speaking like this, I am going to end the call." At this point, users who really want help will stop, while those who are more interested in attacking you will continue to do so.

If the abuse continues after you have told the user that the behavior will not be tolerated, terminate the call and report the incident to the appropriate person in the department. It is possible that the user will call and complain about you, so it is wise to report all abusive incidents when they happen. Nothing may come of it, but at least the incident has been reported and documented. If another help desk employee reports a problem with the same user, someone from the help desk may speak to the individual about appropriate behavior when requesting service from the help desk.

Did You Know?

Who is responsible for the famous customer service quote, "Nobody ever won an argument with a customer"?

Answer: L. L. Bean

The Talkative User

Sometimes it may seem like a user is more interested in chatting than in finding a resolution to a problem. In reality, the problem must take priority, or else the user and the help desk analyst waste valuable time. When working with this type of caller, the analyst must take control of the call. Closed-ended questions can be quite effective when trying to focus a user on the problem. The following example illustrates the use of closed-ended questions.

> **USER:** I can't seem to dial out to the Internet this morning.

> **ANALYST:** What error message did you receive?

> **USER:** Something about a TCP/IP error.

> **ANALYST:** What is on your screen right now?

> **USER:** Oh, a bunch of icons. Some are for programs, others are documents I use regularly, and some, well, and I'm not sure what they are. Do you have any idea what this one is—it looks like an arrow pointing to the right with a yellow flame going through it.

> **ANALYST:** Let's focus on the problem you called about—you are unable to get on the Internet.

> **USER:** Okay. You know lately I have noticed that when I am connected to the Internet, it is very slow. Someone from tech support recently installed a new sound card in my computer; do you think that would cause my slow Internet access?

> **ANALYST:** Actually, I think for now we should take one problem at a time. Tell me exactly what you did when you tried to access the Internet this morning.

> **USER:** Well, I was having my coffee when my wife called to say I left my cell phone at home. I did the same thing I do every morning—clicked the icon for Internet Explorer. By the way, I heard Netscape just came out with a new version of their browser—should I be using that instead of Explorer?

As the conversation continues, the analyst recognizes that she must take control of the conversation, or it will go on for hours. At this time, she switches to closed-ended questions, in an attempt to focus the user on the current problem and minimize the chatter.

ANALYST: Did you check that all the cables are plugged in to the back of your computer

USER: No.

ANALYST: Please look at the back of your computer and see that everything is plugged in. Do you see cables that are not connected?

USER: No, unless you mean the phone line.

ANALYST: Are you sure it is a telephone line?

USER: Well, not exactly. It looks like one but it is a little bigger.

ANALYST: It sounds like the cable that connects you to the network has come unplugged.

The call ends soon after it is discovered that the Ethernet cable had come unplugged from the back of the user's computer. This example illustrates the value of using closed-ended questions when responding to users who spend time talking about issues other than the main problem.

✓ READING CHECK

1. **READING REVIEW** Should help desk analysts try to defend themselves against users' anger? Why?

2. **CRITICAL THINKING** What should a help desk analyst do if a user continues to be abusive?

Audio Exercise 4.4

Listen to Audio Exercise 4.3 on the CD in the back of this book. Then, answer the question below.

❶ What should the rep have done to guide the user toward providing the information needed to solve the problem?

Dealing with Difficult Users

Angel Reese, a first-level help desk analyst for Huron Insurance Company, took a call from a user who was experiencing a problem with a monitor. Following the help desk's standard script, Angel first asked the user's name, telephone number, and office location. Then he asked for information about the user's computer setup and operating system.

The user responded angrily. "Operating system? What difference does it make? Just bring me a new monitor!" Then the user hung up.

Angel waited a few minutes, then called the user. When Angel identified himself, the user snapped, "Where's my new monitor?" Angel explained that the help desk's standard procedure for diagnosing and solving problems required him to ask a few questions before installing a new monitor. He said he needed to know about the operating system because problems that appeared to be signs of hardware malfunction were often the result of software corruption or conflicts.

"Okay, okay, I'm using Windows 2000," the user replied. "Now can I get a new monitor?" Angel asked him to describe the problem with the monitor. "I already told you," the user said. "The screen is blank!" Angel asked if the monitor seemed to be getting power. When the user said it did, Angel asked what the user was doing when the screen went blank. "I wasn't doing anything," the user replied. "I turned on the computer, went to get some coffee while it booted up, and when I came back all I had was a blank blue screen."

Angel then asked him to reboot the computer. As he did so, Angel asked the user if any error messages appeared on the screen. No, the user replied impatiently, the screen was blank, just like before. When Angel asked him to check the monitor's connection to the computer, the user said he had done that before he called the help desk.

Angel decided to connect a new monitor to the user's computer. If it functioned correctly, he would assume that the problem was indeed with the user's monitor and not with the software. If the new monitor did not work either, Angel would transfer the call to a level-two analyst.

As Angel began to disconnect the user's old monitor, he noticed that the connection was loose. He tightened it and rebooted the computer. This time, the monitor showed the operating system's startup screen. Angel had solved the problem without replacing the monitor. However, it had taken him 45 minutes, more than twice as much time as he was supposed to spend on a call.

APPPLYING SKILLS

1. Did Angel follow the correct procedure to solve the user's problem? Outline the procedure he followed, and point out what, if anything, he should have done differently.

2. Do you think Angel handled the user's impatience well? Write a paragraph that states your opinion and your reasons for it.

4.10 Resolving Calls

Call resolution occurs when a solution that is implemented results in the elimination of the problem. Note that the sentence does not say that calls are resolved when symptoms are eliminated. As discussed earlier in this chapter, eliminating a symptom will not prevent the problem from recurring; the root cause must be identified.

A small percentage of calls involve issues that cannot be resolved. There are a number of reasons why problems are not successfully resolved. The user may have discovered a bug in a software program that will not be fixed until the next version of the program is released. Sometimes a workaround is the only option. For example, a user complains of numerous system freezes while running two particular programs at the same time. After troubleshooting the problem and contacting both vendors, the analyst concludes that the two programs are incompatible. The only way the user can avoid the crashes is to run the programs one at a time.

Closing Calls

Once the resolution or outcome has been communicated to the user, the next step is to close the call. Closing refers to the process of explaining why the problem occurred and the steps required to resolve it. It is paramount that the user understands what is going to happen next, whether the help desk will carry out the steps, or if the user must be involved. If the user is to participate in the resolution, it is important to walk the user through the steps required for implementation.

Determining User Satisfaction

Confirming that the user is satisfied with a solution is an essential part of the incident management process. Listen closely to make sure the user is comfortable with the solution. This includes determining whether the user is confident that the solution will resolve the problem, and whether the problem is being eliminated within the user's preferred time frame. Of course it is not always possible to satisfy a user, but showing concern and interest can go a long way toward establishing a positive image of the help desk.

Be sure to thank the person for providing the help desk with the opportunity to be of service, and remind the caller that the help desk is always ready to assist should the current problem recur or another problem arise.

Following-Up

Even though it is referred to as closing a call, the analyst–user interaction does not end with the closing phone call. Within a specified period of time, usually a few days, the analyst follows up with the user to make certain that everything is working as it should. If the response is positive, thank the user and remind him or her that the help desk is there if future problems develop. If the problem persists, reopen the case and engage additional resources in order to provide a timely solution for the user.

✓ **READING CHECK**

1. **READING REVIEW** When is a call considered resolved?

2. **CRITICAL THINKING** Analyze why it is important for a help desk analyst to follow up after a call is resolved.

Computer Practice 4.7   Close a Service Request

Complete the following exercise using the HelpSTAR software that is on the CD in the back of the book.

1. Start HelpSTAR.

2. Login as John Keyser. To login as John Keyser, click the 'Find User' magnifying glass icon to the right of the 'User Name' field. Locate John Keyser in the list and double-click on his entry. Then enter the password (helpstar) and click the Login button.

3. Click OK to close the 'Tips' window that is displayed.

4. Select *Service Requests > My Workspace > In Service* from the main menu.

5. The 'My Workspace – In Service (I'm the Support Rep) – All' window will be displayed.

6. Click the 'Find' button.

7. Select "Shortcut Not Working" and click the 'Update Service Request' button (🖹).

8. In the 'Forward to:' drop-down box, select 'Close'.

9. Enter the following text in the memo field: *Network drive not properly mapped in the login script. Updated user's login script, problem resolved.*

10. Click the 'Save' button. The 'Update Request' window will close.

11. Notice that the request is still listed as being 'In Service'.

12. Click the 'Refresh' button (🔁). The request will disappear from the 'In Service' list. The 'No Items Were Found' Message is displayed as there are no longer any items in the list. Click OK.

13. Confirm that the request has been closed.

14. Select *Service Requests > All Requests > Closed* from the main menu.

15. The 'All Closed Requests – All' window will appear. Click the 'Find' button.

16. The 'Date Range' dialog box will be displayed.

17. Accept the default dates or change as necessary. Click the 'OK' button.

18. The list of closed requests will be displayed.

19. Locate the desired request (you may sort the list by clicking on a column heading).

20. Exit HelpSTAR.

4.11 Documenting Calls

Some help desk analysts dislike documenting call resolutions. Once the problem has been solved and the user is up and running, the challenge is over. The documentation process is seen as extraneous paperwork. However, the information obtained as a result of the help desk intervention is not useful to others until it is documented.

Information and Knowledge

Information by itself is not the same as knowledge. Information may or not be useful to another person. If the other person is able to apply the information in a useful manner, the information is then considered **knowledge**. It follows that documenting the cause of a problem and the steps taken to resolve it is an important aspect of the analyst's job. No help desk call is complete until the problem has been appropriately documented. This is especially important when a problem is a new one that has not been reported to the help desk in the past. By recording information about the problem, its cause, and its solution, the information becomes available to other analysts who may be trying to solve similar problems. The key to successful problem documentation on the help desk is recording information in a way that makes it useful to others.

Analysts should always record the following primary information about a help desk incident.

- A description of the problem, including information about the caller, the hardware and software configuration, and the problem itself
- A list of the troubleshooting steps that were taken, including successful and unsuccessful attempts to solve the problem
- The actual problem resolution, including steps taken to fix the problem and follow-up contact with the user

Benefits of Documenting Calls

One of the major benefits of call tracking is the ability to identify trends. For example, management can review the call logs and determine the time of day when the call volume is at its peak; it may be necessary to add additional staff members during that period of time. By studying how often a problem has been reported over a period of time, help desk personnel can determine whether a problem is increasing or decreasing in frequency. If the problem is occurring more often, a team is assigned to determine the reason for the rise in incidents, and a solution can be implemented. If many users are experiencing the same problem, and if that problem is a user error rather than a technological error, there may be a need for user training in that area.

Problem tracking data are also used to create management reports. Help desk reporting is described in detail in Chapter 7. Reports contain information such as the number of times a problem has been reported, the number of support calls from a particular department, and the length of time until a problem was resolved.

Clearly, the information recorded about a call is of great value to the help desk. However, this information is only as good as the data that are recorded by the analyst. If others cannot understand the problem description and the steps taken to fix the problem, they are of little value to the help desk. Solutions that are written poorly may be misunderstood by others and result in incorrect problem diagnoses.

✓ **READING CHECK**

1. **READING REVIEW** Summarize why it is important for help desk analysts to document the calls they handle.

2. **CRITICAL THINKING** List the information that a help desk analyst records about each call, and explain why this information is important to document.

>> Summary

The following points were covered in this chapter:

1. The five steps in the problem-solving process are identifying the problem, determining the root cause, generating options, evaluating and prioritizing options, and determining a course of action.

2. It is important to collect appropriate data because identifying the cause of the problem is very difficult if the information collected is not complete and accurate.

3. Techniques that are used to find the root cause of a problem include open-ended and closed-ended questions, replication, and root cause analysis.

4. Creativity plays an important part in problem solving because it can be used to generate solutions to problems that have never occurred before and to problems that for one reason or another cannot be solved using other methods. Brainstorming to produce an uncensored collection of possible solutions is an example of the use of creativity in problem solving.

5. Three techniques used to evaluate and prioritize solutions are module replacement, hypothesis testing, and configuration management.

6. An action plan takes into account issues such as how quickly a solution can be implemented, the availability of resources to implement the plan, the cost of the proposed solution, and the likelihood that the solution will eliminate the problem.

7. Throughout the problem-solving process, a help desk employee must take ownership of the problem, which means seeing it through to its resolution. This includes providing the user with frequent status reports so he or she does not feel ignored.

8. It is important to notify other help desk analysts about problems because they may be working on the same problem, and joint problem solving can be beneficial. If multiple users call in with the same problem at the same time, notification alerts the help desk staff that they are dealing with a more widespread problem than one affecting a single user.

9. Call escalation is when a call is transferred from one analyst to another analyst who can help resolve the problem more quickly. Common reasons problems are escalated are that the problem is not being solved within the preset time frame, the user has not received a response, the problem is serious and time critical, the user holds a high position, and the user is unable to understand the analyst.

10. Three types of difficult users are angry users, abusive users, and talkative users.

11. The three components of problem resolution are closing the call, determining user satisfaction, and following-up on the call.

12. Documenting calls helps other analysts who are dealing with the same problem. It aids help desk management in spotting trends and challenges as they develop. It also provides others on the help desk with valuable information, because most problems reported to help desks have already been dealt with earlier.

>> Key Terms

The following terms were defined in this chapter:

<table>
<tr><td>a</td><td>action plan</td><td>k</td><td>module replacement</td></tr>
<tr><td>b</td><td>brainstorming</td><td>l</td><td>notification</td></tr>
<tr><td>c</td><td>call resolution</td><td>m</td><td>open-ended questions</td></tr>
<tr><td>d</td><td>closed-ended questions</td><td>n</td><td>problem data</td></tr>
<tr><td>e</td><td>decision making</td><td>o</td><td>problem solving</td></tr>
<tr><td>f</td><td>fishbone diagram</td><td>p</td><td>replication</td></tr>
<tr><td>g</td><td>hypothesis testing</td><td>q</td><td>right brain</td></tr>
<tr><td>h</td><td>intermittent problems</td><td>r</td><td>root cause analysis</td></tr>
<tr><td>i</td><td>knowledge</td><td>s</td><td>user data</td></tr>
<tr><td>j</td><td>left brain</td><td></td><td></td></tr>
</table>

>> Reviewing Key Terms

Write the letter of the key term that matches each definition below:

_____ **1** The process of removing suspected faulty components and replacing them with components that are known to be working.

_____ **2** A process used to arrive at a solution to a situation that is difficult or disruptive.

_____ **3** A list of the steps required to solve the problem as well as a timetable for implementation.

_____ **4** Information about the problem, including the component affected, the symptom, the time the problem first occurred, and a description of the problem.

_____ **5** Questions that can be answered with a simple yes or no.

_____ **6** A process of deliberately taking steps to recreate the problem.

_____ **7** A process used for identifying the underlying factors that are causing a problem.

_____ **8** A graphic representation used to identify all possible causes of a situation that shows the relationships between processes and solutions.

_____ **9** A group technique used to generate as many solutions as possible without judgment.

_____ **10** Questions that require answers with explanations.

_____ **11** A process of evaluating each possible solution through logical testing.

>> Reviewing Key Terms *(continued)*

_____ 12 A process of choosing among a number of alternatives.

_____ 13 The side of the brain that is the site of rational and analytical thinking.

_____ 14 Information about the person who is experiencing the problem, such as name, title, department, and hardware and software configuration.

_____ 15 Implementation of a solution that eliminates the problem.

>> Reviewing Key Facts

True/False

Identify whether each statement is True (T) of False (F). Rewrite the false statements so that they are true.

_____ 1 Help desk analysts may return a computer to a more basic configuration to help determine the cause of a problem.

_____ 2 Problems are easier to solve if they can be replicated.

_____ 3 A fishbone diagram shows an office layout and is a useful tool for showing the location of the user's computer.

_____ 4 The time a problem occurred can provide valuable clues about the cause of a problem.

_____ 5 One of the first things an analyst does when approaching a problem is to determine whether information about the problem is stored in a knowledgebase.

_____ 6 Information becomes knowledge whenever it is shared with another person.

_____ 7 Better customer service would prevent most nontechnical escalations of help desk calls.

_____ 8 A help desk analyst need not continue trying to help a caller who has become abusive.

_____ 9 Call resolution occurs when the symptoms of the user's problem have been eliminated.

_____ 10 Closing a call is the process of explaining to the user why the problem occurred and the steps required to resolve it.

Completion

Write the answer that best completes the following statements:

1 Creativity is a function of the _____ side of the brain.

2 _____ is a technique that tries to find the cause of a problem by intentionally recreating the problem.

3 Altering a user's hardware or software to return it to a more basic state is known as _____.

4 A help desk analyst can ask _____ questions to keep a talkative user focused on the problem.

5 The primary information the help desk should record about each call includes description of the problem, a list of the _____ that were taken, and the ultimate resolution of the problem.

Chapter 4 Review

>> Understanding Key Concepts

Provide brief answers to the following questions:

1. What are the benefits of asking closed-ended and open-ended questions, respectively? In root cause analysis, what are the three steps of information processing, in order?

2. What can a help desk analyst do to ensure that a user is satisfied with the resolution of a problem, and why is it important to do it?

>> Critical Thinking

As directed by your instructor, write a brief essay or discuss the following issues in groups.

1. Why are some problems harder to solve than others?

2. Which step of the problem-solving process do you think is most important? Why?

3. The problem is that a CD player located in the trunk of a car will not play. How would you test each of the following hypotheses about this problem?
   - The car's battery is dead.
   - A fuse is blown.
   - The CD player has become unplugged from the wiring harness.

>> Help Desk Projects

Complete the projects listed below:

1. **Ask a classmate, friend, or family member to describe a recent problem with a computer.** (Make sure you tell them not to tell you the resolution of the problem.) Using the problem-solving tools and techniques described in this chapter, identify the root cause of the problem.

2. **If your school has a help desk, see if you can obtain permission to observe an analyst who is taking calls from users.** Listen closely, and identify the problem-solving techniques used by the analyst. List the actions that were performed during each stage of the problem-solving process.

3. **A user reports that when she sends a report to the printer, the pages are blank.** Create a fishbone diagram to identify all possible causes of the problem.

4. **As an exercise in using the right side of your brain,** develop a 10-minute explanation of how a computer works that would be clear to someone who has never used a computer.

>> Help Desk Projects *(continued)*

5 **Imagine that a user is trying to access a Web site and gets the message "The page cannot be displayed."** Form a brainstorming team to develop all possible reasons for the failure. Appoint one person to write down all suggestions on a flipchart as quickly as possible. Once there are no more suggestions, decide as a group which two reasons are the most likely cause of the problem.

6 **Team up with a classmate, and take turns playing the roles of an angry user and a help desk analyst who takes the user's call.** Each call should take no more than five minutes. Afterward, discuss whether the responses of the person in the help desk analyst role were likely to make the user more angry or less angry and what responses, if any, might have been more productive.

7 **A user calls to report that his laptop computer will not work on battery power.** Make a list of the questions you would ask him. Note whether each question is open-ended or closed-ended.

8 **Compose a brief paragraph noting the information that you would record about the following situation.** A user calls the help desk because her laptop computer will not run on battery power. You ask her to check its power-use settings and tell you what they are, and they turn out to be correct. Next, you ask her to leave the computer's power cord plugged in for an hour to charge the battery and to call you back before she tries to use the battery again. When she calls back, you ask her to detach the power cord from the computer and tell you what happens. She says the computer shuts down. You then ask her to try restarting the computer without plugging it in, and she tells you that it does not start up. You replace the battery, and that solves the problem.

9 **Write a description of your own personality and temperament in terms of your aptitude for a help desk career.** For example, would you describe yourself as a methodical or as a creative person? Would you rather work alone or as part of a team? How do you generally deal with difficult people and tense situations? Do you think clearly under pressure? Use examples to support what you say about yourself.

>> Help Desk Strategies

Review the following case studies and respond to the questions:

1 A help desk analyst takes a call from a frantic user who is afraid she has lost all the data on her hard disk. She reports that her computer is on but that she sees nothing on the screen. She seems to be in a panic and not thinking clearly, because she has made several contradictory statements.

- What could the analyst do to calm the user?

- What closed-ended questions could the analyst ask to rule out an obvious cause of the problem?
- If closed-ended questions did not provide enough information to solve the problem, what are some open-ended questions the analyst might ask?

2 An hour after the office opens, a user calls the help desk to report that he has been unable to log in to the network since he arrived at work. When he enters his ID and password, he gets an error message telling him that either the ID or password is invalid. He has tried this several times, always with the same result. On the previous day, he was able to log in with no problem. The analyst can see from her own computer that the network is operating normally, and no other users have called the help desk to report problems logging in today.

- What are some possible causes of the user's problem?
- How could the analyst determine which of the possibilities is the most likely cause?

3 An analyst takes a call from a user who cannot upload photographs from his digital camera to his PC, as he has done in the past. The call is directed to a first-level analyst, which is company policy for an initial call about any problem. The first-level analyst has no experience with digital camera connections, but the help desk has a senior analyst who specializes in problems with peripheral devices, including cameras. The first-level analyst collects information about the user's hardware, operating system, and the application he uses to upload photographs. The analyst also obtains a description of what happened when the user tried to upload the photographs, but the description does not provide the analyst with any ideas about how to solve the problem. The analyst has not yet reached his time limit for solving the problem, but he is not confident that he can find the solution.

- What other steps might the analyst take to find a solution?
- What tools might the analyst use?
- What can the help desk do for the user if the analyst cannot solve the problem in a short time?

Chapter  5

Computer Telephony Integration

Objectives

After reading this chapter, you will be able to:

1. Explain the need for automated help desk telephone systems.
2. Describe the functions of an automated call distributor (ACD).
3. Describe the benefits of skill-based routing.
4. Discuss the features of Interactive Voice Response (IVR) applications.
5. Explain how Automatic Speech Recognition (ASR) is used in a help desk.
6. Discuss the importance of computer telephony integration (CTI).
7. Describe the benefits of a unified queue.
8. List common statistics captured by a computer telephony integration (CTI) application.

Chapter Overview

Help desks have been under increasing pressure to support greater numbers of users with fewer resources. To effectively respond to the growing demands placed on the modern help desk, new telephone systems were required. This chapter provides an introduction to telephone-based tools and technologies that the help desk relies on to meet the needs of computer users.

In the past, most user requests reached the help desk via the telephone, and the primary technology was the telephone system. Incoming calls were handled by a switchboard operator, who manually connected the caller with a help desk agent.

Over time, as more people began using technology on the job, the number of user calls began to increase. To be successful, help desks had to be able to efficiently receive and route large numbers of incoming calls. Due to the sheer volume of calls, this had to be accomplished without human intervention. To manage and route a large volume of incoming calls, help desks began to use automated telephone systems.

Private Branch Exchange (PBX)

Telephone systems in businesses are much more complex than home telephones. In a home system, one line connects the telephone to the telephone network. If a family has more than one phone line, each phone line connects separately to the telephone network. It would be very expensive for a company to follow this home system model and connect each employee's line to the network.

To avoid these high costs, companies use PBX systems. A **private branch exchange (PBX)** is an internal telephone network in which users share a certain number of lines for making telephone calls outside the company. In a similar fashion, a PBX allows calls coming into the company from external telephone lines to be routed to internal employees using shared local lines (see Figure 5.1).

In a PBX system, blocks of telephone numbers are assigned to a company. The company in turn assigns a unique phone number to each employee. While the phone numbers are different, the physical telephone lines carrying the calls are shared. For example, if there were 500 separate

FIGURE 5.1

A diagram of a PBX network

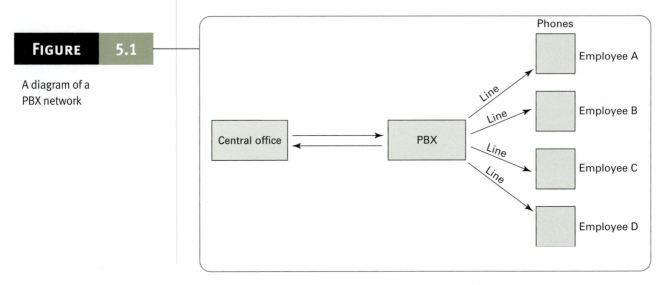

employee phone numbers, there might only be 125 physical lines. The number of internal-external lines in use at any one time would be limited to 125. If all 125 lines were in use, employees would not be able to dial out, and outside callers would receive a busy signal until one of the 125 lines became available.

A PBX is much less expensive than connecting an external telephone line to every telephone in the organization. It also allows internal users to communicate with each other by dialing extension numbers, such as 4409, rather than complete phone numbers. It is easier to call someone within a PBX because the number to dial is typically just 3 or 4 digits long. The PBX is the backbone of most companies' telephone systems.

Centrex Systems

An alternative to a PBX system is a **Centrex** (central exchange services) system, in which a pool of telephone lines is leased at the phone company's central office. All the equipment is at that central office, rather than within the company, and the call routing takes place there.

The single most important difference between the PBX and Centrex systems is the ownership and location of the equipment. In a PBX system, the company owns and maintains the equipment on its site. A Centrex system is a service provided by a telephone company, which owns and houses the equipment at their location.

Advantages of a Centrex system include the following.

- The company does not have to purchase and maintain equipment or provide floor space.
- There is no limit to the number of employees who may request an outside line at any given moment.
- It is easy to set up and can easily be upgraded.
- There is high reliability of services.
  Disadvantages of a Centrex system include the following.
- The company lacks control over the system—all requests for changes must be made to the telephone company.
- It has fewer features than many PBX systems.
- There is little control over the quality of service provided.
- Over the long-term, it costs more to lease equipment than to purchase a system.

✔ **READING CHECK**

1. **READING REVIEW** List the components of a PBX system.

2. **CRITICAL THINKING** Evaluate whether you would rather work in an office with an automated phone system or one in which human beings route calls from a switchboard.

5.2   Automated Call Distributors

The next major change in help desk telephone technology was the implementation of automatic call distributors. **Automated call distributors (ACDs)** are telephone systems that route calls, prioritize calls, and play recorded messages. These systems also record statistics, such as the number of calls in the system, the number of dropped calls, and the average hold time. ACD systems are in widespread use in large part because of the many features they offer, including the ability to

- Inform callers of the current hold time to reach an agent
- Route calls based on specific caller or agent criteria
- Place a call in more than one queue
- Allow agents to receive calls from more than one queue
- Allow managers to monitor live calls
- Allow managers to view real-time data
- Collect call data
- Produce management reports

In a user-support environment, two of the most important functions of an ACD system are call routing and data collection.

Call Routing

One of the major benefits of an ACD system is its ability to route a call to the appropriate help desk analyst without the need for human intervention. The system uses the telephone keypad for information input that routes the call to a particular support group. The call routing feature of an ACD requires callers to listen to a menu of choices. Using the Touch-Tone keypad on the telephone, they select from the choices and push the corresponding button on the telephone keypad. Most people are familiar with this basic form of routing—press 1 for sales, press 2 for services, press 3 for warranty information, and so on.

Routing systems are also used to ensure that calls are answered within an acceptable period of time. The rules for this aspect of the routing system are determined by the help desk's Service Level Agreement (SLA). Service Level Agreements (SLAs) are discussed in Chapter 7. Using data from the SLA, the system is programmed to take the length of the queues into account and to route calls accordingly. For example, if the wait in a queue exceeds a set amount of time, a team of overflow agents is activated, and new calls are routed to them until the queue reaches an acceptable level.

An ACD system allows calls to be routed in any number of ways, depending on the resources available as well as the needs of the users. Before an ACD system is implemented, the organization develops a routing map and a corresponding set of rules that specify the path of calls depending on whether certain conditions are met. In the sample map in Figure 5.2, calls are routed according to the nature of the problem. One group of agents receives all PC hardware calls, another group receives network hardware issues, and so on.

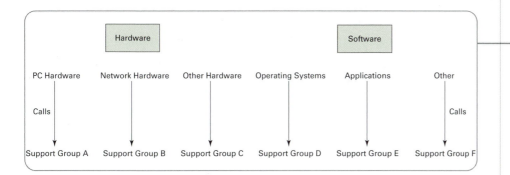

FIGURE 5.2

Call routing with an ACD system

Even in smaller help desks, routing systems are rarely that simple. For example, most routing software is programmed to consider

- The priority level of the call (based on urgency, caller's position, and other factors)
- The skills needed to resolve the call and the agents who possess those skills (specific skills such as network troubleshooting, knowledge of *Excel* macros)
- The length of time an agent has been idle (minutes of talk time versus idle time in a given period)

Routing software is also dynamic; it is capable of responding in real time to an exception to the rules. If there are five calls waiting in a queue and a new call comes in from a senior vice president, the routing system is capable of moving that call ahead of the other five already in the queue. Likewise, in a corporation with international offices, calls can be routed according to the user's language preference.

Methods for Routing Calls

One very popular method of routing calls is **skill-based routing (SBR)**. The purpose of SBR is to forward the call to the agent who can best handle the request, with the goal of solving the problem as efficiently as possible. In the past, ACDs could transfer calls from one queue to another when wait times exceeded an allowed limit. This did not necessarily provide faster service, since the waiting just continued in another queue. With skill-based routing, help desk managers can now determine in real time which group of agents is best equipped to handle a unique caller, given the characteristics of the caller, the waiting time in the various queues, and how fast calls are being routed. The key is to find the routing arrangement that provides maximum efficiency, productivity, and user satisfaction.

A secondary purpose of skill-based routing is to keep the agents at maximum productivity. An SBR system takes into account individual agent skills as well as call priority in assigning tickets to an agent. SBR technology offers the promise of increased efficiency and better utilization of help desk resources.

The SBR features of today's ACD systems allow companies to define a set of rules for call handling. A sample rule set is pictured in Figure 5.3. The most common types of SBR are described below.

Skills-Based Routing with Multiple Agent Groups

Some ACDs provide skill-based routing by allowing an agent to belong to more than one group simultaneously. For example, an agent with skills in *Windows* operating systems area would belong only to that agent group. An agent with skills in *UNIX* would belong only to the *UNIX* agent group. Agents with skills in *Windows* and *UNIX* would be members of both agent groups.

Skills-Based Routing with User Defined Rules

Another way ACDs can provide skills-based routing is through custom rules developed by the company. These rules may be as simple or as complex as desired. For example, a call can be routed to

- A specific agent with whom a user has a positive history
- A different group depending on the time of day
- A different group depending on the severity of the problem
- A different group based on the hold times in the other agent group queues

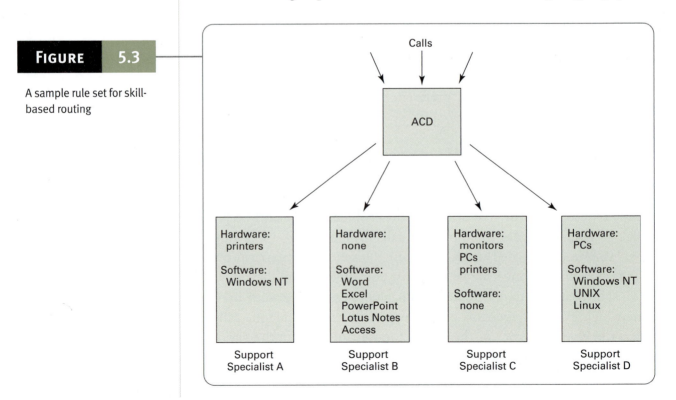

FIGURE 5.3

A sample rule set for skill-based routing

Developing SBR rules is a time-consuming process made up of a number of steps.

- Identify and define the skills required for each type of call.
- Identify and define individual agent skills.
- Prioritize agent skills based on individual competency levels.
- Devise and program into the ACD an appropriate routing plan.

One of the biggest challenges of SBR is distributing the call volume evenly across agents. Based on their particular abilities, some agents are placed in more than one skill group, while agents who specialize are placed in a single skill group. Rules must be established and programmed into the system to prevent the multiskilled agent from being overworked.

Complex Skills-Based Routing

Some ACDs allow for a very large number of routing rule sets. However, more is not necessarily better. As every help desk manager knows, the more ACDs and routing rules that are in place, the more complicated call routing becomes. The company with too many routing rules may be just as inefficient as the company with too few rules.

Data Collection

In addition to sophisticated routing capabilities, ACDs collect and store data about each call. Using these data, the ACD creates management reports that are used to monitor and evaluate help desk efficiency. Managers can determine how many calls are abandoned, the average hold time of calls, and other data such as

- Average talk time (the time spent actually talking with a user)
- Average after-call work time (the time an agent spends wrapping up a call once disconnected from the user)
- Average time per call (average talk time plus average after-call work time)
- Average time unavailable (breaks, lunch)
- Average idle time (waiting for requests)

This type of information can be used to ensure that agents are performing within acceptable SLA guidelines.

 READING CHECK

1 **READING REVIEW** What is the primary purpose of skill-based routing (SBR)?

2 **CRITICAL THINKING** If you were writing a set of rules for an SBR system, how would you balance the goal of routing calls to the agent most likely to solve the user's problem with the goal of connecting the caller with an agent as quickly as possible?

5.3   Interactive Voice Response

Interactive Voice Response (IVR) networks are telephone-based systems that allow individuals to interact with a telephone using the buttons on the telephone keypad. Callers dial a telephone number, listen to a prerecorded list of choices, and make a selection by pressing a key on the telephone keypad. This technology has been in widespread use for years. Today, most people have had the experience of placing a phone call that was answered by an IVR system.

For example, an individual may use IVR to find the balance in a checking account. In this instance, the IVR might sound like this:

> **BANK:** Welcome to XYZ Bank's automated information service. If you are calling from a Touch-Tone phone, press 1 now. If you are calling from a rotary phone, please stay on the line, and an operator will assist you.
> Customer presses 1 on keypad.

> **BANK:** You have reached the main menu. Listen closely to the selections, as the menu options have changed.
> Press 1 for checking account information.
> Press 2 for savings account information....

In a help desk setting, IVR applications perform several important functions. They provide automated help to users, collect caller information, and route calls to the appropriate help desk agents.

With an IVR program, users have the option of receiving immediate information either by listening to a recorded message or by requesting a fax on a particular topic. These 24-hour-a-day services provide information such as installation guides, fixes to common problems, and basic troubleshooting tips. If a call cannot be resolved using the automated help information, users have the option of being transferred to an analyst or leaving a voice mail message.

An Interactive Voice Response system also allows a user to initiate an action. For example, a user experiencing a problem with an unresponsive printer can enter data that will reset the printer. Similarly, users can perform their own password resets without the need for agent intervention.

If an IVR is integrated with other help desk technology, users can report problems, make requests, or check request status via the IVR prompts. Many standard queries formerly answered by help desk agents can now be handled by IVR systems, freeing agents for more complex problems. The greater the number of problems solved by automated voice programs, the greater the cost and time savings to the help desk and the company as a whole.

Making the Most of IVR

Suppose you call your bank to find out when the funds will become available from a check you recently deposited in your checking account. When you are connected with the bank's customer service system, you hear a recorded 20-second welcome message and the following options.

- For a list of branch locations and business hours, press 1.

- For account balances, press 2.

- To request a loan or credit card application, press 3.

- For information about opening an account, press 4.

- To order checks, press 5.

- To apply for a safe deposit box, press 6.

- To report a lost or stolen bankcard, press 7.

- To repeat these options, press 8.

You press 2. You are then asked to press 1 if you are inquiring about a savings account, 2 if you are calling about a checking account, and so on. When you press 2, you are asked to enter your account number. Next, you are asked to enter the personal identification number that you use with your bankcard. After that, you hear the following.

"Your account balance is $2,813.37. For more information, press the pound key. To return to the last menu, press the star key."

When you press the pound key, you are told that the amount of your account balance that is available at present is $743.37, and you are again invited to press the pound key to hear more. You do so and are told the date and amount of your last deposit. Although you are not given an option for more information, you press the pound key again. This time you are told to press star to return to the previous menu. Not wanting to repeat the

account information menu, you press 0, hoping to speak with an operator who will connect you with someone who can provide the information you need. Instead, you are returned to the welcome message with the original list of options. When you press 0 once more, the welcome message repeats.

REVIEWING CONCEPTS

1. The bank's customer service line is an example of what kind of network? Would another kind of customer service line be more helpful? If so, specify which one and state the reasons for your opinion.

2. How would you describe your experience with the bank's customer service line? Although it did not provide you with the information you wanted, do you believe that it probably does satisfactorily answer most callers' questions? Rewrite the customer service line's script (without changing the technology) in a way that would have enabled you to get the information you wanted and that would also provide efficient service to customers in general.

Voice Applications

Recent advances in speech recognition technology have made it possible for users to interact with the help desk by speaking their requests rather than entering them using the telephone keypad. This type of application is called a **voice application**. In a voice application, users respond to prompts from an IVR system, such as "Please press or say 1." This is the technology that is used for the voice dialing feature found on wireless telephones. Rather than using the keypad to dial the number they wish to reach, users say the name of the person or place they are calling based on a personal telephone directory. For example, if someone wanted to call work to check voice mail messages, they would say "call work," and the telephone would dial the number.

In the following example of voice-based IVR, a caller dialed a help desk number and was routed to the correct agent based on speech selections.

SYSTEM: Welcome to [Company Name]'s Help Desk Support Line. Please speak the type of product you need help with, such as printer, keyboard, or software, or say "other."

USER: Software

SYSTEM: Please name the software application you need help with, such as *Windows*, *Excel*, or *Netscape*, or say "other." To go back, say "previous menu."

USER: Other

SYSTEM: You are being transferred to a software support specialist. Please stay on the line.

Advantages of Voice Applications

Voice applications offer a number of advantages over traditional IVR systems. First, callers find it much easier to speak into the telephone in response to a prompt than to press a key on the keypad. This is natural.

Second, voice applications provide users with more hands-free options than keypad-dependent systems. For example, if a salesperson is driving to an appointment and wants to retrieve voice mail messages from an office phone, it is much easier speak a password or PIN than it is to enter the digits using the keypad.

Third, voice applications save time. Rather than listening to a long list of options and making a selection using the keypad, users can speak their request into the phone. The voice application uses sophisticated technology to recognize the caller's words. Once the words have been identified, the system searches a database to locate an appropriate response. Consider the time saved by the voice-based system in the following examples.

Traditional IVR

Welcome to the Huntstown Multiplex Theatre. Today is Friday, November 14th. The following movies are currently showing in our theater:

[FIRST MOVIE TITLE.] To hear show times for today, press 1. For Saturday, press 2. For Sunday, press 3. For Monday through Thursday show times, press 3.

[SECOND MOVIE TITLE.] To hear show times for today, press 1. For Saturday, press 2. For Sunday, press 3. For Monday through Thursday show times, press 3.

[THIRD MOVIE TITLE.] To hear show times for today, press 1. For Saturday, press 2. For Sunday, press 3. For Monday through Thursday show times, press 3.

[FOURTH MOVIE TITLE.] To hear show times for today, press 1. For Saturday, press 2. For Sunday, press 3. For Monday through Thursday show times, press 3.

Voice-Based IVR

Welcome to the Huntstown Multiplex Theater. Today is Friday, November 14th. For a list of movies currently playing, say "List." If you would like to hear show times for today, say "Today."

CALLER: Today
Which movie would you like to hear show times for? Speak the name of the movie now.

CALLER: [Fourth movie title.]

Notice how, in the voice-based example, it took the user much less time to reach the desired information, since it was not necessary to listen to a long list of menu options.

Many companies already using IVR for help desk services have found that adding voice applications improves customer satisfaction. In addition, voice technology reduces the costs associated with providing support, since it does not require a live attendant.

Voice over Internet Protocol (voIP)

Voice over IP (voIP), also known as **Internet Protocol (IP) telephony**, is a technology that allows voice calls to be routed over the Internet or a corporate intranet. In the mid-1990s, new software applications made it

would say "control vee." In response to the voice command, the computer implements the control-enter keyboard action—in this case, pasting the text into the form.

Obtain Status of Most Recent Open Request

Speech recognition technology enables users to track their open requests in the problem management system. Without the technology, a user who wanted a status update would call the help desk, respond to a series of prompts, and wait to be connected to a live agent, who would then look up the status in the same system. The use of speech recognition technology saves time for the user and for the help desk.

This is an example of a status request made using speech recognition technology:

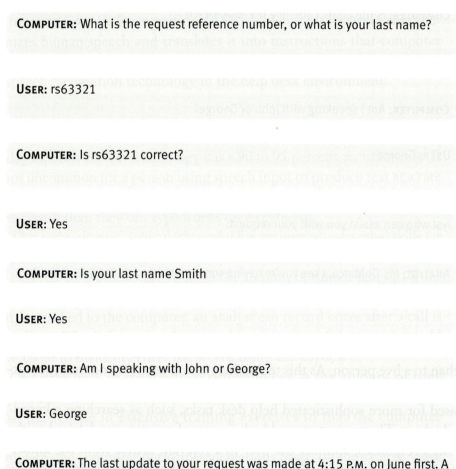

COMPUTER: What is the request reference number, or what is your last name?

USER: rs63321

COMPUTER: Is rs63321 correct?

USER: Yes

COMPUTER: Is your last name Smith

USER: Yes

COMPUTER: Am I speaking with John or George?

USER: George

COMPUTER: The last update to your request was made at 4:15 P.M. on June first. A desktop technician was dispatched to service the PC. The desktop technician is expected to arrive at the customer's desk at 9:10 A.M. on June second. Would you like to speak with an analyst? If not, then thank you for calling the support center.

USER: Yes, I would like to speak with an analyst.

COMPUTER: Please hold for a moment while I find an analyst who can help you.

Talking World Wide Web

Today's state-of-the-art help desks use voice applications that free users from the need to press telephone keys to enter information. Soon, newer technology will allow help desk analysts to carry on spoken conversations with users through their user-support Web sites. Moreover, using the sites will not even require a screen for displaying Web pages. A voice browser, for example, would provide access to the Web through telephones and other voice-transmission devices without requiring the use of a screen for visual display.

Two new extensions of HTML, which is the markup language used to build Web pages and applications, provide the means of making the Web accessible from telephones. One of them, called Speech Application Language Tags (SALT), adds speech capabilities to HTML. The other is called VXML, which stands for Voice Extensible Markup Language.

This first public version of SALT includes tags for enabling speech output, speech input, and call control in Web applications. SALT enables developers to build Web applications that can place, answer, transfer, and disconnect telephone calls and even initiate and control conference calls. SALT can be used with voice-only browsers, or it can be used to add speech and call-processing capabilities to visual displays on the Web. It is designed to interact with a variety of computers, telephones, wireless personal digital assistants (PDAs), and other communication devices.

Because SALT's founders include some of the most dominant computer technology companies, SALT could replace VXML as the standard for developing speech-based user interfaces for Web applications. Either way, spoken conversations between users and help desk Web sites may soon be commonplace.

LOOKING AHEAD

1. What three kinds of features can developers add to Web applications with SALT?

2. Using the Web, magazines, and any other resources you choose, find out more about speech interaction with the Web. Write a paragraph about how a help desk could use this productively.

The application automatically updates the request ticket rs63321 to show that the customer requested a status update.

Authenticate Callers

Some voice applications also offer a speaker verification/authentication feature. A **speech authenticator** is a biometrics-based system that provides secure access to a company's telephone and computer resources. Users first register their voices in a database. Once registered, they can call into the system and simply identify themselves to gain access. Again, all of this is accomplished without intervention of a live agent.

 READING CHECK

1 **READING REVIEW** What device does a caller use to interact with an Interactive Voice Response (IVR) network?

2 **CRITICAL THINKING** Explain why, as a caller, you would rather use a traditional IVR network or a voice application.

5.4 Computer Telephony Integration (CTI)

Recent advances in technology make it possible to integrate many different help desk technologies into one system. The most significant of these developments is the integration of telephone and computer-based systems, known as **computer telephony integration (CTI)**. A familiar example of a CTI application is the caller ID feature offered on home and cellular telephones. When a call is received, the incoming telephone number is matched against a computer database of phone numbers. If a match is found, details such as the caller's name are displayed on the call recipient's telephone.

CTI is made possible by **middleware** applications, software that connects two or more otherwise separate applications across a computer network. In a help desk application, middleware resides between the help desk application and the telephone interface, enabling data to be shared between the computer databases and the telephone system.

Widespread Availability

The cost of linking computer data systems with telephone communications systems used to be prohibitive for all but the largest help desks. Hardware and software had to be upgraded, and data links were expensive to set up and maintain.

A number of developments, however, led to the widespread availability of CTI systems. First, more and more help desks began using servers instead of mainframe computers to process and store information. This made it possible to create and maintain CTI systems without the expense of mainframe programming.

In addition, standards have been established that govern how computer equipment can communicate with telephone systems. The **Telephony Application Programming Interface (TAPI)** standard was created jointly by Microsoft and Intel. In a TAPI environment, the physical connection between the computer and the telephone system is made at the desktop level. The phone on a user's desk is physically connected to the PC, just as a telephone line for a modem is connected to a PC. The **Telephony Services Application Programming Interface (TSAPI)** standard was created by AT&T (Lucent) and Novell. In a TSAPI environment, the telephone system is physically connected to a server on the network, which in turn is connected to a user's PC.

These standards make it possible for developers to write applications that run on a wide range of platforms. Prior to this, developers would have had to write programs for many different computer platforms. There was little incentive to invest hours and hours of time to create a program for a small, segmented market. As development costs are spread over more installations, CTI becomes more affordable. In addition, the development of off-the-shelf CTI applications from vendors has also reduced the need to write custom program code.

Features and Benefits

Computer telephony systems can be programmed to deliver a very wide range of functions and services. The following four features are among the most significant in a help desk environment.

- Displays caller and call details automatically
- Routes voice, fax, e-mail, text messaging, and live chat into a unified queue
- Enables voice, fax, and e-mail to be retrieved from a single location
- Delivers automated responses
- Handles data analysis and reporting

Automatic display of caller and call details

When a user calls the help desk, the support specialist sees a screen that displays information about the user, including hardware and software configuration, recent upgrades, and prior problems. This is referred to as a **screen pop** (see Figure 5.4).

Help desks rely on screen pops to deliver instantaneous information about a caller. With screen pop technology, agents can familiarize themselves with callers before picking up the call. Knowing who is calling and viewing a summary of a caller's open tickets can help an agent provide faster, more effective service.

FIGURE 5.4

A sample screen pop

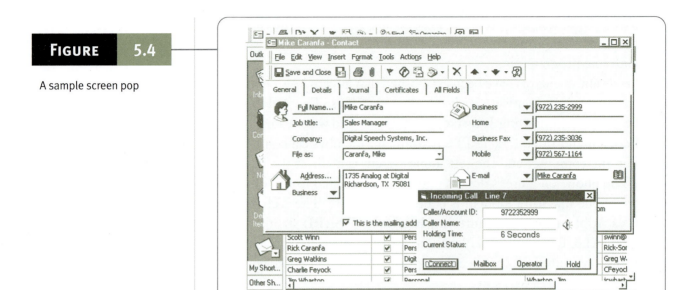

When customers contact the help desk, they are often asked to repeat certain information a number of times. For example, users might be asked to repeat a problem ticket number, the details of their system, and the details of the current problem. Through the use of CTI technology, this situation can be avoided. By linking information in computer databases with incoming call information, the agent knows the user's recent history of problem reports. If the call needs to be transferred to another agent, the most recent update on the problem is also transferred. This process results in significant time saving for the agent and the user.

Routing of voice, fax, e-mail, text messaging, and live chat into a unified queue

As employees have becomes more comfortable with multiple channels of communication, they expect these same channels to be available when they interact with the help desk. In order to provide the level of service expected, help desks must be able to route and respond to e-mail, fax, live chat, Web forms, and other channels. This presents a number of challenges to the help desk, including the issue of queuing. In the past, help desks received the majority of user requests via the telephone. Today, requests come in to the help desk in many different formats.

To respond effectively to multiple media requests, universal queuing is required. A **unified queue** is a system through which all incoming requests pass. All users' inquiries—whether in the form of e-mail, live chat, telephone, or other—enter the same system (see Figure 5.5). Each request is analyzed against a set of rules established by the help desk. These rules determine the priority of the call and where it will be routed. At a minimum, unified queuing rules take into account the urgency of the problem and the skills of the available agents. All requests are handled in the same manner. This system ensures that the most critical problems receive attention first, regardless of how they arrived at the help desk.

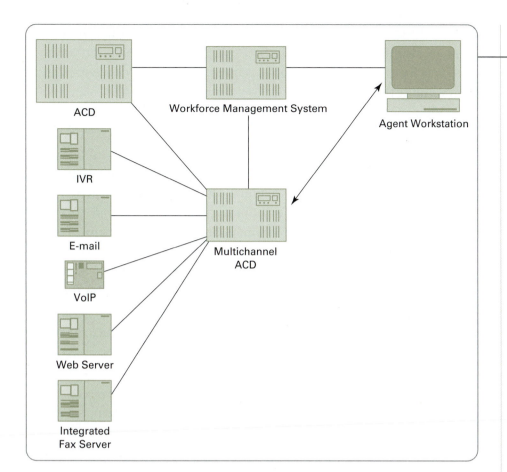

FIGURE   5.5

An example of a unified queue

Unified routing and queuing also provides valuable data to the help desk manager, including real-time queue data. Managers can see at a glance how many calls are in each queue and how long the average wait time is. This information can be sorted by queue, type of media, and urgency of the call, among other factors.

Using historical data, managers are also able to evaluate the quality and timeliness of help desk responses across each type of media. For example, suppose a manager wants to determine whether e-mail requests take less time to resolve than telephone requests. The manager thinks that e-mail is the more efficient way of handling a problem, since no direct interaction with the user is required. The report may show just the opposite—that problems reported by telephone are resolved more rapidly since the user and agent are able to work on the problem in real-time. With an e-mail request, the same five-minute exchange of questions and answers might require fifteen minutes of back-and-forth messages. As this example demonstrates, the data-gathering features of a unified queuing program are invaluable.

A unified queue also leads to an increase in user satisfaction. The primary benefit to users is that however they choose to contact the help desk for assistance, they know that their request will be prioritized and routed to the agent best able to assist them. In addition, since historical data about each user is stored in the system, an agent can quickly become familiar with the history of an event, eliminating the need for users to repeat background information. This results in a shorter overall resolution time.

Consider the following example. A user calls the help desk with a problem, while at the exact same time, another user submits a problem report via a Web site, and yet another user sends an e-mail request for support. Now imagine that there is one queue for telephone calls, one for Web site problem reports, and another for e-mail requests. Complicating the picture even further is the fact that requests are prioritized within each queue, without taking requests in any other queue into account. An urgent request in the telephone queue might wait until the analyst responds to several less urgent e-mail messages. Without a single, unified system that analyzes, routes, and queues each and every request, the task of responding quickly becomes unmanageable.

Suppose a user's call is put through to the help desk agent after the problem was initially reported via e-mail. The agent views basic information about the user in a screen pop and begins asking questions to discover the nature of the call. The user is annoyed that the agent has no idea what he is calling about, since he already sent an e-mail report of the problem. Without an integrated system, the agent had no way of knowing about this report, since the e-mail application does not communicate with the telephone system.

In a unified system, a user's e-mail address can be linked to a telephone number, so when a call or e-mail message comes in, the program automatically checks for prior contact from either medium. In this system, agents know whether the user has reported the problem before and whether that contact was made via e-mail, telephone, or Web. If a prior history exists, agents also can read the original report of the problem.

Retrieval of voice, fax, and e-mail from a single location

In today's corporations, people use a variety of different channels to communicate with one another, including e-mail, voice mail, fax machines, wireless phones, and pagers. **Unified messaging** saves time and increases productivity by enabling agents to access all messages and requests in a single location, regardless of whether they were originally sent via voice, fax, e-mail, or pager.

Some of unified messaging's capabilities in a help desk environment are described below.

- *Listening to voice, e-mail, and fax messages on a telephone:* Unified messaging depends on a number of other technologies, including several of the voice applications discussed earlier. In this instance, text-to-speech software is used to convert e-mail into spoken words. Using this technology, agents are able to listen to their e-mail messages from any telephone.
- *Listening to voice messages on a PC:* Similarly, using standard voice protocols, agents can listen to their voice messages through the speakers of a PC.

- *Sending voice messages via e-mail:* The technology also makes it possible to record a voice message and send it via e-mail to one or more recipients. This is delivered as an e-mail with a voice message attachment.
- *Sending e-mail via fax:* Agents can send e-mail to a fax machine that receives and prints the message. Help desk analysts use this method to get written instructions to a user who is unable to receive e-mail because of a PC problem.
- *Listening to voice, e-mail, and fax messages via wireless phone:* Wireless phones can also be used to access all varieties of messages. Using the display and the keypad, agents can access their mailbox and view a list of their voice, fax, and e-mail messages. They can then use the keypad on the phone to listen to messages.
- *Distributing a message to many recipients:* Unified messaging technology also allows a message to be sent to a large number of people, whether or not they are using the same device to communicate. This is referred to as **broadcast messaging**. Using a distribution list, the system sends the message in whatever format it finds available on the recipient's connection, whether it be voice mail, e-mail, wireless phone, or another format.

Delivery of automated responses

An **auto attendant** is a phone system that answers calls with a recorded message. The user selects from the choices listed, and the program routes the call based on the caller's selection. Once the call has entered the system and been logged and assigned, the user can call the system to check the status of the help request. Another feature of an auto attendant is the ability to provide the caller with prerecorded solutions to common problems.

Data analysis and reporting functions

CTI is constantly monitoring the telephone systems, so it is easy to collect all kinds of data on help desk performance. It provides real-time information on the status of the entire telephone system. It provides real-time data on every agent, every user, and every outstanding request. Using these data, reports can be created from within many CTI programs, and the data can also be imported into a spreadsheet or database.

Reporting tools enable managers to examine incoming and outgoing calls over a period of time with a variety of information. For example, they can look at a list of lost requests—users who called the help desk but hung up before their call was taken—or users whose e-mail requests have gone unanswered for more than 24 hours. Common statistics captured by a CTI system include the following:

- Agent statistics
- Log on and log off times
- Call time
- Idle time

- Other-work time
- After-call work time
- Busy time
- Calls handled by agent
- Call statistics
- Call type
- Inbound source
- Call duration
- Times placed on hold and total hold time
- ANI (digital equivalent of Caller ID)
- Call date
- Call start and end times
- Ring start and end times

Advantages of CTI

Computer telephony applications offer a number of advantages over telephone systems that are not connected to a computer database:

- Provision of services such as caller identification, call routing, and automated response
- Integration of different user access methods (telephone, fax, e-mail, text messaging)
- Efficient use of available help desk resources
- Integration of technology systems, resulting in a working environment that is easier to maintain and staff

Today's help desks are actively working on the seamless integration of telephone and computer technologies. Once the integration is complete, there will be dramatic increases in help desk productivity, since all requests and responses will flow through one system. Until then, the integration of different forms of help desk technology will continue to be an issue that must be addressed.

 READING CHECK

1 READING REVIEW Summarize the purpose that middleware serves in a help desk application.

2 CRITICAL THINKING What do you consider the greatest advantage that CTI provides to a help desk?

>> Summary

The following points were covered in this chapter:

1 Automated telephone systems enable help desks to receive and route a large number of calls more efficiently than they could with manual switchboards.

2 Automated call distributors (ACDs) are widely used business telephone systems that route calls, prioritize calls, play recorded messages, and record data about calls. In a user support environment, an ACD's two most important features are call routing and data collection. ACDs can provide skills-based routing through a custom set of rules developed by the company. Managers can use the data ACDs collect to make sure the help desk is responding to calls as efficiently as possible.

3 The benefits of skill-based routing include the capability to forward the call to the agent who can best handle the request with the goal of solving the problem as efficiently as possible. Skill-based routing also keeps the help desk staff at maximum productivity.

4 Interactive Voice Response (IVR) networks, which are in widespread use, allow users to select options from recorded lists by pressing buttons on their telephone keypads. In a help desk setting, IVR can provide automated help to users, collect caller information, and route calls to the appropriate help desk agents. Many IVR networks now include voice applications, which enable users to speak their requests instead of using a keypad.

5 Automatic Speech Recognition (ASR) software can convert speech into instructions that computer systems can process. It enables help desk analysts to enter information into the computer faster than they could with keyboards. It can also save time by collecting information about callers before they are connected to analysts, and it can enable callers to get status information without help from analysts.

6 Computer telephony integration (CTI) features important to help desks include the ability to display caller information automatically; unified queuing; unified messaging; and automated response. A CTI system can also collect detailed data about calls to the help desk and how they are handled. The integration of telephone and computer technologies will make help desks more productive.

7 A unified queue ensures that the most critical problems receive attention first, regardless of how they arrived at the help desk. Unified queuing also provides valuable data to the help desk manager, including real-time queue data.

8 The common statistics captured by a CTI application include agent statistics—such as log on and log off times, call time, idle time, other-work time, and after-call work time—and call statistics such as call type, inbound source, call duration, time placed on hold, and total hold time.

Chapter 5 Review

>> Key Terms

The following terms were defined in this chapter:

- **a** auto attendant
- **b** automated call distributors (ACDs)
- **c** automatic Speech Recognition (ASR)
- **d** broadcast messaging
- **e** centrex
- **f** computer telephony integration (CTI)
- **g** interactive Voice Response (IVR) network
- **h** internet Protocol (IP) Telephony
- **i** middleware
- **j** private branch exchange (PBX)
- **k** screen pop
- **l** speech authenticator
- **m** skill-based routing (SBR)
- **n** telephony Application Programming Interface (TAPI)
- **o** telephony Services Application Programming Interface (TSAPI)
- **p** unified messaging
- **q** unified queue
- **r** voice application
- **s** voice over IP (voIP)

>> Reviewing Key Terms

Write the letter of the key term that matches each definition below:

____ **1** A telephone-based system that allows a caller to interact with it by using the buttons on the telephone keypad.

____ **2** A system in which a business leases a pool of telephone lines at the phone company's central office and call routing takes place at the phone company's office.

____ **3** A phone system that answers calls with a recorded message that offers a list of choices, routes the call based on the caller's selection, enables the user to check the status of a help request, and offers the caller recorded solutions to common problems.

____ **4** A system enabling agents to access to all messages and requests in a single location, regardless of whether they were originally sent via voice, fax, or e-mail.

____ **5** An automated method of forwarding each call to the agent who can best handle the request.

____ **6** An internal business telephone network in which users share a certain number of lines for making telephone calls outside the company.

>> Reviewing Key Terms (continued)

____ 7 A telephone system that route calls, prioritizes calls, and plays recorded messages.

____ 8 A standard that allows a computer and a telephone system to be physically connected on a desktop application.

____ 9 A technology that allows voice calls to be routed over the Internet or a corporate intranet.

____ 10 Instantaneous delivery of information about a caller on an agent's computer screen, so the agent can become familiar with the caller's background before picking up the call.

____ 11 Another name for voice over IP (voIP).

____ 12 The integration of telephones and computer-based systems.

____ 13 A system through which all incoming help requests pass, regardless of the means by which they arrive, and are analyzed against a set of rules.

____ 14 Software that recognizes human speech and translates it into instructions that computer programs can process.

____ 15 A standard whereby a telephone system is physically connected to a server on the network, which in turn is connected to a user's PC.

____ 16 Software that connects two or more otherwise separate applications across a computer network.

____ 17 A biometrics-based system that provides secure access to a company's telephone and computer resources.

____ 18 A type of application that enables users to enter their requests by speaking rather than by using the telephone keypad.

____ 19 The distribution of a message to a large number of people, whether or not they are using the same device to communicate.

>> Reviewing Key Facts

True/False

Identify whether each statement is True (T) or False (F). Rewrite the false statements so that they are true.

____ 1 A successful help desk must be able to receive and route large numbers of incoming calls efficiently.

____ 2 In a PBX system, blocks of e-mail addresses are assigned to a company.

>> Reviewing Key Facts *(continued)*

____ **3** In a Centrex system, a pool of telephone lines owned and maintained by the telephone company is sold to a business.

____ **4** An automated call director (ACD) system uses information input by a telephone keypad to route the call to a particular support group.

____ **5** Routing software can be set up to route calls according to the caller's language preference.

____ **6** An Interactive Voice Response (IVR) application can route calls to the appropriate help desk agents.

____ **7** Middleware is hardware that connects telephones with computers.

____ **8** On a help desk that uses skills-based routing (SBR), agents are each assigned to only one skill group.

____ **9** The development of off-the-shelf computer telephony interface (CTI) applications reduced the need to write custom program code.

____ **10** Voice over IP (voIP) eliminates almost all long-distance billing charges for telephone calls.

Completion

Write the answer that best completes each of the following statements:

1 An ACD system can route a call to the appropriate help desk analyst without the need for _____.

2 Users of a voice application that features a speech authenticator must first register their _____ in a database so that the system can recognizes them.

3 Caller ID is an example of _____.

4 Help desks rely on _____ to deliver instantaneous information about users so that analysts can familiarize themselves with the users before picking up their calls.

5 With the seamless integration of telephone and _____, help desks will see dramatic increases in productivity.

>> Understanding Key Concepts

Provide brief answers to the following questions:

1 Why have help desks automated their call systems?

2 In what ways can help desks benefit from using Automatic Speech Recognition (ASR)?

3 What are the main advantages that a unified queue offers to a help desk?

›› Critical Thinking

As directed by your instructor, write a brief essay or discuss the following issues in groups:

1. You are the manager of a help desk with a CTI system that collects the following data.
   - Log on and log off times for all help desk analysts
   - The total time each analyst spends on calls
   - The total time each analyst spends on other tasks
   - The amount of time each analyst spends resolving each call, and the analysts' average resolution time per call
   - The number of calls each agent handles
   - The date, time, and duration of each call that the help desk receives
   - The amount of time each caller waits to be connected with an analyst
   - The number of callers who hang up before they are connected to analysts
   - Each caller's identity

   How would you use this information to make sure that the help desk is performing as well as possible?

2. You work on a help desk with automated skills-based call routing. As the only analyst who is familiar with *Linux*, *Unix*, and *Windows*, you are so busy handling service requests that you barely have time to eat lunch. Most of the other analysts apparently have a lot of idle time between calls, and some of them even seem to be bored. You have decided to talk with your manager about this problem. What solutions might you suggest for distributing work more evenly among you and the other analysts?

3. You see in a screen pop that the user whose call you are about to take is Fred Jackson, who calls the help desk often. The last time you took a call from him, he hung up angrily because you did not have an immediate solution to his problem. How would you deal with Jackson this time?

›› Help Desk Projects

Complete the projects listed below:

1. **In small groups, investigate your school's telephone system.** Find out such information as the following:
   - Is it a PBX, a Centrex system, or some other alternative?
   - How many telephone numbers or extensions does it include?
   - Does it use automated call distributors?
   - What other features does it have (such as caller ID, voice mail, and unified messaging)?

2. **Investigate the features of the telephone you use most often, which might be a home telephone, a cell phone, or the telephone at a job.** What features do you find most helpful? What features do you dislike or seldom use? Are there features you would like to add to that telephone?

›› Help Desk Projects *(continued)*

3 **Make a call to a business or other organization that has an Interactive Voice Response network.** This might be a call to a movie theater to find out this week's movies and show times, a call to a chain store to find out the nearest location, or a call to a credit card company to determine your available credit line, to name just a few possibilities. Take notes about your experience, including how many options you had to listen to, whether you had to use a keypad or could use speech, and how long it took you to get the information you wanted. Write a report in which you evaluate your experience, including any ways in which the business you called could improve its IVR network.

4 **Search the World Wide Web for information about computer telephony integration (CTI) systems.** Then write a brief report listing three companies that produce CTI systems and comparing and contrasting the features of their products.

5 **Suppose you are setting up a skill-based routing (SBR) system on a help desk that has four analysts on each shift.** One of the analysts specializes in hardware problems. Another knows only *Unix*; a third analyst knows only *Windows*; and the fourth knows both *Unix* and *Windows* as well as your company's word processing and spreadsheet programs and other common applications. Developing a list of rules for call-routing rules so that users reach the most appropriate help desk analyst as quickly as possible.

6 **As a group, discuss the advantages and disadvantages of caller ID, which is a common feature of CTI systems.** Discuss the benefits and drawbacks caller ID offers to businesses, their customers, and users of private home telephones or cell phones.

7 **Suppose you are a help desk manager.** What data would you most want to collect about incoming calls and the help desk analysts who handle them? How would you use each piece of information?

8 **Use the Web to research voice over IP (voIP) services for consumers.** Would you consider using voIP for all of your personal calls? Give reasons for your answers.

›› Help Desk Strategies

Review the following case studies and respond to the questions:

1 Quicksilver Courier Service started out with 5 employees, including a receptionist who routed all incoming calls. It now has 15 employees and is growing rapidly. The business now gets so many incoming calls that the receptionist has trouble answering them promptly, and some callers hang up before she gets to them. Most of the incoming calls are from customers who want to schedule pickups or deliveries, although a significant number are from people checking the status of pickups or deliveries they have already scheduled.

- Would hiring a second receptionist be the most effective way to solve the problem?
- Should Quicksilver consider installing an ACD?
- What advantages and disadvantages do you see in each of the above solutions?

>> Help Desk Strategies *(continued)*

2. Abacus Payroll Processing is about to upgrade its ACD system. Of the company's 800 employees, about a third are recent immigrants from all over the world. Many of the employees, including some of the analysts on the internal help desk for employees, speak with heavy accents. Because of this, the help desk analysts and the callers sometimes have difficulty understanding each other.

   - What voice applications, if any, might be useful to Abacus?
   - What other features might Abacus include in its new telephone system that would help make communication with the help desk less of a problem?

3. Millenium Properties, a large real estate agency, has scores of brokers. The brokers all spend a lot of their time outside the office, visiting properties and conducting other business in a geographic area that includes two states and half a dozen different area codes. While they are working outside the office, the brokers frequently call the office from their cell phones to check on whether they have received e-mail, telephone messages, or faxes they are expecting. The employees in the office are constantly interrupting their other work to check the callers' e-mail and fax machines, for them and then calling them back with the messages. Including calls to brokers in the field and calls to customers throughout its business area, long-distance telephone charges are among Millenium's biggest business expenses.

   - Can you suggest a more efficient way for the brokers to pick up their e-mail and telephone messages and faxes?
   - How might Millenium reduce its long-distance telephone charges?

Chapter 6

Web-Based Support

Objectives

After reading this chapter, you will be able to:

1. Explain the concept of self-service support.
2. Summarize the advantages of self-service support.
3. Describe the four stages of support provided on a help desk Web site.
4. Identify common user problems easily solved by self-service technology.
5. Discuss the major types of self-service tools found on a support Web site.
6. Discuss the role of assisted support in a help desk Web site.
7. Describe two challenges associated with Web-based support.

Chapter Overview

Cost and efficiency pressures are forcing companies to find new ways of providing support. The costs associated with traditional support have increased dramatically as more people use technology to perform their jobs. As technology becomes more complex, users are calling the help desk with more challenging questions. As a result, help desk analysts are taking longer to provide solutions. In addition, many organizations are realizing that the demand for services is outpacing their ability to hire additional help desk technicians. These realities have prompted businesses to create Web-based support sites that save money and reduce overload on the help desk.

6.1 Self-Service Support

Many of the tools and technologies discussed in this chapter provide users with the ability to solve problems on their own through the use of a support Web site. This is known as **self-service support** and is also referred to as e-support or self-help. Figure 6.1 illustrates an example of a support Web site.

FIGURE   6.1

A support Web site

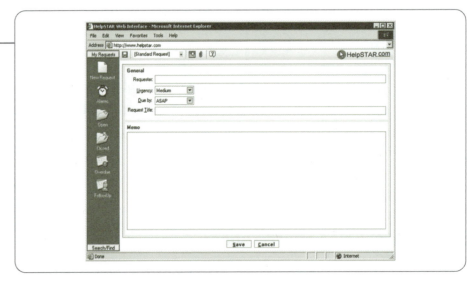

Self-service technology gives users the power to solve problems on their own, 24 hours a day, 365 days a year, from any location. It is less costly to provide support options other than telephone support (see Table 6.1).

TABLE   6.1

Transaction Cost by Support Method (Source: Forrester Research)

Support Method	Average Cost per Transaction
Telephone	$32.74
E-mail	$9.99
Live chat	$7.80
Web self-service	$1.17

A basic example of a self-service technology is online problem ticket submission. Rather than calling the help desk, users can simply complete a trouble ticket on a Web site and submit it to the help desk. The request is routed to an analyst who diagnoses and resolves the problem. A sample Web-based submission form is pictured in Figure 6.2.

Another example of a self-service tool is a searchable knowledgebase. A user experiencing a problem enters a few key words in a form, and a knowledgebase searches for relevant information. Once the knowledgebase has located possible solutions, they are displayed to the user. If the user is still unable to solve the problem after reviewing this information, additional help is readily available. With a single click of the mouse, all relevant data are entered into a problem ticket and submitted to the help desk.

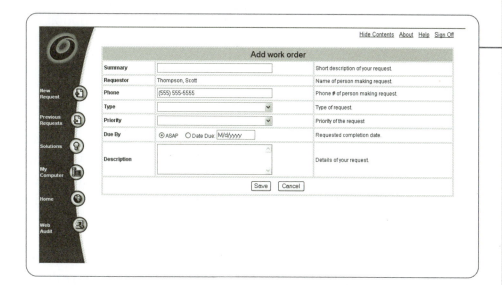

FIGURE 6.2

A form for submitting help requests via a Web site

Evolution of Self-Service Support

Self-service support is possible because of several key developments in the field of information technology. Until these advances were made, self-service support was simply not feasible. The developments include

- Growth and popularity of the Internet
- Standards for secure online activities
- Technologies that enable users to interact with a Web site
- Simplicity of deploying a Web site

The Internet has become as familiar to people as a television set. Few users have not visited a Web site for information or to make a purchase. This makes a Web site an excellent method of providing support, since it requires no user training.

Some companies were initially hesitant to place information on a Web site that could be prone to attacks from intruders. The creation of standards for secure online transactions and the development of firewalls meant that individuals outside the company could not view protected information placed on a Web site. In addition, most support Web sites are located on a company's **intranet**, which is a network similar to the Internet, except that the information is accessible only to employees within an organization or others who have been granted access rights.

The development of other technologies, such as Java Script and ActiveX, made it possible for users to interact with a Web site rather than merely read content and search for information. By selecting different options and filling in forms, users can interact with the site in real time, making it much more efficient to request the information they require.

Finally, creating and maintaining a support Web site is less cumbersome than installing support software on each user's PC. Since no special software is installed, there is no need for costly software updates.

All of these developments helped make self-service a viable option for today's modern help desk.

Advantages of Self-Service Support

Self-service tools offer tremendous advantages to the user and to the help desk. A well-designed support site provides answers very quickly, and help is always available. The tools presented on the site are easy to learn and to use, as most users are already familiar with the navigation used in Web browsers. Self-service support also results in better educated, more confident users, as they gain experience researching and solving problems on their own.

As more and more users become comfortable using self-service support, call volume to the help desk drops off. In turn, users who do call the help desk are likely to have their problems resolved more quickly than in the past. In many cases, Web-based initiatives are reducing costs by driving service and support toward less expensive methods such as knowledgebase, e-mail, and discussion forums.

The idea behind Web-based support is simple. If help desks are able to practice call avoidance and deflection by driving problem resolution to self-service channels, support staff can focus on more difficult technology problems that are having a major effect on business productivity.

Characteristics of an Effective Support Web Site

Developing a successful user support Web site is a major undertaking. To be effective, Web-based support must

- Be easy to use
- Provide fast and accurate service
- Offer a variety of support options
- Be consistent across all pages
- Offer assisted help
- Be updated often
- Be easy to administer

For any self-service solution to be successful, it must be easy to use. The site design and layout should be clean and simple, and pages should load quickly. Users must be offered a variety of support options from which they can select the one that is most likely to provide the help they need. If at any time during a site visit a user would like to switch to live or assisted support, this should be easy to accomplish. The user must be able to fill out forms without any special training.

Above all, the material on the site must be accurate and timely. If these criteria are not met, the site will create more problems than it solves. Support sites require a high level of maintenance. New information must be added regularly, and outdated information has to be updated or removed from the site. For this reason, the site must be easy to administer.

Problems Suited to Self-Service Solutions

Four types of problems typically make up more than half of all of help desk requests: password resets, problem status calls, break/fix inquiries, and how-to questions. A Web-based support site easily handles these issues. Self-service tools are most appropriate for routine problems and procedures that do not require a high level of technical expertise to resolve. Password resets, problem status calls, break/fix inquiries, and how-to questions typically make up more than half of all help desk requests. These four problems are well suited to self-service tools.

- *Password resets* enable the user to reset a password at any time, from any location, without contacting the help desk.

  Example: A user forgets his or her password. The user logs on, responds to several authentication prompts, and requests a new password. The program automatically e-mails a new password, and the help desk is automatically notified of the password change.

- *Problem status automation* allows the user to enter a problem ticket at any time and to check its status at any time.

  Example: A user calls the help desk to report a problem. Thirty minutes go by, and the user would like to know the status of the case. This information is obtained by accessing the support Web site and entering the ticket number. The user can edit existing information and add new information to the case file.

- *Break/fix problem resolution* provides users with access to file recovery, system rollback, virus recovery, and other break/fix solutions.

  Example: A user is experiencing a problem that is already known, so the resolution is thoroughly documented in the knowledgebase, complete with a link to a software patch that can be downloaded.

- *How-to instructions* provide the user with step-by-step instructions to resolve common PC problems.

  Example: A user is not certain how to print a sales presentation to a special large-format color printer located on a different floor. A quick search of the online documentation uncovers instructions for this procedure. The user prints the instructions and makes the setting changes so as to direct output to the color printer.

Table 6.2 lists some other common user needs and the Web-based solutions that can be offered to meet them.

TABLE 6.2

Common User Actions and Web-Based Solutions

User Actions	Web-Based Solution
Find solutions to problems	FAQs, knowledgebase, discussion forums, document library
Check status of a request	E-mail updates, Web accessible case information
Provide additional information on a case	E-mail, Web case form
Request live assistance	Live chat, Web case submission
Reset password	Web password reset utility
Download and apply software updates	Download library

 READING CHECK

1 READING REVIEW How does the cost per transaction of Web self-service compare with that of live chat, telephone service, and e-mail? Rank these methods in order of their cost per transaction, starting with the most expensive.

2 CRITICAL THINKING What Web-based solutions might be used to resolve each of the following service issues?

- An employee cannot open a document because he has an out-of-date version of the word processing software the company uses.

- A user who called to report a printer is out of toner.

- A user who called about a problem two hours ago wants to know why it has not been solved yet.

6.2 Progressive Support Options

An effective Web-based support site offers users options other than self-service. Help is offered in four progressive stages, moving from complete self-service to fully assisted service.

Stage 1: Automated Help

In stage 1, no action is required on the part of the user. The help is provided by programs that run unassisted, performing regular checks of the user's computer. A common example of a stage 1 program is an antivirus program. The application runs in the background while the user is performing other tasks. When a virus is detected, an alert is sent to notify the user of the problem.

Stage 2: Self-Service

In stage 2, users actively seek help via a Web site. They use a variety of tools such as a knowledgebase, online documentation, and a discussion forum to try to resolve the problem without contacting the help desk.

Stage 3: Real-Time Assisted Support

Real-time assisted support involves live contact between a user and a help desk agent. Live chat is an example of this mode of support; the user and the agent write messages back and forth in real time as they try to determine the cause of a problem.

Stage 4: Delayed Assisted Support

Just as in stage 3, stage 4 requires contact between a user and a member of the support staff. However, in this case, the assistance is delayed, not live. E-mail is a familiar example of a delayed method of communication. The user sends the e-mail and has to wait for a response from the help desk.

READING CHECK

1 **READING REVIEW** Identify the first stage of successful Web-based user support, and give an example of this type of support.

2 **CRITICAL THINKING** Explain why, as a user, you might prefer delayed assisted support rather than real-time assisted support.

6.3 Web-Based Support Tools

A variety of different tools can be posted on an Internet or intranet support site. Figure 6.3 lists the major tools and technologies used in each stage of Web-based support. This section of the chapter provides an overview of several of these tools.

Automated Support: Self-Healing Programs

Self-healing programs automatically restore desktop applications to their original state by reinstalling components that have been damaged, removed, or modified. These programs function autonomously, without user or help desk intervention. The software takes a snapshot of the user's configuration and stores it on a server. At regular intervals, the program checks the user's computer for changes and problems. If a problem is found, a **rollback** can be implemented. A rollback involves restoring a program or computer to an earlier configuration that is known to work effectively.

FIGURE 6.3

Stages of Web-based support and appropriate tools

Stages/Tools of Web-based Support

I. Automated Support:
Self-Healing Programs

II. Self Service Support:
Knowledgebase
Frequently Asked Questions (FAQs)
Online Documentation

III. Real-Time Assisted Support:
Live Chat
Remote Control Programs
Diagnostic Programs

IV. Delayed Assisted Support:
E-mail
Discussion Forums

Did You Know?

The market for remote control and self-healing applications is expected to grow to $1.1 billion in 2006.

Did You Know?

More than 60 percent of help desk calls are from users who are unable to access their applications, according to Hurwitz Group, Inc., a research firm in Framingham, Massachusetts.

Some companies have policies that specify the acceptable use of both software and hardware and define standard software and hardware equipment. These are known as **standards**. One important element of this policy is an up-to-date list of what software and hardware is standard on company computers. The help desk is responsible for supporting only programs that are part of the standard configuration. This is logical; it would be impossible for a help desk to support the thousands of programs that users can download from the Internet. Most of the programs users download from the Internet and install on their PCs are not part of the standard PC configuration in the organization. Self-healing programs monitor user PCs and detect the installation of unapproved software. When an unapproved application is found, the program automatically uninstalls it and restores the computer to a previous setting.

Self-healing programs offer a number of benefits to the user and to the help desk. These applications identify and repair problems before a worker's performance is affected. Many times the program becomes aware of a problem and fixes it before the user even knows a problem exists. Reports of incidents are automatically sent to the help desk for analysis to determine the causes . However, unlike in traditional live support, the worker is up and running before problem diagnosis begins.

In addition, software failures can be repaired without resorting to traditional time-consuming tasks such as reinstalling entire applications. Instead, the self-healing program restores only the application items that are damaged or missing. For example, suppose a corporation experienced a major system outage in its accounting department when upgrading to a new version of an application. The upgrade included a driver that prevented other applications from loading completely. Without self-healing technology, specifically the ability to perform a rollback, a problem such as this one could take hours to fix. In the meantime, the help desk would be swamped with calls from users reporting problems.

Self Service: Knowledgebase

A knowledgebase is a collection of information stored on a network that is used to answer questions and solve problems. A support knowledgebase enables users to search for answers to their questions 24 hours a day via the Internet or a company-wide intranet. See Figure 6.4 for a sample knowledgebase page from a support Web site.

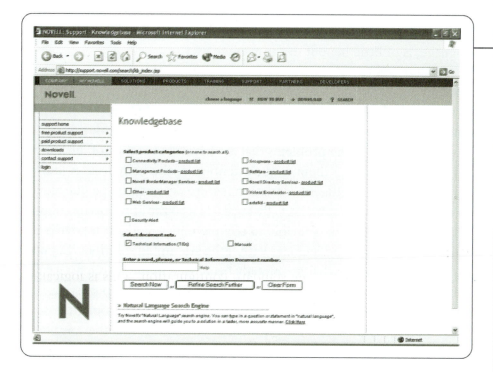

FIGURE 6.4

An example of an online knowledgebase

When a search is initiated, a knowledgebase

- Analyzes the query
- Searches for related information
- Retrieves entries and sorts by relevance
- Returns the sorted results to the user

An online knowledgebase is continually updated with new information based on user problems and other data. As support analysts resolve user problems, solutions are added to the knowledgebase. Procedures must be in place to get information from support agents into the knowledgebase. (The topic of knowledge management is discussed in more detail in Chapter 8.) The next time a user searches the knowledgebase for information on this issue, a solution will be displayed. As more and more solutions are added, the number of problems that users can solve on their own increases.

As with other help desk tools, knowledgebases have advantages and disadvantages. A major advantage is easy access to information at any time and from any location with Internet access. Another benefit is the quality of the information that it contains. All articles in the knowledgebase have been checked for accuracy and are updated on a regular basis. In addition, since all users and help desk agents use the same knowledgebase, information is consistent.

One of the primary challenges associated with a support knowledgebase is maintenance. To be effective, a knowledgebase requires continual updating. Outdated information must be deleted; existing information must be updated; and new solutions must be added. A balance must be achieved between the level of information provided and the ease of using the site. A site with too much information, especially if written in highly technical language, is of little benefit to the average user.

Intelligent Escalation

Even with the best knowledgebase solution, there will always be questions that cannot be resolved using the system. **Intelligent escalation** is the capability of identifying problems that are beyond the scope of the knowledgebase and bringing them to the attention of the help desk. A knowledgebase with an intelligent escalation feature detects when a question is beyond its ability and automatically escalates it to the appropriate support level. When the system is unable to complete its agenda, it forwards the question to support, and includes with it the attempted solutions. Support analysts can easily see what has already been tried in the search for a solution. This saves time, since the analyst does not have to repeat steps that have already been performed. The customer receives automatic e-mail updates on the issue. Once the problem has been resolved, the solution is communicated to the user and added to the knowledgebase, so the benefits of that work are available to everyone. Intelligent escalation also provides valuable information to the help desk about the current limitations of the knowledgebase. These areas can be targeted for improvement through the addition of relevant material.

Self-Service: Frequently Asked Questions (FAQs)

A **FAQ** is a list of **frequently asked questions** (and answers) about a topic. Almost all support Web sites offer several FAQs. Figure 6.5 illustrates a FAQ on the Microsoft support Web site. Notice that the FAQs have been organized into a number of categories, such as Getting Started, Working with Music and Video, and Install and Troubleshoot Hardware. Within each category, quite a few different questions are listed. When a user clicks on a question, a relevant support page that is designed to provide an answer is displayed.

The most effective FAQs list the most common questions at the top, so users do not need to scroll down the page and look through a large number of questions before finding what they need. Categories are a critical element in designing effective FAQs. Look again at Figure 6.5 and imagine the page without categories. It would not be nearly as effective without categories that organize the information by topic.

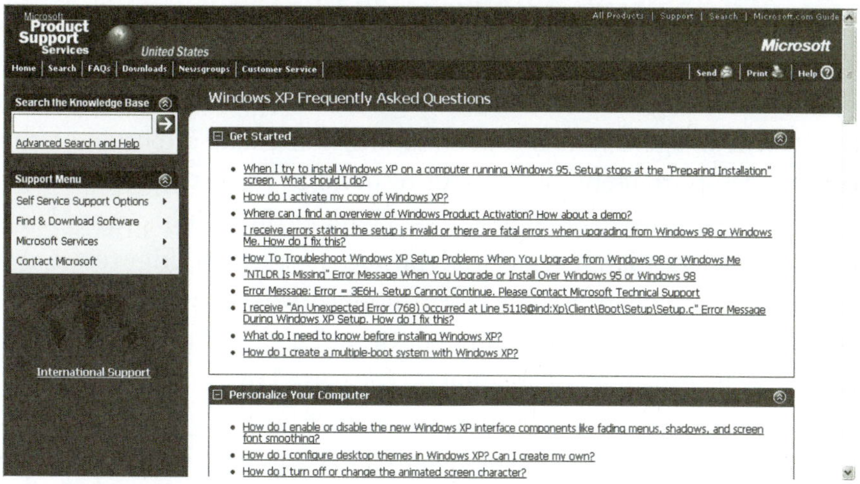

FIGURE 6.5

An example of a FAQ feature on a Web site

The primary benefits of FAQs are availability and convenience. Placed on a Web site, FAQs can be available 24 hours a day, 7 days a week, 365 days a year. They can be accessed from any location around the world; all that is required is an Internet connection. Another advantage of FAQs is consistency; all users access the same information. Unlike in a telephone call, with a FAQ there is no possibility that one user will be told one solution and another user will be told another solution. It is also relatively easy to maintain and upgrade FAQs. When new issues arise, the help desk can edit the FAQ to reflect the changes. For example, some help desks routinely update FAQs on a weekly basis in response to the most common user problems. If a new software patch has been installed and many users are reporting difficulties, the help desk may decide to include questions pertaining to this issue at the top of the list.

The downside to this support method is not inherent in the FAQs, but rather in the quality of the effort put into developing, updating, and maintaining them. The information is only of benefit to users if it is well written and current.

Self-Service: Online Documentation

Many support sites have **online documentation** as a help feature. Documents such as user manuals, installation instructions, and training materials are typically available in a number of formats. The dominant format for online documents is Adobe's Portable Document Format, known as PDF. Users download *Acrobat Reader*, a program required to open, view, and print PDF documents. Some sites also offer files in plain text, rich text format (RTF), *Word*, *PowerPoint*, and *Excel*.

As with other Web-based support methods, an online documentation library provides users with the opportunity to solve problems without contacting the help desk. Besides this cost saving, there is an additional saving as fewer documents must be printed and distributed to employees. A user can print documents stored on a Web site if desired.

Real-Time Assisted Support: Live Chat

Live chat establishes immediate, two-way communication between a user and a help desk agent. Without having to pick up the phone, users can interact with an agent in real time, focusing immediate attention on their problems. Support agents are able to respond to more than one user at a time, often handling as many as four chats at once. This provides far greater efficiency than a typical telephone interaction. Figure 6.6 is an example of a window from a live chat support program.

Chat applications provide a number of timesaving features. Many programs have the capability of creating preformatted responses to commonly asked questions. When appropriate, these responses can be inserted into a live chat, saving the agent the time required to retype this information every time it is needed. For example, suppose that within one 24-hour period, 20 users engaged in live chat and required instructions on importing data from a specific spreadsheet program into a presentation program. The agent without a set of preformatted responses would have to key this information 20 times. With the preformatted response feature, it can be inserted into a chat with one click of the mouse. This list of responses is easily modified. As new questions come up, answers can be added to it. This type of semi-automated dialogue makes chat more efficient and allows agents to conduct multiple chats at one time, or even take phone calls and chat concurrently.

Help desk agents are able to monitor Web site activity in real-time, and can initiate chat with a user who seems to be having difficulty finding help on the Web site. For example, if an agent notices that a user has already read two FAQs and is now searching the knowledgebase, the agent may offer live help by sending an instant message to the user.

Chat applications also save transcripts of all live chats. These transcripts are often e-mailed to users so they can refer to them if needed after the chat has terminated. This is known as transcript forwarding.

The reporting features of chat programs provide information such as average wait times and length of chat sessions.

Web-based live chats are second only to telephones when it comes to problem resolution times. As a result, user satisfaction with live chat as a support method is usually high.

FIGURE 6.6

An example of a live chat feature on a Web site

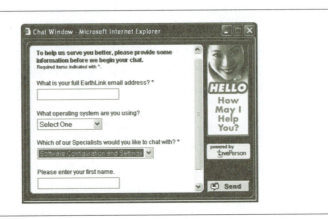

Real-Time Assisted Support: Remote Control Programs

Remote control programs allow support personnel to take over and manage user PCs without leaving the help desk. Using remote control software, help desk analysts have the ability to

- Log in to a user's PC
- Display configuration options of a user's PC
- Reboot a user's PC
- Transfer files to or from a user's PC
- Initiate live chat with the user

Remote control applications are used for problems that the user cannot solve without hands-on assistance. Many remote control applications can operate in three different modes—watch, share, and control. In the watch mode, the analyst is able to observe exactly what the user is doing when a problem occurs (assuming it can be replicated). This can provide important clues about the cause of the problem. In the share mode, the user is still able to access the computer, but the technician also has access and can make changes. The control mode gives the support specialist total control of the user's PC.

Diagnostic programs are a specific type of remote control software that collect PC configuration information, analyze the diagnostic data, and troubleshoot problems, all from a remote location.

In any remote access program, security is a major concern. For this reason, remote control programs provide a wide range of security features to ensure that systems are protected. They include

- Providing different levels of remote control, from observing to sharing access to total control
- Requiring passwords at each level of access
- Recording all activity during the remote session to provide an accurate audit trail

The primary benefits of remote control software include the ability to solve complex problems without visiting a user's desk. This results in improved help desk efficiency, since no travel time is required. User satisfaction is usually very good, since the analyst's hands-on intervention usually results in a relatively prompt solution.

Delayed Assisted Support: E-mail

On many Web support sites, questions can be sent to the help desk via e-mail. This is an appealing option for users and analysts alike. The user composes and sends the e-mail when it is convenient. The analyst has time to read the information and think about it before responding to the user.

E-mail messages, unlike telephone calls, do not require real-time interaction with users.

However, the ability to respond to e-mail requires other skills and abilities. Help desk analysts who provide e-mail support must be good writers who are able to translate technical information into content that is easy for users to understand. Some help desks assign a special team of agents to handle e-mail inquiries because of this skill requirement.

When the help desk receives an e-mail message, an agent chooses the method of response, depending on the nature of the problem. If the agent needs more information, it can be obtained by e-mail or telephone. It is often more efficient to call a user to gather information or to clarify a point than to begin a round of back-and-forth e-mail.

If the problem is one that the user will be able to solve with instructions, the agent might e-mail or fax a list of instructions. E-mail and faxes also provide the option of including graphics, which can be especially helpful to users. For example, if a user is having problems with a device, it may be necessary to delete the driver and install a new one. The user is much more likely to perform this procedure successfully if a written document with screen captures is provided.

When e-mail messages are sent to the help desk, they are analyzed and routed to the agent most likely to provide timely resolution. The user receives a confirmation that the e-mail has been received. In organizations that use unified queuing systems, e-mail is routed into the same queue as phone calls and faxes. In a company without a unified queue, e-mail is routed as a separate entity.

Some sophisticated help desk systems provide automatic responses to user e-mail messages. The system analyzes the content of the message and searches for keywords. Then, the system searches a knowledgebase for occurrences of these keywords and sends a list of relevant knowledgebase articles to the user. In case the user prefers live help, an option to contact an analyst is included in the reply. Typically, the user clicks on a link in the e-mail, and the program automatically submits a problem report based on the user's original message.

The major advantages of e-mail include convenience and usability, since most individuals are familiar with and adept at using e-mail to communicate. In addition, analysts can work on e-mail problems at their convenience (within limits, of course). In some help desks, agents work on e-mail problems during slow periods of the day.

There are several disadvantages to using e-mail as a support tool. First, response time is typically slower than with telephone support. E-mail should not be used for urgent problems, since a quick response is unlikely. Standard response times are listed in a company's Service Level Agreement. For example, a company may state that the help desk will resolve telephone inquiries within four hours, and e-mail requests within eight hours. Another disadvantage is that problems may require multiple exchanges to obtain information and arrive at a solution. If an agent is on the telephone, questions can be asked when necessary. By the end of the phone call, the agent probably has most of the information required to work on solving the problem. With e-mail, the agent may have to respond a number of times before all the information has been gathered. Finally, while less expensive than telephone support, e-mail is not inexpensive. In fact, next to phone support, it is the most expensive method of providing user support.

Delayed Assisted Support: Discussion Forums

Discussion forums are online message boards in which individuals post and respond to text messages (see Figure 6.7) for an example of an online support community at Adobe.com). A discussion forum allows users to interact with each other and help solve problems. Users post problems that can be viewed by other users visiting the forum. If the other users have experienced similar problems or questions, they can share their resolution to the problems. Any user can respond to any message. Many times a discussion forum has several "power users"—individuals who have considerable experience with computers—who regularly post responses to messages.

Users are also able to use keywords to search the discussion forum for messages pertaining to the problem they are experiencing. From time to time, older messages are removed from the message board and stored in archives. Users are given the choice of searching messages from the last 30 days, 60 days, or earlier.

 READING CHECK

1 **READING REVIEW** Summarize how the most effective FAQ lists are organized, and explain why this is the most effective form of organization.

2 **CRITICAL THINKING** In addition to e-mailing transcripts of live chat sessions to users, how might a help desk make use of the transcripts?

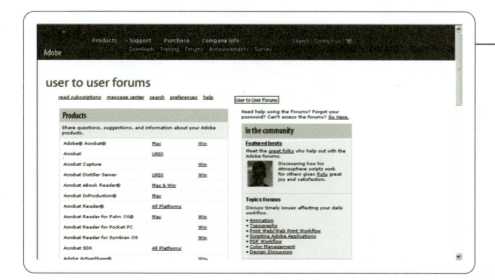

FIGURE 6.7

An example of discussion forums on a Web site

Help Desk Analysts as Writers

Help desk analysts spend most of their time dealing with people who have problems, so they need strong communication skills as well as technical and analytical skills. In a telephone-based support environment, the most important communication skills for an analyst are the abilities to listen carefully and speak clearly. As help desks shift to Web-based support solutions, many analysts spend less time talking and listening, but that does not mean communication skills are becoming less important. What it does mean is that help desk analysts increasingly need to develop their writing abilities as well as their conversational skills. According to the 2002 Help Desk Institute Best Practices Survey, five years ago, 36 percent of help desk managers thought that writing was an important skill for support reps to possess. By 2002, that number had increased to 49 percent.

Thea Johnson works in the customer service department of a company that makes medical devices such as thermometers and blood pressure meters. She handles service requests not only from consumers who use the devices at home but also from physicians, nurses, and other health care workers who use them professionally. Most of the telephone support requests she handles are from consumers, many of whom do not have Internet access at home. Medical professionals increasingly use the company's support site, which includes FAQs, a knowledgebase, and live chat as well as e-mail responses to low-priority requests. Thea is careful to use correct grammar and spelling and a formal tone in e-mail messages and live chat. Errors could easily cause misunderstanding about the products and their use. They could also create a negative impression of the company and its products and services.

In addition to handling customer requests directly, Thea is responsible for keeping the FAQ list up to date. Also, when she solves a problem, she must write up the solution and add it to the site's knowledgebase. That way, users who have the same problem in the future will be able resolve it without calling the help desk.

Thea's company has a technical communications department with professional writers and editors who review documents before they are added to the knowledgebase. They check the documents to ensure clear language and organization as well as correct grammar and spelling. Thea's documents require few changes before they are published in the knowledgebase. One editor even suggested that Thea consider technical writing as the next move on her career path.

EXPLORING CAREERS

1. Why is writing ability increasingly important for a help desk analyst?

2. Use the Web, newspaper advertisements, job postings in your school's placement office, and other resources to find descriptions of help desk jobs. What percentage of the job descriptions mention writing tasks or specifically list writing skills as a requirement? What kinds of writing do they involve? For example, do they require writing e-mail, contributing articles to a knowledgebase, or writing installation instructions for software? Write a report about what you find.

6.4 Web-Based Support: Benefits and Challenges

The field of Web-based support is evolving on an almost daily basis. The rapid pace of change is accompanied by both major advances and major challenges. In coming years, the addition of tools that are even more intelligent and efficient promises to change the help desk as we know it today.

Benefits

The tools and technologies available in today's support environment should not be underestimated. There are numerous benefits to the user and also to the help desk.

Benefits to the User
- Support is available 24 hours a day, 7 days a week, 365 days a year.
- Support is available from any location with Internet access.
- Access to information is instant, with no busy signals and no wait for support.
- The user receives expert, tested advice.
- The user can track the status of the problem online.
- Time savings are afforded by eliminating the step of describing the problem to a help desk analyst; instead the user goes directly to the process of resolving it.
- Users are more productive because they are not relying on people and resources that may not be immediately available when needed.
- A wider choice of options meet their support needs (e.g., Web, telephone, desk-side).
- Service quality for other support requests is increased because help desk staff members are not occupied with repetitive calls.
- Support can be provided in multiple languages without increasing staff.

Benefits to the Help Desk
- Key information about the user, existing applications, and hardware configuration is electronically collected, eliminating the need to gather information each time a user submits a problem.
- The job is more interesting because self-service tools handle simple, repetitive issues.
- There are cost savings.
- The volume of calls is reduced.
- Support staff are better able to respond to critical, time-sensitive problems such as system outages.
- Callbacks, status requests, and repeat calls are greatly reduced.
- The single point of distribution for all contact types ensures consistent information.

Chapter Review

›› Summary

The following points were covered in this chapter.

1 Self-service support enables users to solve problems at any time, from any location, without calling the help desk. Examples of self-service support include Web sites for submitting service requests and knowledge-bases where users can search for solutions to problems.

2 Self-service support is easy to use, and it provides fast, accurate service with a variety of options. In addition, the information provided is consistent and up-to-date, and it is also less expensive than traditional methods of support.

3 An effective Web-based support site offers other support options in addition to self-service. The options can be sorted into four stages: automated help that requires no action on the user's part, self-service support, real-time assisted support, and delayed assisted support.

4 Self-service tools are most appropriate for routine problems that do not require a high level of technical expertise to resolve. On a typical help desk, more than half of service requests are for password resets, problem status reports, help with problems such as recovering lost or corrupted files, and instructions on how to perform tasks. These requests can generally be resolved quickly with self-service support.

5 A number of tools can be posted on support Web sites. These include self-healing programs for restoring applications to working condition, searchable knowledgebases, lists of frequently asked questions (FAQs), online documentation, live chat, e-mail, and discussion forums.

6 Help desk Web sites also offer assisted support if a user is unable to solve a problem using self-service tools. Assisted support can be real time or delayed.

7 Challenges presented by Web-based support include difficulties integrating it with other help desk programs, such as traditional call management systems, and motivating employees to use it. Even the best-designed Web site must be marketed to users if it is to succeed.

›› Key Terms

The following terms were defined in this chapter:

a diagnostic programs

b discussion forums

c frequently asked questions (FAQ)

d intelligent escalation

e intranet

f live chat

g online documentation

h remote control programs

i rollback

j self-healing programs

k self-service support

l standards

Chapter 6 Review

›› Reviewing Key Terms

Write the letter of the key term that matches each definition below:

_____ **1** These Web-based tools and technologies enable users to solve problems on their own through the use of a support Web site.

_____ **2** A network similar to the Internet, except that the information is accessible only to employees within an organization or others who have been granted access rights.

_____ **3** Programs that automatically restore desktop applications to their original state by reinstalling components that have been damaged, removed, or modified.

_____ **4** Policies that specify the acceptable use of both software and hardware and define standard software and hardware equipment.

_____ **5** In a knowledgebase, the ability to identify problems that are beyond its scope and bring them to the attention of the help desk.

_____ **6** A list of common queries and answers on a topic.

_____ **7** Software that allows support personnel to take over and manage user PCs without leaving the help desk.

_____ **8** Software for collecting PC configuration information, analyzing the diagnostic data, and troubleshooting problems.

_____ **9** Online message boards in which individuals post and respond to text messages.

_____ **10** A type of Web-based support in which a user and a support agent write messages back and forth in real time as they try to determine the cause of a problem.

_____ **11** The restoration of a program or computer to an earlier configuration that is known to work effectively.

_____ **12** Software and hardware manuals and other user guides that are available through Web sites.

›› Reviewing Key Facts

True/False

Identify whether each statement is True (T) or False (F). Rewrite the false statements so that they are true.

_____ **1** Web-based self-service support costs less than telephone service but more than live chat and e-mail support.

_____ **2** Most support Web sites are located on the Internet for use by the general public.

_____ **3** As users become comfortable with self-service support, the help desk receives fewer calls about routine problems and can focus on difficult technical problems.

>> **Reviewing Key Facts** *(continued)*

____ **4** Requests for password resets are the most frequent type of support call.

____ **5** An effective self-service Web site requires all users to resolve their own problems without involving the help desk.

____ **6** In case of problems with a user's software configuration, a self-healing program can implement a rollback to a configuration that worked well.

____ **7** A support knowledgebase enables users to search for answers to their questions only during business hours.

____ **8** An effective knowledgebase solution can resolve all questions that users have.

____ **9** Intelligent escalation saves time by not requiring a help desk analyst to repeat steps that have already been taken in an effort to solve a problem.

____ **10** In live chat support, help desk analysts have to type the answers to questions whenever they are asked, even if the same questions are asked several times a day.

Completion

Write the answer that best completes each of the following statements:

1 Self-service support was made possible, in part, by the growth and popularity of _____.

2 Self-service support results in better educated, more confident _____.

3 Live chat is an example of _____ help for users.

4 To be effective, a knowledgebase requires continual _____.

5 A remote control program allows a support staff member to take over and manage a user's _____ without leaving the help desk.

>> **Understanding Key Concepts**

Provide brief answers to the following questions:

1 What is the idea behind Web-based support?

2 When a company has standards that specify what hardware and software employees may use for business, how does this affect the company's help desk?

3 How does a support agent work with live chat?

›› Critical Thinking

As directed by your instructor, write a brief essay or discuss the following issues in groups:

① Why are online security standards a basic requirement for Web-based support?

② Why are progressive stages of support provided on a Web site?

③ Why would a help desk put product documentation on a support site?

›› Help Desk Projects

Complete the projects listed below:

 ① **Use a Web browser to visit and evaluate support sites for two different organizations, using criteria discussed in this chapter.** Report on your findings to the class.

 ② **Suppose you are on the technical support staff of an airline.** The airline has developed an intranet support site that provides a knowledgebase, online documentation for various devices and applications, and online forums for requesting help. In a group with several of your classmates, brainstorm strategies for promoting the use of the support Web site to employees.

 ③ **Think of a specific problem with a program or device that you use.** The problem can be real or imagined. Examples might include trouble starting your word processing or spreadsheet software, inability to turn on a PDA or cell phone, or a digital camera that crashes your PC whenever you attempt to upload pictures. Visit the Web site of the company that makes the software or device and try to find help with the problem. Describe the experience in a written report. Provide details about what support options were available from the Web site and how easy or difficult they were to use. Was the problem resolved? If so, in what way? How much time did you spend attempting to resolve the problem? Specify whether this support experience included telephone conversation, e-mail exchanges, or live chat with a member of the support staff.

 ④ **Invite the manager of your school's support staff to speak to your class about the school's user support.** Follow the manager's talk with a question-and-answer session. Find out why the school does or does not use Web-based support. If it does provide support through a Web site, find out what support options the site offers, what benefits and challenges it has presented, and what plans, if any, the support department has to expand the site.

 ⑤ **Register as a user at a Web site that is accessible only to people with passwords, or visit a site where you are already registered.** Suppose you have forgotten your password or need to change it. What must you do to reset the password? How long does it take? Did resetting the password require a telephone call or live chat exchange with a help desk analyst? If you received a new password by e-mail, what indications do you have that it was sent automatically or that it was sent manually?

⟫ **Help Desk Projects** *(continued)*

6 **Visit the Web site for this book and locate the link to the New York Public Library's Web site.** In what ways does this site save time for the library's cardholders? In what ways might it save money for the library? Evaluate the site's ease of use.

7 **Explore the applications and operating system on your computer to determine which ones, if any, have self-healing features.** What applications on the PC, if any, provide automated help such as software updates that require no action on your part?

8 **Locate an application on your PC that features online documentation, which might be on your hard disk, on a network server, or at a Web site.** Then locate an application for which you have (or can borrow) a printed manual. Compare and contrast the use of online documentation with the use of a printed manual for instructions for specific tasks, such as creating a formula in a spreadsheet or changing the layout of a document page. As a user, what advantages and disadvantages do you see in printed manuals and online documentation?

9 **With the class instructor as moderator and judge, divide into two teams.** Ask the teams to research and then debate this question: Do remote control programs pose serious threats to user' privacy and their control over their computers?

10 **Suppose you work for a company that makes printers.** With a group of classmates, develop a plan for a customer service Web site.

⟫ **Help Desk Strategies**

Review the following case studies and respond to the questions:

1 The law firm of Davis, Levine, and Huang employs about 400 attorneys and administrative employees. For technical support, they either call or e-mail the firm's help desk. Technical support requests fall into these general subject categories, in order of their frequency: procedures such as synchronizing a PDA with a PC-based calendar and address book; using the firm's network and databases from remote locations; difficulty finding specific directories and files on the firm's servers; inability to start specific applications; PCs and related devices that will not start or have otherwise malfunctioned; problems caused by missing or corrupt device drivers; and conflicts between drivers and other system components. The help desk's manager receives many complaints from attorneys and other employees about delays in resolving problems that prevent them from working efficiently.

- In general, what could the firm do to shorten the time it takes to resolve users' problems?

- What alternatives to telephone and e-mail support might it provide for the categories of requests it receives most often?

- Are these alternatives likely to be more costly or less costly than telephone support?

>> Help Desk Strategies *(continued)*

2. Employees at Inkwell Publications often use their office PCs to browse the Web during their lunch breaks and slow times. Many of them have downloaded games and other applications from Web sites. An administrative assistant even downloaded a shareware spreadsheet application that she prefers to the one that most other employees use.

   - In your opinion, should employees download programs to company computers? Why ?

   - What are the advantages and disadvantages of employees' choosing their own spreadsheet applications or other business applications for use at work?

   - What steps could the company take to limit the applications that employees install on company PCs?

3. A customer initiated live chat with an electronics company's help desk analyst to obtain help with connecting a digital camera made by the company to her laptop computer. The agent diagnosed the problem as a missing device driver and directed her to a page on the company's Web site where she could find it. The next day, the user received a routine e-mail asking her to evaluate her experience with the help desk. She replied that the analyst had taken too long to figure out the solution to her problem. She also complained that his writing contained so many grammar errors and misspellings that she had trouble understanding his questions, that he used too much technical jargon, and that he was rude to her when she asked him to use nontechnical language.

   - How can the help desk manager determine whether the analyst handled the request correctly?

   - In you opinion, is live chat the best means of providing the kind of help this customer needed? Why ?

Performance Management

Objectives

After reading this chapter, you will be able to:

1. Explain the purpose of a Service Level Agreement.
2. Describe common help desk performance metrics.
3. Explain some of the difficulties in interpreting metrics.
4. Explain the importance of reporting results in business terms.
5. Describe how metrics are used to evaluate help desk performance.
6. Discuss the importance of customer satisfaction surveys.
7. Describe some mechanisms for call monitoring.
8. List common help desk operating costs.
9. Explain the relationship between cost per call and help desk performance.

Chapter Overview

Measuring the performance of a help desk is challenging, because statistics that seem impressive at first glance are often misleading when examined more closely. How would you view an analyst who receives more calls then other analysts? The number of calls a help desk analyst answers is not always a good representation of performance. The time it takes to effectively resolve an incident varies greatly, depending on the nature of the problem. A simple question, such as "Is the network down?" takes far less time to answer than a more complex problem, such as a computer that will not reboot. How would you perceive an analyst who has the greatest number of closed requests? The number of closed requests can also be deceptive. An analyst who closes a large number of calls in a short amount of time may not be providing adequate responses. Users may need to call the help desk again once they find out that the suggested solution does not fix the problem. This chapter examines different approaches to measuring help desk performance.

7.1 | Service Level Agreements

More and more employees rely on technology to help them perform their jobs. As a result, help desks must commit to providing a specified level of service. A Service Level Agreement (SLA) is a written agreement between the help desk and its customers (users) that defines the nature and levels of service provided. SLAs set expectations by explicitly defining the products, services, and support structure that the help desk will provide. A sample page from a SLA is shown in Figure 7.1. **Service-level management** refers to the set of people and systems that allows the organization to ensure that SLAs are being met and that the necessary resources are being provided efficiently.

The purpose of a Service Level Agreement is to specify, in mutually acceptable terms, what users can expect from the help desk in regard to the

- Scope of services provided (hardware and software supported)
- Level of services offered (for example, response time and hours of operation)
- Method for measuring and reporting compliance with the agreement
- Process for dealing with conflict between a user and an analyst

FIGURE 7.1

Sample page of a service level agreement

Service Level Agreement

Objectives
This agreement sets out the minimum level of service that Support Services is required to meet and the corresponding penalties for not meeting such levels. Our objective is to provide a continuously operating service that is well beyond the minimum levels specified.

Uptime
The target up-time for primary services is 99.8% each month.

Support
All support requests will be handled as soon as possible, the target time to action all support requests is within 15 minutes. Telephone and email support is provided Monday to Friday 8am – 10pm and on Weekends from 10am to 6pm.

Performance
All services are continuously monitored to ensure rapid response to any faults, which may occur. Monitoring is carried out on all primary services. Monitoring feedback is provided to technical support staff via email and paging services 24 hours, 7 days.

Service Level Guarantee
The service level guarantee will be measured by Support Services and is based on the up-time. If we determine that primary services were unavailable for period exceeding the maximum allowable under the prescribed up-time target, and extending for a continuous duration of 1 hour or more per instance, upon the customers request, we will credit the customers monthly invoice the prorated charges of one (1) day of the Support Services fee for each consecutive hour, up to a maximum of 7 days per month. To receive credit if this guarantee has not been met, the customer must contact us within 30 days of the end of the month for which credit is requested.

Definition of Terms
Primary services: Network availability, Operating system, Web server, Email server, Database servers.

Up-time: the total percentage of hours each month not affected by down-time.

Down-time: the total duration each month for which the primary services are not operating at a reasonable level. Down-time does not include periods for which the primary services are not operating as a result of scheduled outages or outages which can reasonably be determined as resulting from the customers actions.

Customer: Persons to whom the client has authorized access to the web hosting for the purposes of configuration, testing or development or those persons authorized/requested to act on behalf of the client.

Scheduled outages: From time to time upgrades to hardware and or software may be required, such upgrades will be performed outside of business hours. The client will be notified as far as practicable in advance of such upgrades. Scheduled outages under normal conditions should not exceed 5 hours per
year. Under normal conditions the client will be advised via the technical news mailing list no less than 24 hours in advance of any scheduled outage.

Client: The company or individual so named on the web hosting order or hosting agreement.

Most SLAs include the following topics:

- Customers—who is specifically supported by this SLA
- Mission—what the application or service supported does
- Location—where the services and support are located
- Contacts—who provides technical support
- Services covered—specific description of the application or service provided
- Service goals— measurable tasks, deadlines, or milestones
- Hours of support—specific coverage hours provided
- Environments supported—hardware, software, and release levels covered
- Environments not supported—hardware, software, and release levels not covered
- Method for requesting services and reporting problems—telephone numbers, e-mail IDs, and Web addresses for contacting support
- Support levels—specific escalation levels provided in the agreement
- Service metrics—specific measurable events covered by the agreement
- Customer satisfaction—measurable method for ensuring customer satisfaction (such as a survey) and the schedule to be followed

Characteristics of Effective Service Level Agreements

The services covered by an SLA must be built around measurable events (such as 50 percent of software-related trouble tickets will be closed during the initial call, 25 percent within two hours, 15 percent within one business day, and 10 percent within five business days). This ensures that SLAs can be monitored for meeting performance standards, and that user expectations are met. To ensure measurability, basic terms such as *response* and *resolution* must be defined, as must types of problems and corresponding response levels. Users need to know how to categorize a problem before they know what type of response to expect from the help desk. Performance standards should be set conservatively in the beginning, then increased as more experience with delivering the service is developed.

Effective SLAs have been found to share a number of characteristics, including

- Based on an understanding of business objectives and user requirements
- Developed with input from the help desk and the users
- Simple and easy to understand, with clearly defined terms that are not subject to misinterpretation
- Roles and responsibilities of all parties defined
- Levels of services defined
- Response times for levels of service defined
- Criteria for service evaluation defined

7.4 Call Monitoring

Call monitoring is the process of observing and evaluating agent performance for quality assurance and training purposes. Call monitoring confirms that users are receiving courteous and efficient service and keeps abusive users in check by informing them that their calls may be monitored. Call monitoring is also used for staff training purposes.

Monitoring Formats

Help desk managers use a combination of call monitoring methods to evaluate agent performance. The most commonly used techniques are real-time remote monitoring and call recording. In addition to telephone calls, many help desks monitor e-mail responses, fax correspondence, and Web chat sessions.

Real-Time Remote Monitoring

In **real-time remote monitoring**, a manager listens to calls without being present at the agent's workstation. Remote monitoring tends to produce an accurate portrait of agent performance, since the agent is usually unaware of precisely when monitoring takes place. Feedback can be provided immediately after a call or during regularly held feedback sessions. A sample call monitoring form is displayed in Figure 7.2.

Side-by-Side Monitoring

Side-by-side monitoring takes place at the agent's workstation. This type of monitoring is used most frequently with new agents who benefit from instant feedback on their performance. Once an agent gains experience, more accurate results are achieved through the use of remote monitoring, since the agent's behavior is not influenced by a manger's presence.

Call Recording

One of the newer methods of call monitoring is the use of sophisticated call recording systems. **Call recording** uses various technologies to record actual help desk calls for later analysis. These systems can record all calls of all agents, or they can be set up to selectively record calls from different agents at different times and days so management can analyze a random sample. Later, the recording can be listened to by both the manager and the agent. Some of these systems also capture the computer screens the agent uses during a call so the manager and the agent can determine whether the entries were made accurately and efficiently.

Call Recording: Beyond Metrics

For many help desk managers, monitoring analysts' handling of calls takes more time than any other single task. Technology has provided tools that help managers monitor calls more efficiently. A digital call recording and monitoring system, for example, can be set to alert a manager to calls that exceed a specified time limit. The manager can then listen to long calls to evaluate how the analysts could have handled them in less time.

Call length and other standard metrics can help managers identify which calls they want to evaluate, but metrics alone do not tell the whole story of whether analysts are handling calls in ways that produce customer satisfaction. While playing back a recorded call, an effective manager will listen for clues to call-handling skills and techniques that cannot be measured in minutes. These include

- **Duplication**
A help desk analyst who asks a caller's name when the caller has already stated it should pay more attention. Making the customer repeat the information annoys the customer and lengthens the call.

- **Interest**
Calls in which analysts show interest in the callers and their problems are more likely to produce positive outcomes than those in which analysts seem distracted or inattentive.

- **Assumptions**
When a caller presents a problem that sounds like hundreds of others the analyst has heard, the analyst can easily assume that it calls for the same solution. Such assumptions, however, can keep the analyst from listening closely enough to determine whether this caller's actual needs are different.

- **Responsibility**
An effective help desk analyst will take responsibility for a problem and its resolution. Evasions such as "This isn't really my territory" waste time and undermine the caller's confidence in the help desk.

- **Control**
Efficient call handling requires that the help desk analyst to stay in control of the discussion so that it stays focused on the problem. Allowing it to wonder off point will lengthen the call and can make it more difficult to obtain the information that will lead to a solution.

- **Friendliness**
Analysts should speak to callers in a friendly tone but should not overdo it. A genuinely friendly, helpful manner fosters customer satisfaction, but insincerity has the opposite effect.

Based on what they hear in recorded calls, managers can help individual analysts improve their customer relations skills and resolve problems more efficiently. Managers can also identify examples of successful call handling and use them as models in training classes.

Call recording systems can benefit help desk analysts as well as their employers. For example, a recording of a call from a disgruntled customer can protect an analyst against an unfair accusation of rudeness or ineptness. Some digital call recording systems also allow analysts to flag calls that they found troublesome. For instance, an analyst could flag a call that went off course because the caller wandered from one subject to another. The analyst could then take the initiative of asking her manager to review these calls with her and discuss ways in which she could have kept the conversation on track.

REVIEWING CONCEPTS

1. How do call recording systems help managers identify calls they want to review?

2. On help desks that use call recording, what information should analysts be given about it?

FIGURE 7.2

Sample call monitoring form

CALL MONITORING FORM

Date: _____

Help Desk Employee: _____

Evaluator: _____

Ratings: 5=Outstanding   4=Above Average   3=Average   2=Needs Improvement   1=Unacceptable

Category	Call 1	Call 2	Call 3	Call 4	Call 5	Total
Identifies self						
Uses positive tone of voice						
Speaks clearly						
Offers assistance						
Practices active listening						
Uses open-ended questions						
Uses closed-ended questions						
Listens without interrupting						
Conveys empathy						
Develops a plan of action						
Gains user agreement						
Uses customer's name						
Reviews action plan steps						
Thanks customer						
Total per Call						

Signature of Help Desk Employee _____ Date _____

Signature of Evaluator _____ Date _____

Comments: _____

Drive-Bys

A **drive-by** takes place when a manager overhears an agent's phone conversation with a user while passing by and stops to provide feedback. Drive-bys should not be relied on for regular agent evaluation, since they are unplanned events.

Characteristics of an Effective Call Monitoring System

Call monitoring, when performed effectively, is perhaps the best metric for evaluating the quality of service provided by help desk agents. In practice, effective monitoring is a time- and labor-intensive activity. To ensure that the effort is worthwhile, a monitoring system must possess the following characteristics:

- Analysts are informed that they may be monitored (may be required by state law).
- Analysts understand the purpose of monitoring and how results will be used.
- Analysts are told which lines are not monitored (can be used for personal calls).

- Only qualified designated personnel are permitted to monitor.
- Evaluation criteria are objective and standardized, and are applied consistently.
- Feedback is given promptly.
- Results are reported in such a way that an individual cannot be identified.

✔ **READING CHECK**

1. **READING REVIEW** Why do help desks monitor calls?

2. **CRITICAL THINKING** If you were a help desk manager, which types of call monitoring would you use? Why?

7.5 Quality Versus Cost

The ability to consistently provide a high level of service is key to achieving customer satisfaction. **Quality assurance** is the process of monitoring whether services being provided meet the needs of users. To determine whether quality levels are met, management uses metrics, customer satisfaction surveys, and call monitoring. Some of the questions considered in evaluating the quality of service include the following.

- Are users satisfied with the level of service the help desk is providing?
- Is the help desk meeting the requirements of the Service Level Agreement (SLA)?
- Are help desk staff and management satisfied with the service they are providing?

The quality of service must be balanced against the cost of providing the service. **Cost per call** is the average cost of each call coming in to the help desk. The standard cost-per-call formula is annual operating and overhead costs divided by number of calls received for the year. For example, if total costs were $3,000,000 and 100,000 calls were received, the average cost per call would be $30. The Help Desk Institute's Best Practices Survey for 2002 found that the average cost per call was $29.58.

While the formula itself is relatively simple, identifying all of the costs involved with operating a help desk and interpreting the results of the cost-per-call calculation are much more complicated. Costs fluctuate widely as a result of the structure of the help desk, the services provided, and the definition of *call*. For example, a help desk that uses a dispatch structure will generally have a lower cost per call than a help desk that emphasizes first call resolution.

Determining Operating Costs

Within the confines of a limited budget, the help desk tries to satisfy the service levels set in the SLA. The higher the budget, the more the help desk can procure the resources required to meet user expectations. The main expense of all help desks is staff. The second most expensive resource is usually telephone costs, particularly if a toll-free phone number is provided for callers. In general, the following elements are considered in calculating help desk operating costs:

- Salaries and benefits for help desk staff (salary and wages, benefits package, incentive compensation, recruiting fees, and temporary staffing costs)
- External services provided to users (contracts for hardware maintenance, off-the-shelf software support, and outsourced help desk functions)
- Training for help desk staff (cost of internal and external training programs)
- Help desk software maintenance (purchasing and updating all types of help desk software, including call tracking systems, knowledge bases, remote control, reporting software, and self-healing software)
- Hardware purchase or leasing (purchasing or leasing hardware used by help desk)
- Yearly ACD and telecommunications equipment maintenance costs
- Facilities overhead (office space rent, furniture, wiring, telephone service, telephone equipment, office equipment leasing, subscriptions, resource material, customer communication and marketing, office supplies, and travel expenses).

Once total costs have been established, the term *call* must be defined before cost per call can be calculated. Help desks define a call in many ways. Some help desks use the total number of incidents rather than calls. An incident could have originated by e-mail, Web, fax, or phone. Other help desks track each type of incident separately, resulting in average cost per call, average cost per e-mail message, and average cost per Web incident.

Comparing the figures from a cost per incident help desk to the figures from a cost per call help desk can be very misleading. For example, a cost per incident calculation takes into account all contacts related to the incident until it is closed. If this requires three phone calls and an e-mail message, the total cost for the incident would include all four contacts. On the other hand, if cost per call is calculated, the total cost would be reported for each of the four contacts. The cost per call result would clearly be lower than the cost per incident figure.

Cost per call also varies depending on the services provided, which can range from the simple (password resets) to the complex (software and/or hardware conflicts). A help desk that has implemented self-service tools will most likely have a higher cost per call than a help desk that has not. Using self-service technology, users can resolve many simpler problems on their own without contacting the help desk. As a result, the calls that are made to the help desk tend to involve more-complex problems that require more time and lead to increased costs. The help desk that does not provide self-service options receives calls for simple problems along with more-complex calls. The simpler calls are resolved quickly, lowering the average cost per call.

Interpreting Cost per Call

Meaningful cost-per-call data require careful interpretation. It is overly simplistic to assume that a lower cost per call is desirable. In reality, higher cost-per-call figures can be indicative of an extremely effective help desk. There are a number of reasons why greater costs are associated with higher performing help desks.

- *Calls are longer in duration.* First call resolution requires the analyst to spend more time speaking with the user to ensure that the exact nature of the problem is well-defined.
- *More staff members are required.* If more time is spent on each initial call, there must be enough analysts available to answer calls that come in while the other analysts are busy on first contact calls.
- *Training costs are higher.* A high rate of first call resolution requires well-trained, experienced analysts.

When interpreting cost-per-call figures, first call resolution rates and customer service ratings must be considered. A high cost-per-call figure coupled with high first call resolution and high customer satisfaction does not indicate a problem. On the other hand, a low cost-per-call figure coupled with low first call resolution and low customer satisfaction does demand attention. Table 7.6 explores the impact of cost per call, first call resolution, and customer satisfaction on help desk effectiveness.

Cost per Call	First Call Resolution	Customer Satisfaction	Overall Effectiveness (1–5 scale, 5 = highest)
High	High	High	5
High	Low	High	4
High	High	Low	2.5
High	Low	Low	1
Low	Low	Low	1
Low	High	Low	2.5
Low	Low	High	4
Low	High	High	5

TABLE 7.6

Impact of Cost per Call, First Call Resolution, and Customer Satisfaction on Overall Help Desk Effectiveness

Like all statistics that are available to management in operating the help desk, cost per call must be interpreted along with all available metrics to determine the overall value and success of the help desk. Factors such as how quickly phones are answered, how long it takes to resolve a problem, and how users perceive the service being provided should all be taken into account when evaluating help desk performance.

Understanding and correctly using performance metrics is crucial to the success of a help desk. Used appropriately, performance metrics are a powerful way of demonstrating the help desk's value to the organization. When the metrics used by the help desk accurately reflect the service levels promised in the SLA, chances are that the goal of customer satisfaction will be met.

✓ READING CHECK

1. **READING REVIEW** What is the standard formula for calculating cost per call?

2. **CRITICAL THINKING** Last year, the help desk at Armbruster Manufacturing introduced Web-based self-service support in an effort to reduce support costs. Now, the average cost per call is higher than it was when all contact with the help desk was via telephone calls. Does this mean the self-service support is ineffective? Why?

>> Summary

The following points were covered in this chapter:

1 As more employees rely on technology to perform their jobs, help desks are increasingly required to provide specified levels of service. A Service Level Agreement (SLA) is a written definition of the nature and level of service a help desk is obligated to provide.

2 Support managers use standard metrics, such as the average time to answer and average call handling time, to evaluate the performance of the help desk and of individual support specialists. The metrics used by a help desk correspond closely with the terms and conditions defined in its SLA.

3 The interpretation of common help desk metrics is challenging; many times a result that initially appears positive or negative may actually be just the opposite. A decrease in call handling time may indicate a more efficient help desk, or it may suggest that analysts are not spending sufficient time to resolve user problems. A decrease in the number of calls to the help desk could mean users are more able to solve problems on their own, or it could indicate that users have such a low perception of the help desk that they do not bother to call.

4 Reports on how the help desk contributes to the company's success are more effective than metrics for demonstrating performance to senior management. Developing this kind of information requires the help desk to have a keen understanding of the business and to collect information about contributions it has made, such as the number of times an analyst has helped an employee close a sale or meet a critical deadline.

5 Companies use surveys, questionnaires, and evaluation forms to measure customer satisfaction. They may also use informal methods such as telephone calls and e-mail to users. To measure event-based satisfaction, they generally use one-time surveys completed by users soon after service encounters; the results are used to evaluate the performance of individual agents. To measure general satisfaction, they survey all users or a cross-section of the user base annually or at other regular intervals.

6 Customer satisfaction surveys are a critical component of a help desk quality assurance program. User surveys provide valuable information about areas in which the help desk is performing well and areas that need improvement. The most common method is to survey users immediately after they have completed calls to the help desk.

7 Call monitoring helps ensure that users receive courteous and efficient service from the help desk, and it is useful for training purposes. The most commonly used monitoring techniques are real-time remote monitoring and call recording. Many help desks monitor e-mail and fax correspondence and Web instant chat sessions as well as telephone calls. Side-by-side monitoring by a manager at a support specialist's workstation is most often used to provide immediate feedback to new agents.

8 Common help desk operating costs include staff salaries and benefits, external services, training, equipment purchase or lease, hardware and software maintenance, and facilities overhead.

9 The quality of service must be balanced against the cost of providing service. The standard way to determine cost per call is to divide annual operating and overhead costs by the number of calls received for the year. Costs fluctuate widely according to help desk structure, the services provided, and the definition of *call*.

›› Key Terms

The following terms were defined in this chapter:

- **a** auxiliary time
- **b** available time
- **c** average abandon rate
- **d** average handling time (AhT)
- **e** average hold time
- **f** average speed to answer (ASA)
- **g** average work time (AWT)
- **h** call monitoring
- **i** call recording
- **j** cost per call
- **k** customer satisfaction
- **l** drive-by
- **m** event-based satisfaction
- **n** first call resolution (FCR)
- **o** overall satisfaction
- **p** performance measurement
- **q** quality assurance
- **r** real-time remote monitoring
- **s** return on investment (ROI)
- **t** service-level management
- **u** side-by-side monitoring
- **v** total number of calls

›› Reviewing Key Terms

Write the letter of the key term that matches each definition below:

_____ **1** A measurement that compares the cost of providing support to the value of a support group's services and benefits.

_____ **2** A metric that measures the average time callers are on hold.

_____ **3** The customer's perception of the service that is being provided by the help desk.

_____ **4** A type of monitoring that takes place at an agent's workstation to give agents immediate feedback on their performance.

_____ **5** A metric that measures the amount of time an analyst spends out of the queue performing work required to complete the call after hanging up the telephone.

_____ **6** A metric that indicates the percent of incidents that are resolved by the help desk on the initial contact.

_____ **7** The process of observing and evaluating agent performance for quality assurance and training purposes.

_____ **8** A type of call monitoring in which a manager overhears an agent's phone conversation with a user while passing by and stops to provide feedback.

>> Reviewing Key Terms (continued)

____ **9** A metric that reflects the amount of time each help desk analyst is unavailable to receive calls due to time spent performing non-phone support tasks.

____ **10** A metric that measures the average time it takes an agent to resolve a user problem.

____ **11** A metric that reflects the amount of time each help desk analyst is logged into the ACD system waiting to take calls.

____ **12** A relatively new type of call monitoring that uses various technologies to record actual help desk calls for later analysis.

____ **13** A measure of customer satisfaction obtained from one-time surveys completed by users soon after service encounters.

____ **14** A metric that measures the average amount of time from when a call is placed until it is answered by the help desk.

____ **15** A type of call monitoring in which a manager listens to calls without being present at the agent's workstation.

____ **16** A metric that reports the percentage of calls that come into the help desk but are not answered by a help desk analyst.

____ **17** A metric that indicates the number of distinct user problems a help desk receives in a fixed period of time.

____ **18** The people and systems that allow an organization to ensure that it meets the terms of its SLA and that necessary resources are provided efficiently.

____ **19** A measure of customer satisfaction determined through the use of ongoing surveys conducted at regular intervals.

____ **20** The process of monitoring whether services being provided meet the needs of users.

____ **21** The average cost of responding to each service request.

____ **22** The monitoring of help desk performance to determine the level of service provided

>> Reviewing Key Facts

True/False

Identify whether each statement is True (T) or False (F). Rewrite the false statements so that they are true.

____ **1** Effective SLAs are developed with input from users as well as the help desk.

____ **2** Creating an effective metrics program requires minimal time and effort.

____ **3** A measurement of the total number of calls should include tickets generated by e-mail, voice mail, and a Web site.

____ **4** A low average handling time (AHT) means that a help desk is performing efficiently.

>> Reviewing Key Facts *(continued)*

____ 5 Help desk analysts assigned to telephones should spend all of their time answering calls from users and resolving their problems.

____ 6 If a help desk exceeds its service level goals every month, its goals may be set too low.

____ 7 Best practices indicate that at least 90 percent of the customer base should rate their overall satisfaction with the help desk as "satisfied" or better.

____ 9 The results of annual customer satisfaction surveys are used to appraise the effectiveness of individual help desk agents.

____ 9 In an effective monitoring system, analysts are told which lines are not monitored.

____ 10 The standard cost-per-call formula is the number of calls received divided by the total salaries of the help desk staff.

Completion

Write the answer that best completes each of the following statements:

1 The services covered by an SLA must be built around _____ events.

2 Some help desk metrics, including the average abandon rate, are obtained directly from the _____ system.

3 The selection of performance metrics should be _____ periodically.

4 Customer satisfaction surveys are a regular part of a help desk _____ program.

5 The main expense of a help desk is its _____.

>> Understanding Key Concepts

Provide brief answers to the following questions:

1 What are the benefits of Service Level Agreements to help desks and users?

2 Help desk metrics are obtained from what sources?

3 What tools does management use to ensure that help desk service quality levels are being met?

>> Critical Thinking

As directed by your instructor, write a brief essay or discuss the following issues in groups:

1 Should an SLA for a new service use aggressive service standards or conservative service standards? Why?

2 When should a support manager consider adjusting the help desk's performance goals?

3 What is the relationship between customer satisfaction and standard metrics?

›› Help Desk Projects

Complete the projects listed below:

 1 **Use a Web browser to find two ACD products.** Compare them in terms of the metrics they provide, and discuss how those metrics would be useful to a help desk.

 2 **Interview your school's technical support manager about the metrics the school uses for evaluating help desk performance.** Find out where the manager obtains the metrics, how the metrics are used, and how often performance goals are reevaluated. Write a report about your findings.

 3 **Invite one of your school's help desk analysts to speak to your class about how much time he or she spends handling (a) telephone calls and (b) other duties.** As a class, interview the analyst about the risk of burnout and the importance of spending some work time away from the phone.

 4 **Use a Web browser to find Service Level Agreements for two different organizations.** Evaluate and compare the agreements in terms of what you have learned in this chapter.

 5 **Work with several classmates to create a questionnaire for users that would measure event-based satisfaction.** Decide how and when you would distribute the questionnaire and how you would use the responses in managing a help desk.

 6 **Work with several classmates to create a survey that would enable a help desk to measure overall customer satisfaction.** How often would you distribute the survey? To whom would you distribute the survey, and by what means? How would the results be useful?

 7 **Imagine that you are the help desk manager for your school.** Using what you have learned in this chapter, create a draft of a Service Level Agreement that you would present to the school's directors as a starting point for negotiating a final agreement.

 8 **Form a team with two classmates.** While two of the team members play the roles of caller and help desk analyst during a service call, the third should use the call monitoring form in Figure 7.2 to evaluate handling of the call. Switch roles so that each person on the team acts as both an analyst and an evaluator.

 9 **Use a Web browser to research help desk management software products.** Identify two products from different companies, and compare them in terms of features that would help with metrics and Service Level Agreements. If you were a help desk manager, which product would you select? Why?

>> Help Desk Strategies

Review the following case studies and respond to the questions:

1 At Rayden Equipment Corp., sales rose 18 percent last year and set a new record. Help desk metrics show that the average time on hold has decreased from 70 seconds to 40 seconds in the past year, and the average call handling time is now 11.6 minutes, nearly 20 percent lower. The total number of service requests is up slightly, and most of the calls come from the sales and marketing departments. The last annual survey found that 88 percent of the employees who used the help desk were satisfied with the service they had received. Seventy-one percent of the help requests were resolved on the first contact with the user. The average abandon rate is about the same as last year's, at 6 percent. Agents now spend 21 percent of their logged-in time on auxiliary tasks and 10 percent waiting for calls.

- If you were the help desk manager, what information would you emphasize in a report on the help desk's performance to the company's senior management?

- In your report, would you suggest that the help desk staff be increased? Explain.

- Do the metrics indicate that the help desk should receive additional training? Explain.

2 The help desk at Foodsmart, a large regional grocery store chain, sends the following questionnaire to users immediately after their calls to the help desk are resolved:

> Thank you for contacting the Foodsmart Help Desk. To help us in our effort to continue providing the highest level of service, please take a moment to answer these questions about your most recent experience with us.
>
> Did the Help Desk succeed in helping you resolve the problem?
>
> Were you treated courteously?
>
> Please rate the Help Desk's response to your request as one of the following: (a) Excellent; (b) Satisfactory; (c) Somewhat disappointing; (d) Completely unsatisfactory. _____
>
> How many times per year do you call the Help Desk, on average?

- Is the number of questions appropriate?

- If you were the help desk manager, would you make any changes to the questionnaire? Explain.

3 The help desk supervisors at Bridgeport Pharmaceuticals monitor at least two calls handled by each help desk analyst on every shift. The supervisors use electronic monitoring equipment to listen in on the calls. The analysts know that some calls are monitored, but they do not know when the supervisors are listening. While monitoring each call, a supervisor uses a form to evaluate the analyst's handling of it. The supervisors do not share their findings with the analysts. Instead, they give the forms to the department's manager, who uses them as the basis of analysts' twice-yearly performance ratings. The manager also reviews the information for patterns that indicate a need for more training of individual analysts or the help desk as a whole.

- What type of call monitoring does this represent?

- Is the information gathered from the monitoring being used as effectively as possible? Explain.

Knowledge Management

Objectives

After reading this chapter, you will be able to:

1. Discuss the benefits of a knowledge management system.
2. List the characteristics of an effective knowledge base.
3. Explain the difference between reactive and proactive knowledge management.
4. Describe the four components of a solution.
5. Discuss the knowledge management process.
6. Describe methods of searching a knowledge base.
7. Discuss the effect of knowledge management on help desk metrics.
8. Discuss barriers to effective knowledge management.

Chapter Overview

In most support organizations, expertise grows over time and is related to ability, background knowledge, and problem-solving skills. Some agents know more than others and can therefore handle a wider range of queries. An experienced help desk staff is a valuable resource. When staff members leave the company or switch to different assignments, their knowledge and experience leave with them. The help desk team must handle an increased workload until replacements can be hired.

Finding and hiring a new staff member who possesses communication skills, interpersonal skills, and technical ability is not easy. Many help desks must hire entry-level personnel to fill positions left open by the departure of experienced agents. Entry-level agents must learn and master large amounts of information while developing communications and relationship skills. It takes time and effort for a service and support agent to come up to speed and assume a full workload. These problems can be reduced by efficient knowledge management.

Knowledge management is the process of gathering, structuring, refining, and delivering knowledge that is of value. In a help desk setting, knowledge is stored in a database known as a knowledge base. Analysts use the knowledge base to look up answers to users' questions, and users access the knowledge base to try to solve problems without contacting the help desk.

Help desks that implement knowledge management systems realize many benefits to both users and analysts. The section below describes some of the significant benefits, including

- Decreased call volume
- Shared expertise
- Reduced training time
- Reusable solutions
- Enriched job content
- Personal empowerment
- Continuous improvement

Decreased Call Volume

A self-service knowledge base allows users to search for answers to their questions 24 hours a day via the Web. By providing this type of support, fewer calls are made to the help desk. As a result, help desk analysts can devote their time and resources to answering more complex questions.

As using the Web has become as familiar as turning on a television to many people, more individuals prefer self-service to a live-service encounter, at least for some problem types. The primary reasons are speed and efficiency. There is no waiting time; the user can look for a solution as soon as a problem is detected. For example, a user receives an error message about a driver being corrupted. Rather than call the help desk and wait for a live agent, it is possible to immediately search the knowledge base for a solution—in this case, a solution that provides a link to a specific driver for downloading.

Shared Expertise

A knowledge base not only captures information and expertise, but also makes that expertise available to a broad range of individuals, from end users to support staff. In the help desk itself, this sharing of expertise reduces the impact of employee turnover. In the past, when an agent left the help desk to take a different position, everything the agent knew was lost. It existed in the agent's head, not in a computer database. With a knowledge base in place, agents write up solutions and workarounds to problems as they occur, and if appropriate, these solutions are added to the knowledge base.

In addition to the problem of turnover, help desks also struggled with differences in analysts' knowledge levels. There were always some analysts who knew how to solve problems that others did not know how to solve. If a user called with a problem, the timeliness of a solution would depend on which analyst took the call. With a knowledge base in place, any analyst who received the call can search the knowledge base and find the solution. Because information included in a knowledge base is accessible to all agents, individuals can reach the same level of expertise by building on one another's experience and knowledge.

Reduced Training Time

When support agents are trained to effectively use a knowledge base, they quickly become productive. They are able to search for solutions to user problems in the knowledge base instead of exclusively relying on the information they learn on the job. Once agents are comfortable using the knowledge base, they become much more efficient.

Reusable Solutions

Once a problem has been analyzed and solved, the benefits of that work are available to anyone who needs access to the information. This results in increased productivity, allowing agents more time to deal with new queries. It also improves user satisfaction, since answers are delivered in less time. In addition, the reuse of existing knowledge lowers costs due to repeated searches of the same topics and repeated development of the same solutions.

Enriched Job Content

Some of the top reasons for burnout and departure cited by analysts include having to support old products, supporting products for which insufficient knowledge is available, and repeatedly solving the same problems. Analysts who have access to a knowledge base are able to solve routine problems quickly (in fact, many are solved by users themselves), so they spend their time researching new and novel problems instead of responding to the same queries over and over.

Personal Empowerment

The analyst is transformed from someone who provides answers over the phone to someone who creates organizational knowledge. As creators of knowledge, analysts become recognized for their abilities to diagnose and resolve problems. The valuable work and knowledge of the analyst is recognized as an important asset and is preserved so that it can be used to improve the productivity of the help desk and its users.

Continuous Improvement

As a knowledge base is used over time, continuous feedback from agents and users helps the system improve. Existing solutions are revised, new solutions are added, and outdated solutions are removed. This continuous evaluation increases the value and usability of the knowledge base.

✓ READING CHECK

1. **READING REVIEW** What are some significant benefits of knowledge management?

2. **CRITICAL THINKING** How might individual help desk analysts contribute to the continued improvement of their company's knowledge base?

8.2 Characteristics of an Effective Knowledge Base

To be a useful tool, a knowledge base must be
- Easy to use
- Simple to maintain
- Relevant
- Accessible

Easy to Use

Above all, the knowledge base must be easy to use. It must be intuitive, possess a simple interface, and be developed with commonly accepted Web tools. The system must not place any constraints on the end user or require special abilities or training. A key to ease of use is to have strong search capabilities.

Simple to Maintain

The knowledge base site must be easy to administer, especially since content changes on a daily basis. A knowledge base is not very useful if it is not kept up-to-date. If the process of administration is complex and time-consuming, information is less likely to updated frequently. At the same time, the ability to make changes to the knowledge base must be restricted to ensure that the information is accurate and conforms to standards for quality, style, and format.

In addition, maintenance and administrative tasks must be kept to a minimum to avoid unnecessarily high expenses. The knowledge base should interact with the problem management system, so new solutions are easy to add to the system.

Relevant

The knowledge base must be relevant to the needs of the help desk and the users. Relevancy is established primarily through the content of the solution, particularly the context in which a problem occurs. When the context of a situation is contained within the solution, the solution is reusable by a very wide audience.

The solution's ability to be found is as significant as its relevance. Analysts and users do not have time to perform multiple searches that lead to answers that are not relevant. The solutions in the knowledge base must be categorized and prioritized relative to the details of a situation presented by a user.

Accessible

Access to the knowledge base via the Web gives both users and remote staff the ability to capitalize on the available knowledge. The knowledge base can provide self-service support via the Web, giving customers direct access to the most up-to-date information on a 24-hours-a-day, 7-days-a-week, 365-days-a-year basis. This releases analysts from resolving minor issues and allows them to focus on bigger issues.

 READING CHECK

1. **READING REVIEW** What are four characteristics of an effective knowledge base?

2. **CRITICAL THINKING** What difference does it make to a knowledge base's users if the knowledge base is difficult to maintain? Why?

8.3 Proactive and Reactive Knowledge Management

One of the primary decisions an organization must make when implementing a knowledge management system is whether to adopt a reactive or proactive methodology. Many of the decisions made later in the implementation process are based on the type of methodology that will be used.

Reactive Knowledge Management

In a **reactive knowledge management** process, the task of capturing new knowledge is part of the problem management practice—that is, new knowledge is captured when a case is closed. Reactive knowledge management is also referred to as solution-centered support or knowledge-centered support.

Processes must be in place to ensure that the relevant knowledge is captured and is presented in a way that makes it usable to the greatest number of people. The knowledge management process consists of four steps (see Figure 8.2).

1. Capture
2. Structure
3. Review
4. Release and maintain

Capture

Capturing knowledge is the first step of the process and involves identifying and collecting information that will be included in the knowledge base. When an organization is creating a knowledge base from scratch, it is necessary to identify the information that users and the help desk staff require. Initial entries in the knowledge base are derived from existing help desk requests. By studying existing call records and logs, it is possible to discover the most frequently reported problems. These issues should all be included in a list of problems and solutions to be added to the knowledge base.

Information is also obtained by interviewing help desk staff at all levels. The problem-solving information required for a new first-level analyst differs greatly from the information used by an experienced second-level analyst. Other information resources can be used to create knowledge, such as manuals and cases stored in problem management systems. These sources are reviewed to determine which information would be of value in the knowledge base.

FIGURE   8.2

The knowledge management process

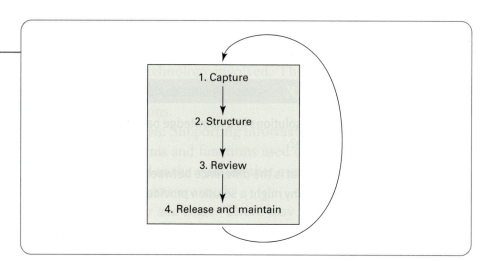

Once a knowledge base exists, content is added, revised, or deleted as needed. When a new problem has been solved by an analyst, that analyst writes a draft of the situation, which is then placed in an existing structure.

Structure

Once knowledge has been captured, it must be structured. **Structuring** is the process of indexing, categorizing, and classifying information. An unstructured knowledge base is a collection of documents in various formats. The document contains words, but the search engine has no means of determining the context of the words. The lack of structure minimizes the ability of the search engine to provide the right answer. A search for "printing problem" will yield solutions that have nothing to do with printing. Somewhere in the document the word "print" and "problem" may have been used, like "To see his name in print" or "A test print will be performed so it can be documented on screen what the problem might be" This does not mean that unstructured knowledge has no value. Most companies maintain Web sites with documentation, manuals, and other files that, when combined with a search engine, permit the support analyst or user to find a solution.

Structuring information establishes relationships between pieces of information. The solutions in a support knowledge base are usually classified into different levels for easy retrieval. For example, a search on the term "macro" would result in a subset of choices such as macros in *Microsoft Excel* and macros in *Microsoft Access*. The same search in an unstructured knowledge base would display all information that contained the word *macro*. To find the desired information, a user would have to sort through hundreds of unrelated articles.

The first level is broad and encompasses a grouping of products, such as software. The second level narrows the classification down to a specific type of software, such as *Microsoft Word*. The third level breaks out a component or feature, such as spell checker. Finally, the fourth level identifies the specific error codes or addresses how-to functionality. Proper categorization is important; broad categorization retrieves too many solutions, while narrow categorization retrieves too few.

A well-defined structure ensures that solutions are easy to find and easy to implement. The structuring process is time- and labor-intensive. It requires a type of work that has not traditionally been part of the help desk analyst's job. However, the time invested in creating this structure is more than compensated for by the time saved in finding reusable solutions. The final product will be of value only if it is easy to use. Once a preliminary structure exists, it should be tested with users. The logical classifications developed by the help desk staff may be too detailed for the needs of end users.

Most support organizations report that as many as 60 to 75 percent of the problems they solve either have already been reported to the organization or are a variation of a recognized problem. If three out of four problems can be solved by reusing a solution rather than by re-solving the problem, the one-time investment in structuring the solution for subsequent reuse is more than worth the effort. Without a content structure, the information contained in a knowledge base is free-form and cannot provide the level of performance required to help users solve technology problems.

Review

Once knowledge has been captured and structured, it must be reviewed before it can be added to the knowledge base. The new solution must be checked to determine

- Whether it accurately describes symptoms, the problem, and its resolution
- Whether it is technically accurate
- Whether it follows the standard format
- Whether it is written so that the user can understand it
- Whether it is a viable alternative that does not yet exist in the knowledge base
- Whether it can be incorporated into an existing case
- Whether it can be combined with another case to form a new one
- Whether the new case would cause an inconsistency
- Whether there is a newer case already available in the knowledge base

First the content is reviewed for technical accuracy, usually by a subject-matter expert. A **subject-matter expert (SME)** is an individual who exhibits the highest level of expertise in performing a specialized job, task, or skill within the organization. The SME is most likely a second-level or third-level support analyst with specific knowledge of the specific content area. It is the SME's responsibility to make sure the solution is correct and that all of the necessary information was collected. If the problem can be replicated, the solution is tested to determine if it resolves the problem. This process is called **validation**.

After the solution has been validated, it is reviewed for grammar, spelling, writing style, and presentation format so that the agreed-to standards are followed. It is always important to remember who will be using the knowledge base when reviewing solutions. This minimizes the possibility of including too much detail or using technical words or jargon. For example, a solution that says to reinstall *Windows* without listing the steps to accomplish this task or providing a link to a document that describes how to accomplish it is probably not going to be very useful. In addition to monitoring language, it can be helpful to include captures of screens the user will encounter while following the steps listed in the solution.

Release and Maintain

Once the review is complete, the new knowledge is ready to be released. Depending on the technology used, this usually involves publishing a copy of the knowledge and moving it to the Web support site where the knowledge base is housed.

To be effective, data in a knowledge base must be kept current. In many companies, new products or services are being offered continually. Therefore, it is critical for users to be able to find answers and solutions for the new products and services on the support site. Regular and timely maintenance of the knowledge base is critical to success. If people repeatedly fail to find what they are looking for, they will stop using the system.

To keep the knowledge base current, the help desk must receive up-to-date information in the following areas:

- When problems occur that do not have existing solutions
- When new software is going to be released
- When new product purchases are planned
- When new bugs are discovered

Existing content also must be reviewed on a regular basis to determine whether it is still accurate and relevant. A knowledge base that is not maintained can quickly bog down with hundreds of outdated solutions that have not been removed. Changes are made to the existing information when several circumstances occur, including the following:

- Help desk staff suggest revisions when they encounter problems using a solution during the normal course of their work.
- Users contact the help desk to report a solution that is not working.
- Help desk staff members become aware of changes to systems and services (through meetings, change management reports) and search the knowledge base to identify documents that will require revision.

✓ **READING CHECK**

1. **READING REVIEW** What is the first step of the knowledge management process?

2. **CRITICAL THINKING** Is it better to add solutions to a knowledge base as quickly as possible or to spend time reviewing them first? Why?

Computer Practice 8.1 | Add a New Standard Solution

Complete the following exercise using the HelpSTAR software that is on the CD in the back of the book. *Note: The password for all of the sample users in these exercises is 'helpstar'.*

1. Start HelpSTAR.

2. Login as John Keyser.

3. Select *Administration > Standard Solution* from the main menu. The 'List of Standard Solutions' window will be displayed.

4. Click the 'New Standard Solution' button (🗒). The 'Create a New Standard Solution' window will appear.

5. Enter *Error 512254 - Cannot Print Invoices* in the 'Title' field.

6. Click in the 'Problem Type' field and select "Software – Accounting" from the drop-down menu.

7. Click the 'Add' button next to the 'Keywords' field. The 'Keywords' dialog box will appear.

8. Select 'Application' from the available keyword(s) and click the 'Add' button. The keyword will disappear from the 'Available' list on the left and appear in the list of 'Selected keywords' on the right.

9. Click the 'Save' button.

10. In the 'Problem Description' field, enter *Cannot print invoices from Accounting Software*.

11. In the 'Resolution field', enter *Download latest patch from vendor's website and install on PC experiencing the problem. This is a known issue reported by the vendor*.

12. Click the 'Save' button.

13. A message will appear stating that the solution has been added as a 'Draft' solution. New solutions that are saved in 'Draft' mode can only be accessed by support reps. (Solutions can also be "published" so that they may also be accessed by end users). Click the 'OK' button to continue.

14. To confirm that the solution is listed as a 'Draft' solution, click the arrow at the end of the 'Published List' field at the top-left of the Standard Solutions listing and select 'Draft List'. Only the solutions in draft mode will be listed.

15. To publish the Standard Solution, select the new solution in the draft list and click the 'Publish' button (🖉)on the toolbar. The solution will no longer be visible in the draft list as it has been moved to the published list of solutions.

16. To verify that the Solution has been published, click the arrow at the end of the 'Draft List' field and change the display from 'Draft List' to 'Published List'.

17. Exit HelpSTAR.

8.6 | Knowledge Base Search Methods

Once knowledge has been captured, structured, reviewed, and released, it becomes incorporated into the knowledge base. The knowledge is available to help desk analysts and to end users—if they can find it. To locate desired solutions in a knowledge base, a search is conducted. Many studies have been conducted in an attempt to identify the most effective methods of searching for information in a large database such as a knowledge base. Some of the available search methods include

- Keyword search engine
- Natural-language processing
- Expert systems
- Decision tree

Keyword Search Engine

The simplest search method is a basic **keyword search engine**, into which users enter several key words and click on the Search button. The system then returns a list of answers or pages that contain one or more of the words provided. The more words that matched the contents of the search string, the higher the relevance given the answer.

This basic search method has several major drawbacks. First, the search will result in a large number of documents, many of which will not be at all relevant. For example, a search on a term such as "Windows" will return documents about household windows, automobile windows, the Microsoft operating system, and thousands more. The search will even include all documents in which "windows" appears only once.

Another problem with search engines is the underlying assumption that a user can specify the appropriate keywords to search for the related documents. Users are not necessarily technical workers; more often they are people in other areas of the business who simply want to ask questions in their own words and receive solutions that work. If the user does not have the skill to provide proper keywords, the system may fail to retrieve the relevant documents even though they are in the system.

Finally, documents themselves can be misleading. The true meaning comes from the context in which words are used. Basic search engines do not take into account different meanings and interpretations of words in relation to context.

Natural-Language Processing

Advances in keyword search engines have led to more sophisticated search capabilities that allow the support analyst or user to enter actual phrases or sentences. **Natural-language processing systems** evaluate the words based on their positioning in relation to each other. An exact match of a phrase would have a higher relevancy than phrases with all the same words in a different order. Natural-language processing is the easiest search method for nontechnical users and is widely used on the Web.

Expert Systems

An **expert system** is a program that simulates the interaction a user might have with a human expert to solve a problem. A familiar example of an expert system is *Windows'* troubleshooting "wizards." The end user provides input by selecting one or more answers from a list or by entering data. The program will ask questions until it has reached a conclusion. The conclusion may be the selection of a single solution or list of possible solutions arranged in order of likelihood. Expert systems perform a set of activities traditionally associated with highly skilled or knowledgeable humans—activities like medical diagnosis and stock market analysis.

A **rule-based** expert system is an expert system that uses a set of rules as its knowledge base. **Rules** are statements of the form: *if some condition is true, then do something.* A rule is a concise description of a set of conditions and a set of actions to take if the conditions are true. For example, a rule might be stated as follows:

> *If the printer is plugged in, turn it on.*
>
> or
>
> *If the printer is not plugged in, plug it in now.*

Decision Tree

One type of rule-based expert system is a decision tree. A **decision tree** consists of a series of questions that guide a user to relevant solutions based on his or her responses (see Figure 8.3). By making a selection at each branch point, a tree diagram can help someone make a decision. In a sense, it is a very simple expert system. This type of tree-structured logic can easily be converted to a computerized system that is easier to use, faster, and automated.

An example of a simple form of decision tree is a diagnostic tree, in which a support analyst or user is presented with a question that helps the system identify the actual problem. The answer may lead to a solution or to another question. Diagnostic trees are an easy way to guide the user from a symptom like "I can't print" to a problem like "I can't print because my printer is out of paper," which in turn leads to a solution. Decision trees are most effective when solving relatively simple problems.

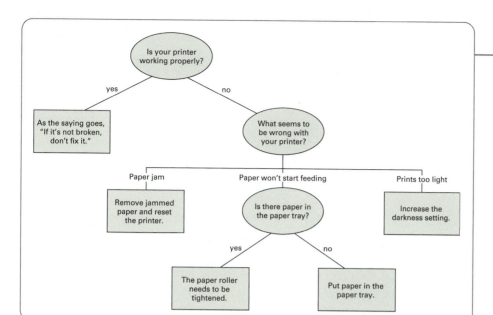

FIGURE 8.3

Sample decision tree

In a help desk environment, expert systems possess a number of limitations, such as the following:

- The process of encoding the knowledge into the system is slow, making it difficult to keep the knowledge base up to date.
- The investment in developing the system is significant, as is the investment in system maintenance.
- Expert systems are limited to certain problems, working successfully only with problems of classification that have few alternative outcomes. In addition, the outcomes must be known in advance.
- Not all problems can be solved through the use of if-then statements. Many times, user problems are solved through the intuitive powers of an analyst who has a hunch about the source of the problem. Expert systems cannot accommodate knowledge that is essentially intuitive.

While rule-based systems have wide-ranging application in business, particularly in financial areas, case-based reasoning (CBR) is frequently used to build help desk knowledge systems.

Case-Based Reasoning

Case-based reasoning (CBR) systems use past cases to solve new problems. **Case-based reasoning** is based on the assumption that human beings use their past experiences to try to solve problems. The approach of CBR is not to find appropriate rules in a knowledge base, but to find similar cases from the database of prior cases (see Figure 8.4).

Elements in a case-based reasoning system are the case database and an electronic "index" that is used to efficiently search and quickly retrieve cases that are most appropriate or similar to the current problem. If no

FIGURE 8.4

Case-based reasoning

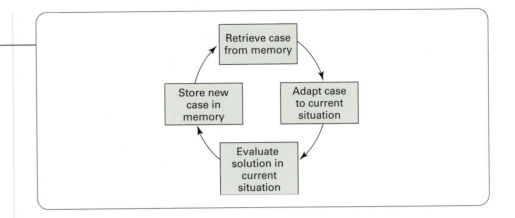

reasonably appropriate prior case is found, then the current case and its human created solution can be added to the knowledge base, thus allowing the system to learn.

Cases consist of information about the problem, diagnosis, and solutions. The problem description is the first information the help desk agent gets from the user. This description is what the user subjectively perceives as the problem. It may or may not have to do with the actual cause of the failure. The diagnosis consists of the questions the help desk agents must ask or the information they must obtain from various sources to arrive at a diagnosis. The diagnosis contains the minimal amount of information that is necessary to diagnose the problem.

The solution contains the fault—that is, what caused the problem—and the remedy—how to solve the problem. Depending on how the system is implemented and what statistical information is needed for further evaluation, some additional data may also be included in the case file.

To be effective, a CBR system needs a good case retrieval mechanism and a good case database maintenance method. If a CBR system lacks either of these methods, it can not solve a problem because it may find irrelevant or outdated cases.

When the support analyst or user enters several words and clicks on the Search button, the system responds with a list of potential solutions. In addition, the system presents a set of questions that will help refine the search. The questions are usually ordered so that the first question relates to more of the solutions provided, as the system reasons that these solutions are the most likely to resolve the problem. Unlike with a decision tree, the support analyst or user can choose to answer any question in any order. Both the selection of questions and the answers provided impact the search results. This technology can provide for a very effective knowledge base.

Some CBR systems use the sentence structure of the problem description to index into past cases. Some use specialized text retrieval technology. One even claims to use fuzzy logic to identify the most relevant cases. **Fuzzy logic** is a rule-based technology that creates rules that use approximate or subjective values and incomplete or ambiguous data. Fuzzy logic represents more closely the way people actually think than traditional if-then rules. For example, if one person states that 85 degree weather is hot and 40 degree weather is cold, then what is 65 degrees? The answer is "fuzzy"—it cannot be answered by responding to if-then questions.

Case-based reasoning systems are relatively easy to learn and use. No expensive initial accumulation and organization of the knowledge is necessary. Knowledge is accumulated in a shared-notebook format, starting with the first case handled. These systems can often be maintained by dedicated staff members who re-index cases that are not being properly retrieved and remove those that are no longer relevant.

✔ READING CHECK

1. **READING REVIEW** Which knowledge base search method most closely resembles consulting a human being about a problem?

2. **CRITICAL THINKING** Why do support knowledge bases often use case-based reasoning (CBR) rather than expert systems?

8.7 Knowledge Management Metrics

When a knowledge management system is implemented in a support environment, it is necessary to add new metrics and reevaluate existing metrics that are used to evaluate performance. For example, if analysts are rewarded for the number of cases they handle in a day, they are going to resist process changes that will lengthen the time to close a case, such as capturing the knowledge.

Development of New Metrics

When analyzing the value of the knowledge management system, new measures of performance are required. Some examples of such measures are

- Total number of solutions available
- Number of cases resolved using the knowledge base
- Percent of cases resolved using the knowledge base
- Number of times users access the knowledge base
- Number of escalations to the support center via the Web
- Most frequently searched key words in the knowledge base
- Number of solutions contributed by various teams or analysts compared to the resolution rates for those same individuals via the knowledge base

Reevaluation of Existing Metrics

Effective knowledge management requires not only new measurements, but also a reexamination of existing metrics and the interpretation of measurement results. Some of the metrics that need to be reexamined when a knowledge management system is implemented include:

- *Average case duration*: When a knowledge management system is first implemented, there is a learning curve resulting in increased time for agents to handle a case. As the support analysts become more comfortable with the tools and as the knowledge base contains more information, this time will begin to decrease . Support analysts are also being asked to do more work (capture the knowledge) when a solution is not in the knowledge base. This will extend the time spent on this case, but the time will be leveraged the next time a customer presents the same problem. If a self-service knowledge base is implemented, users will begin solving more problems on their own, and the help desk will be left with the more challenging cases that may take longer to solve.
- *First call resolution rate*: A knowledge management system that is used by analysts to solve user problems should lead to an increase in first call resolution rates since analysts answer more cases more quickly. When a user self-service option is implemented, the first call resolution rate may decrease since users start answering their own questions, leaving the more challenging cases for the support center.
- *Call volume*: As more and more users become comfortable with a Web-based self-service knowledge base, the number of calls to the help desk should decrease, and the amount of Web site access should increase.

The implementation of quality metrics will help support center management identify content and process areas that need improvement or adjustment. In addition to these types of measurements, it is important to capture the measurements that will be used to define the project's success.

 READING CHECK

1. **READING REVIEW** Should a company continue to use the same help desk metrics when it institutes knowledge management? Explain briefly.

2. **CRITICAL THINKING** How does knowledge management change the ways in which help desk analysts' productivity is evaluated?

Jobs in Knowledge Management

As an analyst on a help desk in an organization that uses knowledge management, you are likely to gain knowledge management experience in at least two ways: by consulting a knowledge base and by contributing to it. You will probably consult the knowledge base for existing solutions to users' problems. When the knowledge base contains no solution for a problem you are handling, you may be responsible for documenting how you solve the problem and adding the solution to the knowledge base. Support specialists may also be involved in maintaining the knowledge base by identifying redundant, conflicting, incorrect, or outdated solutions that need to be removed from the knowledge base.

A job on a help desk can be the gateway to many related fields, and knowledge management is among them. Based on the introduction to knowledge management that support work provides, you might develop an interest in this field. Knowledge management offers a variety of career opportunities for people with a range of skills and temperaments. Knowledge management jobs include the following.

- **Knowledge engineer**
People in this job focus on the technical side of knowledge management. Working as a knowledge engineer requires training or experience with the software available for capturing knowledge, storing it in a knowledge base, and retrieving it from the knowledge base.

- **Knowledge editor**
Knowledge editors are concerned primarily with the quality of the knowledge base's contents. Editing and writing skills are important in this job.

- **Knowledge navigator**
Knowledge navigators are responsible for locating pools of knowledge within their organizations, which might be spread through a multitude of documents and databases.

- **Knowledge manager**
Experienced knowledge workers can become knowledge managers who oversee the work of knowledge engineers, knowledge editors, and knowledge navigators.

- **Chief knowledge officer (CKO)**
A CKO is the most senior knowledge manager in an organization, usually a large company. The CKO creates business plans and financial reports regarding knowledge management and exchanges information with the company's other senior executives about the value of knowledge management to the organization.

People who work in knowledge management are sometimes called knowledge workers. Two organizations that certify knowledge workers are the Global Knowledge Economics Council and the Knowledge Management Certification Board. The certification process for knowledge workers is similar to the certification processes for other specialists, such as systems engineers and network administrators.

EXPLORING CAREERS

1. In an organization with knowledge management, what kind of knowledge management experience does working on a help desk provide?

2. Use the Web, newspaper advertisements, job postings in your school's placement office, and other resources to find descriptions of jobs in knowledge management. How might experience as a support specialist help prepare an applicant for any of these jobs? What skills and aptitudes do they require that are also needed on help desks?

8.8 Barriers to Effective Knowledge Management

The number-one reason most knowledge management implementations fail has nothing to do with technology. Most failures occur because of resistance to change within the help desk itself. An effective knowledge management system requires the organization to take action to manage the change process before, during, and after implementation. There are a number of reasons why support analysts fear the arrival of knowledge management, including fear if job loss and fear of losing value to the organization.

Fear of Job Loss

Support professionals fear they will lose their jobs. They may believe that management is going to use the new technology to reduce staff. Support analysts believe they have job security because they have critical knowledge.

Fear of Losing Value to the Organization

Many analysts believe they are of value to the organization because of what they know. They fear that if they share this knowledge with others in a public way, such as in a knowledge base, they will no longer be important to the company.

Fear of Change

Some analysts may dislike change; they find it easier to maintain current processes and procedures than to learn new ones. This may be true for their jobs and also in their personal lives. The implementation of a knowledge management system is one of many changes a help desk analyst will encounter. Working in the information technology field requires the ability to cope with constant change. Technology changes so rapidly that a good agent will constantly be reading and watching for changes in the field as well as ways to incorporate the new technology into the workload.

New Opportunities

In reality, the implementation of a knowledge management strategy offers many benefits and opportunities to support personnel. An analyst goes from being "someone who answers the phone" to a conduit of knowledge. The job will not be just to transmit knowledge, but instead to transform it into reusable solutions. This requires an analyst to take on the role of a developer—one who creates a product (knowledge) that will be valued by users and the organization as a whole. As solution developers, analysts become recognized for their true competency: the ability to frame, diagnose, and resolve problems. The valuable work and knowledge of the analyst is captured, recognized as a core asset, and preserved in a format that can be used to improve the productivity of the entire organization. As a result of knowledge management, the opportunities for support analysts in this new environment are greater now than they ever have been.

Overall, the successful implementation of a knowledge base protects a company from the vulnerability of staff turnover, eliminates user dissatisfaction arising from poor or inconsistent responses, and improves staff motivation. Web-based access allows the knowledge base to become a tool for both analysts and users, improving the quality of service and the consistency of response. The knowledge base also significantly reduces call volume to the help desk. The cost of implementing a knowledge management solution is quickly recovered by increased productivity, reduced call resolution times, improvement in staff effectiveness, and reduction in staff turnover, recruitment, and training costs.

Did You Know?

By 2002, 25 percent of all organizations had created a new senior executive position focused entirely on managing the organization's knowledge. The person in this position is referred to as a chief knowledge officer, or CKO. By 2005 the number of CKO positions is expected to grow by 80 percent.

✔ READING CHECK

1. **READING REVIEW** What is the biggest obstacle to the success of knowledge management in a company? Explain briefly.

2. **CRITICAL THINKING** What new career opportunities might knowledge management offer to a support specialist? What skills would these opportunities require?

Chapter (8) Review

>> Summary

The following points were covered in this chapter:

1 Knowledge management provides access to solutions for problems so that other people can apply the solutions when the problems recur. With knowledge management, help desks can find solutions efficiently even when the analysts who developed them have moved on to different positions. Knowledge management systems benefit both users and help desk analysts. A self-service knowledge base allows users to find solutions for many of their own problems at any time, which frees help desk analysts to deal with more difficult problems and makes their jobs more interesting. A knowledge base makes solutions available to all help desk analysts, regardless of their experience and skill. Knowledge management reduces help desk training costs, and it increases productivity by making the results of each new problem-solving effort available for reuse.

2 An effective knowledge base is easy to use and simple to maintain. It is also relevant and accessible. Natural-language searching capabilities can make a knowledge base easier to use. A knowledge base that is simple to maintain is more likely to be updated frequently, which is necessary if the information is to be useful. Relevancy depends on the content of the solution, particularly the context in which a problem occurs. Accessibility helps both users and help desk staff capitalize on the stored knowledge.

3 Knowledge management can be proactive or reactive. In reactive knowledge management, new knowledge is captured when a case is closed. Proactive knowledge management involves building knowledge before it is needed. Reactive knowledge management provides the benefit of lower ownership costs, but it also poses some quality problems. A proactive knowledge base, which follows a development process similar to that of software, is especially effective for reducing the volume of calls about new products or major upgrades.

4 Solutions stored in support knowledge base consist of explicit knowledge and tacit knowledge. Each solution involves four elements: analysis, which is the diagnostic process; situation, which is the configuration and other information about the context of the solution; information, which is the data required for understanding why and how the solution works, and resolution, which is the objective of the solution.

5 The four steps of the knowledge management process are capture, structure, review, and release/maintain. Capture involves identifying information to include in a knowledge base. Structuring is the process of indexing and categorizing the information. Review ensures that solutions added to the database are accurate, that they follow a standard format, that they are written in a way that users can understand, and that they do not duplicate or conflict with other solutions already in the database. After review, the solution is released, which usually involves publishing it on a Web support site. It must also be maintained, which involves keeping it up to date.

6 The simplest search method for making solutions in a knowledge base available is the keyword search engine. More sophisticated search methods include natural-language processing and expert systems. Natural-language processing enables users to search a knowledge base using questions or phrases that do not necessarily duplicate text or keywords in the documents. Expert systems simulate the interaction a user might have with a human expert, including a question-and-answer process.

›› Summary *(continued)*

7 Implementing knowledge management for support requires new metrics and reevaluation of existing metrics for analyzing the help desk's performance. New measures of performance can be based on the number of solutions available in the knowledge base, the number and percent of cases resolved with the knowledge base, the most frequently searched keywords, and the number of solutions contributed by support teams or individual members. Metrics that need to be reevaluated include average case duration, first call resolution rate, and call volume.

8 Barriers to effective knowledge management include support specialists' fear of losing their jobs or their importance to their employers and general fear of change. Knowledge management actually offers benefits and opportunities for support personnel. Instead of just answering telephones, analysts become better able to transmit knowledge and transform it into reusable solutions, which increases their value to their employers.

›› Key Terms

The following terms were defined in this chapter:

a analysis

b capturing

c case-based reasoning (CBR

d decision tree

e expert system

f explicit knowledge

g fuzzy logic

h information

i reactive knowledge management

j natural-language processing systems

k proactive knowledge management

l reactive knowledge management

m resolution

n rule

o rule-based

p situation

q structuring

r subject-matter expert (SME)

s tacit knowledge

t validation

›› Reviewing Key Terms

Write the letter of the key term that matches each definition below:

_____ **1** An expert system methodology that uses past cases to solve new problems.

_____ **2** Building knowledge before it is needed.

_____ **3** A program that simulates interaction that a user might have with a human expert to solve a problem.

›› Reviewing Key Terms *(continued)*

_____ ④ Knowledge that can be expressed using language and can be easily transmitted among individuals.

_____ ⑤ The diagnostic process that involves taking a user's description of a problem, reasoning how to further test and confirm what the problem is, and determining the most effective solution.

_____ ⑥ The data required for proper interpretation of how to implement a solution and understand why and how it functions.

_____ ⑦ The objective of a solution, which includes the specific answer and response to a problem and one or more methods of addressing it.

_____ ⑧ Solution-centered support, in which new knowledge is captured when a case is closed.

_____ ⑨ The definition of a problem's context, including what products are being used and the symptoms of the problem.

_____ ⑩ Identifying and collecting information that will be included in a knowledge base.

_____ ⑪ Knowledge based on individual experience—for example, hunches and intuition.

_____ ⑫ Technology that lets people interact with computers in conversational language.

_____ ⑬ The process of indexing, categorizing, and classifying information.

_____ ⑭ An individual who exhibits the highest level of expertise in performing a specialized job or task within an organization.

_____ ⑮ The process of replicating a problem and testing a solution.

_____ ⑯ The simplest method of searching a knowledge base, in which users enter keywords and click on the Search button.

_____ ⑰ A type of expert system that uses a set of rules as its knowledge base.

_____ ⑱ A concise description of a set of conditions and a set of actions to take if the conditions are true.

_____ ⑲ A series of questions that guide a user to relevant solutions based on the user's responses.

_____ ⑳ A rule-based technology that creates rules that use approximate or subjective values and incomplete or ambiguous data.

›› Reviewing Key Facts

True/False

Identify whether each statement is True (T) or False (F). Rewrite the false statements so that they are true.

_____ ① Users as well as help desk analysts can access a knowledge base.

_____ ② Explicit knowledge includes data, facts, and documents.

_____ ③ Tacit experience is usually passed on to others in documents.

>> Reviewing Key Facts *(continued)*

_____ (4) Information is the essence of the diagnostic process.

_____ (5) A resolution will resolve a problem but is temporary, incomplete, or more labor-intensive than desired.

_____ (6) The disadvantages of reactive knowledge management relate to quality.

_____ (7) The process of structuring information is time- and labor-intensive.

_____ (8) The simplest search method is natural-language processing.

_____ (9) Case-based reasoning ‹CBR› systems are based the assumption that people use past experience to try to solve problems.

_____ (10) Fuzzy logic represents more closely the way people actually think than traditional if-then rules.

Completion

Write the answer that best completes each of the following statements:

(1) Natural-language processing enables people to interact with _____ in conversational language.

(2) Analysis, situation, information, and resolution are all elements of each _____ in a knowledge base.

(3) With reactive knowledge management, a knowledge base will cover a _____ range of topics with little depth.

(4) In a knowledge base with a well-defined structure, solutions are easy to _____ and easy to implement.

(5) Implementing a knowledge management system requires adding new help desk _____ and reevaluating those that are already in use.

>> Understanding Key Concepts

Provide brief answers to the following questions:

(1) Why must a knowledge base be simple to maintain?

(2) What is the difference between reactive knowledge management and proactive knowledge management?

(3) How does an expert system work?

>> Critical Thinking

As directed by your instructor, write a brief essay or discuss the following issues in groups:

(1) How does knowledge management in a support environment benefit users?

(2) Ideally, would a help desk use reactive knowledge management, proactive knowledge management, or both? Explain.

(3) How does implementing knowledge management affect jobs on the help desk?

Prevention of Widespread Problems

An asset tracking program also enables organizations to prevent potential problems from developing throughout the company. For example, suppose a configuration problem discovered on one computer has the potential to occur on hundreds of similarly configured workstations throughout the company. Once the problem has been identified, the asset tracking system can scan the database to locate workstations with similar configurations. The help desk can then send a fix out over the network to all affected computers. Using this approach, there are significant savings in both time and money. There is no employee downtime because the problem never actually occurred, and instead of spending an hour resolving each user's problem, the help desk is able to perform a fix on hundreds of computers at once.

Remote Diagnosis of Problems

An asset database can also be a powerful diagnostic tool for the help desk. For example, an examination of a user's hardware and software configuration can be compared against usage prerequisites, corporate standards, and known problems in order to more quickly determine the exact nature of the problem. The database can also be used to ensure that all users are using the most up-to-date versions of software.

Detection of Unauthorized Software

An asset tracking system can detect unauthorized software on users' PCs. For example, suppose an employee is using a copy of *Adobe Illustrator* to create graphics for an annual report. The employee encounters a problem and calls the help desk for support. The help desk analyst reviews the asset database and sees no record of *Adobe Illustrator's* being installed on the workstation. The analyst then requests the registration number of the program from the user and searches the database for a match. The search reveals that the program is actually registered to another employee in the company. This application would then be removed from the employee's workstation, and, if appropriate, a request for the software would be entered in the request management program.

Determination of Total Cost of Ownership

The data collected by the help desk also helps determine the total cost of equipment ownership by incorporating information about trouble ticket and service request costs. Knowing the number of trouble tickets and associated costs generated by a particular model of PC or by a particular version of software aids management when future purchasing decisions are made. For example, data—such as the number of specific models of hard drives or video cards that have been repaired or replaced over the last year—allow management to identify those devices that are most expensive to own and maintain.

The integration of help desk and asset management systems also is beneficial in controlling the costs and usage of assets over their life span. The help desk is the location in the company that becomes aware of mismatches between users and assets. For example, computers that have become obsolete for high-powered users in the finance department may still perform a useful function in the facilities or operations management department.

Implementation of Change Requests

This ability to track assets is crucial when a company is undergoing change. For example, if a department is moving from one area of a building to another , an asset management program can track the movement of hardware and software. Many times the help desk is involved in ensuring that equipment is moved to its correct location and that it is operating correctly after the move.

Tracking of Warranty and Maintenance Information

Aside from assets such as computers and software, most companies also have assets in the form of maintenance and support contracts, warranties, and leases. Companies need to keep track of the maintenance and support contracts and warranties entered into with outside vendors. If a computer has problems and is still under warranty, investing the help desk's time and labor to diagnose and fix the computer wastes valuable resources. The company is wasting not only the money it has spent on support from the vendor, but also the money spent on help desk salaries. A good system for tracking warranties and tying them to individual assets makes it easy to determine whether an individual computer is still under warranty.

✔ **READING CHECK**

1. **READING REVIEW** Is an asset management system a replacement for an existing help desk information system?

2. **CRITICAL THINKING** Briefly discuss the how obtaining configuration information from an asset management database differs from obtaining configuration information from a user.

9.4 Threats to Computer Security

Computer security is the process of planning, implementing, and verifying the protection of an organization's computer-related assets from

An importa[...] cy is ensu[...] their own resp[...] tion's assets. [...] tion in handbo[...] when they are [...] revised. These [...] about the orga[...] cies as well as [...] responsibilitie[...]

The *Ventur[...]* distributes an[...] other compan[...] regarding com[...] Specific polici[...]

E-mail and [...] are company [...] the company'[...]

Personal u[...] discouraged.

Only softw[...] company may[...] may not use c[...] ny's compute[...] freeware, or c[...] works unless [...] advance.

Employee[...] any software [...] the company [...] and the infor[...]

All compu[...] top compute[...] be purchase[...] department.

from the Internet, the request goes to the proxy server, and the proxy server makes the request to the Web server. Similarly, the requested information is delivered back to the proxy server, which then sends the information to user's workstation. While this may seem less efficient than if the browser and server interacted directly, the use of a proxy server provides a great deal of control of network traffic. For example, a proxy server can filter certain types of files, such as those with a file extension of BIN or EXE. With such a filter in place, any requests made for files with these extensions will be denied. Figure 9.4 illustrates the flow of information in a secured network.

Passwords

Passwords are another means of preventing unauthorized users from gaining access to information on a computer or network. Password utilization is a standard practice in most organizations. It is easy to implement, and it can keep unauthorized users from successfully logging onto a system or network. Password logging programs can track all successful and failed log-in attempts, which can be useful in detecting possible break-in attempts or unauthorized logging.

Although password utilization is widely used, it has some disadvantages. Users sometimes forget their passwords, and they tend to choose passwords that are easy to guess.

Cryptography

Cryptography is the protection of information by transforming it into an unreadable format before it is distributed. To read a message, the recipient must have a key that deciphers the information. The act of encoding the contents of the message is known as **encryption**. Cryptography also enables the recipient to determine whether the message has been intercepted and tampered with before final delivery. This allows the message to be checked for authenticity.

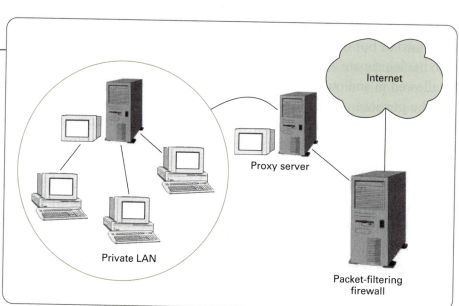

| FIGURE | 9.4 |

The flow of information in a secured network

Internet

Proxy server

Private LAN

Packet-filtering firewall

Cryptography is essential for the transmission of sensitive data over networks. It is widely used to protect e-mail messages, credit card information, and corporate data. Just as with other security methods, cryptography is not perfect. Encrypted messages are vulnerable to cracking, although this is becoming more and more difficult as new standards are developed.

Antivirus Software

Antivirus software scans a system for known viruses. After detection, antivirus software attempts to remove the virus from the system and, in some cases, fix any problems the virus created. Antivirus tools, however, cannot detect and eliminate all viruses. New viruses are continually being developed, and antivirus software must be regularly updated to maintain its effectiveness. While antivirus software will prevent some incidents from occurring, it is just one of many necessary security devices.

 READING CHECK

1. **READING REVIEW** List the basic security tools for keeping intruders out of computer systems.

2. **CRITICAL THINKING** What do natural disasters such as floods and earthquakes have to do with computer security?

9.5 Security Processes

The process of securing a computing system consists of five distinct stages:

1. Identifying assets
2. Assessing risk
3. Preparing
4. Monitoring
5. Responding

Identifying Assets

Before assets can be protected, they must be identified. Asset discovery is commonly performed as part of an asset management plan, as discussed earlier. Once assets have been identified, the next step is to gauge the risk level for each category or asset.

Assessing Security Needs and Risks

An assessment should be conducted to determine the risk level of the organizations' technology assets. Risk assessment takes into account the potential consequences of a security incident. Questions are considered such as "If an area becomes compromised, how will it affect the operation of the organization?" and "Will there be loss of revenue, loss of reputation, or possible lawsuits?"

The following key areas should be addressed during an assessment:

- Physical security
- Exterior security—fencing, lighting, building location
- Secured disposal sites—trash compactors, shredders
- Building security—locked doors, biometric authentication, guards, security cameras
- Computer/data center—environmental controls, fire suppression, cable management, secure consoles
- Data security
- Passwords—effective management, user awareness
- Data classification—confidential, top secret, restricted, general access
- Data access privileges—assigned by user and/or group
- Social engineering—persons pretending to be employees or maintenance workers to gain unauthorized access

Information generated from the assessment process will help the IT staff and management make logical decisions about how to protect company assets. These data will also serve as a reference for creating and/or updating the company's existing security policy.

Preparing for Security Violations

While many people are familiar with threats from outside an organization, in reality most security incidents occur from within. For example, causes of internal security violations can range from a curious employee with unrestricted access exploring files, to a disgruntled employee on probation deliberately destroying data.

A well-written, comprehensive security policy is the foundation for building a secure computing environment. A security policy must state its purpose, identify its scope, define terms, declare the rights of users, delegate responsibility and action, reference related documents, and always change to meet nearly all criteria. It must be easily understandable and recognized as an authoritative document. See Figure 9.5 for an excerpt from a security policy.

As part of a security effort, every employee needs to understand his or her role in the protection of corporate assets. As employees become more comfortable with technology, they begin to make configuration changes, download patches, and upgrade software without approval.

FIGURE 9.5

University Security Policy

1. It is the policy of the University that its computing and networking facilities are intended for use for teaching, learning, research and administration in support of the University's mission. Although recognizing the increasing importance of these facilities to the activities of staff and students, the University reserves the right to limit, restrict, or extend access to them.

2. All persons using the computing and networking facilities shall be responsible for the appropriate use of the facilities provided as specified by the "Codes of Practice" of this policy, and shall observe conditions and times of usage as published by the Administrator of the system.

3. It is the policy of the University that its computing and associated network facilities are not to be used for commercial purposes or non-University-related activities without written authorization from the University. In any dispute as to whether work carried out on the computing and networking facilities is internal work, the decision of the Vice-Chancellor or his delegate shall be final.

4. The user will not record or process information which knowingly infringes any patent or breach any copyright.

5. The University will endeavour to protect the confidentiality of information and material furnished by the user and will instruct all computing personnel to protect the confidentiality of such information and material, but the University shall be under no liability in the event of any improper disclosure.

6. The University will endeavour to safeguard the possibility of loss of information within the University's computing and networking facilities but will not be liable to the user in the event of any such loss. The user must take all reasonable measures to further safeguard against any loss of information within the University's computing and networking facilities.

7. If a loss of information within the system can be shown to be due to negligence on the part of the computing or network personnel employed by the university, or to any hardware or software failure which is beyond the user's means to avoid or control, then the Information Technology Services will endeavour to help restore the information and will not charge the user for computer time spent in such restoration.

8. The use of the computing and networking facilities is permitted by the University on the condition that it will not involve the infringement of any patent or the breach of any copyright and the user agrees to indemnify and keep indemnified the University and each member and every member of its staff against all actions, claims, and demands for infringement of patent and or breach of copyright which may be brought or made against the University or any member of its staff arising out of or in connection with the use of the computing and networking facilities.

9. Users of the computing and networking facilities recognize that when they cease to be formally associated with the University (e.g. no longer an employee, enrolled student or visitor to the University), their information may be removed from University computing and networking facilities without notice. Users must remove their information or make arrangements for its retention prior to leaving the University.

10. The University reserves the right to limit permanently or restrict any user's usage of the computing and networking facilities; to copy, remove, or otherwise alter any information or system that may undermine the authorized use of the computing and networking facilities; and to do so with or without notice to the user in order to protect the integrity of the computing and networking facilities against unauthorized or improper use, and to protect authorized users from the effects of unauthorized or improper usage.

11. The University, through authorized individuals, reserves the right to periodically check and monitor the computing and networking facilities, and reserves any other rights necessary to protect them.

12. The University disclaims responsibility and will not be responsible for loss or disclosure of user information or interference with user information resulting from its efforts to maintain the privacy, security and integrity of the computing and networking facilities and information.

Excerpt from a security policy

Monitoring Networks and Their Use

To ensure security, networks must be monitored at all times. An **intrusion detection system (IDS)** inspects all inbound and outbound network activity and identifies suspicious patterns that may indicate an attack. A **sniffer** is one type of IDS that intercepts and analyzes data packets transmitted over a network. Sniffers can be used to determine whether something looks out of the ordinary. Intrusion detection systems can be very helpful in determining whether an attack is occurring. However, for these systems to be effective, the collected data must be reviewed on a regular and timely basis.

Responding to Incidents

Despite the implementation of appropriate security measures, incidents can, and will, occur. The way in which an organization responds to computer security incidents is known as its **incident handling capability**, and this capability is equally as important as the measures taken to prevent incidents from occurring. Effective incident handling demands the ability to quickly and efficiently react to disruptions in the normal course of events. At a minimum, there must be a written policy that specifies procedures to be followed in the event of a violation or attack. Systems must be in place to record all activity, and to quickly escalate to upper management in the event of a serious attack.

Centralized Reporting

Successful incident handling requires users to be able to report incidents in a convenient, straightforward fashion; this is referred to as **centralized reporting**. A response to an incident depends on timely reporting. If reporting incidents is difficult or time-consuming, the incident handling capability may not be fully used.

Incident handling will be greatly enhanced by mechanisms that enable the quick and convenient dissemination of information. For example, if users are linked together via a network, the incident handling capability can use the network to send out timely announcements and other information. Users can take advantage of the network to retrieve security information stored on servers and receive updates via e-mail.

One way to establish a centralized reporting and incident response capability is to use an existing help desk. Since the help desk is already a central point of contact for users experiencing technical problems, it is a logical choice for reporting security incidents. Some help desks have a special telephone number or e-mail address for reporting security incidents.

Preventing Future Damage

Incident handling capability also assists an organization in preventing damage from future incidents, as the organization can learn from the incidents it has experienced. Data about past incidents can be analyzed to identify specific patterns and potential vulnerabilities. Knowledge about the types of threats that are occurring and the presence of vulnerabilities can aid in identifying the need for additional security measures.

Prior incident information can also be used as examples in a user training program to provide information to users such as measures that can help avoid incidents (for example, virus scanning) and what should be done in case an incident does occur.

 READING CHECK

1. **READING REVIEW** List the five stages of securing information technology assets.

2. **CRITICAL THINKING** Briefly discuss the role of the help desk in incident reporting.

9.6 Additional Security Measures

Organizations rely on several additional measures to ensure the safety and integrity of their computer systems. These include backups, user education, and disaster recovery plans.

Backups

Backing up is the activity of copying files to another medium so that they will be preserved in case the originals are no longer available. A successful backup plan is critical in recovering from either a minor or major security incident that jeopardizes critical data. The use of backups as a security measure requires careful planning. Issues that should be considered when developing a backup plan include the following:

- Which files are to be backed up?
- How often should these files be backed up?
- Who will perform the backups?
- How often are backups tested for accuracy and quality?
- Where and how will backups be stored?
- How long will the backups be maintained?

Backups can take several forms. The most common backup methods are

- *Full backup*: All selected files are backed up, even if they have not been modified since the last backup. While this is the most complete backup, it is also the most time-consuming. However, it simplifies the process of restoring data, since all data will be restored. Most backup software includes a feature to schedule backups, which allows this process to be completed during off-hours when computers are not heavily in use. With this option, full backups should be performed on some type of schedule.
- *Incremental*: Only selected files that have changed since last backup are backed up. This type of backup takes the least amount of time to conduct, but it is the most time-consuming during restoration, since each incremental tape is needed. For example, if a computer crashed today, it would be necessary to use all incremental backup disks since the last full backup to restore data.
- *Differential*: Only files that have changed since the last full backup are backed up. To restore data using the differential method, the last full backup and the last differential backup would be required.
- *Daily copy*: Only files that were changed on that day are backed up.
- *Copy*: This allows for backing up only selected files.

User Awareness and Education

Computer security is not the sole responsibility of the IT department. Users are critical in ensuring the security of computer systems and data. Human actions account for far more computer-related loss than all other threats combined. In order to protect technology assets, employees must receive training in computer security. Through training and awareness programs, users can become knowledgeable about how to prevent, recognize, and report incidents.

The purpose of computer security training is to enhance security by improving users' awareness of the need to protect system resources and enabling them to develop the skills and knowledge to perform their jobs more securely. This includes teaching people what they should do and how they should do it. Users need to understand good computer security practices, such as

- How to protect the physical area and equipment
- How to protect passwords or other authentication data
- How to recognize and report security violations or incidents

Written Guidelines

Users should be informed about the organization's policies for protecting information and computer systems and the roles and responsibilities of various organizational units with which they may have to interact. Any security planning process must include establishing guidelines for what is expected of the users of the system. It is absolutely imperative that, at an early stage in the process of developing a security plan, effort be put into developing a set of written guidelines that will be presented to all users. Such a set of guidelines is referred to as an **acceptable use policy**. Employees cannot be expected to follow policies and procedures of which they are unaware. In addition, enforcing penalties may be difficult if users can claim ignorance when caught doing something wrong. Figure 9.6 presents a sample acceptable use policy.

Individual Accountability

Security training also makes users aware of their security responsibilities and promotes individual accountability, which is one of the most important ways to improve computer security. The major causes of loss due to an organization's own employees are errors and omissions, fraud, and actions by disgruntled employees. Security awareness and training is designed to reduce employee errors and omissions. However, it can also reduce fraud and unauthorized activity by increasing employees' knowledge of their accountability and the penalties associated with such actions.

FIGURE 9.6

Sample acceptable use policy

Acceptable Use Policy

The Corporation owns all Corporate information resources; use of such resources constitutes consent for the Corporation to monitor, inspect, audit, collect, and remove any information without permission or further notice. Personnel shall be trained in what use is acceptable and what is prohibited. Any infraction of corporate acceptable use policies shall constitute a security violation. Personnel shall be held personally accountable and may be subject to disciplinary action or criminal prosecution.

Hardware and Software
Acquiring Hardware and Software
To prevent the introduction of malicious code and protect the integrity of corporate information resources, all hardware and software shall be obtained from official corporate sources.

Complying with Copyright and Licensing
All software used on corporate information resources shall be procured in accordance with official corporate policies and procedures, and shall be licensed, and registered in the name of the corporation. All personnel shall abide by software copyright laws and shall not obtain, install, replicate, or use software except as permitted by the software licensing agreements.

Using Personally owned Software
To protect the integrity of the corporate information resources, personnel shall not use personally owned software on corporate information resources. This includes purchased and licensed applications; shareware; freeware; downloads from bulletin boards, Internet, Intranet, FTP sites, local area networks (LANs) or wide area networks (WANs); and other personally-owned or controlled software.

Protecting Intellectual Property
To ensure the integrity of corporate developed software, all personnel shall abide by the intellectual property protection contract provisions of the corporation.

Electronic Mail and Messaging
Access to the corporate electronic mail (email) system is provided to personnel whose duties require it for the conduct of corporate business. Since email may be monitored, all personnel using corporate resources for the transmission or receipt of email shall have no expectation of privacy.

Acceptable Use
The corporate provides email to facilitate the conduct of corporate business. Occasional and incidental personal email use shall be permitted if it does not interfere with the corporation's ability to perform its mission and meets the conditions outlined in official corporate directives. However, while they remain in the system, personal messages shall be considered to be in the possession and control of the corporation.

Prohibited Use
Prohibited activities when using corporate electronic mail shall include, but not be limited to, sending or arranging to receive the following:
  a. Information that violates state or federal laws, or corporate regulations.
  b. Unsolicited commercial announcements or advertising material, unless approved by management in advance.
  c. Any material that may defame, libel, abuse, embarrass, tarnish, present a bad image of, or portray in false light, the corporation, the recipient, the sender, or any other person.
  d. Pornographic, racist or offensive material, chain letters, unauthorized mass mailings, or malicious code.

Disaster Recovery

Disaster recovery has taken on new urgency in recent years. As companies' reliance on computers has increased, so have the threats of terrorism, hackers, and computer viruses. A **disaster recovery plan** details activities and preparations to minimize loss and ensure continuity of critical business functions in the event of a major disaster. The types of events addressed by a disaster recovery plan typically include

- Natural disasters (earthquake, fire, flood, storm)
- Terrorist acts (explosion, chemical weapons, hostage-taking)
- Power disruptions and power failures
- Computer software or hardware failures
- Computer shutdowns (effects of hacker, virus)
- Labor problems (strike, slowdown, walkout)

At the heart of a computer-related disaster is the loss of corporate servers and their network connections. When the servers and network go down, so do an organization's vital day-to-day operations such as order entry, manufacturing, and accounting. Most disaster recovery plans specify that data and servers are maintained at a physical location separate from the company's main facility, known as a recovery site. Selecting an appropriate type of site is a critical step in disaster recovery planning. There are several types of recovery sites, including

- *Hot site:* In a **hot site** approach, servers, applications, and data are maintained in real-time synchronization with the main facility. In the event of a disaster, there is no loss of processing time, since the alternate systems are already up and running. This approach is costly, since it usually requires duplicate hardware and software.
- *Cold site:* In a **cold site** approach, data, applications, and often servers are maintained on a standby basis with regular updates. In the event of a disaster, it takes time to bring the systems up to speed. This approach is less expensive than a hot site, but it also makes recovery less efficient.
- *Off-site data storage*: In an **off-site** approach, data are stored off-site, but no hardware is off-site. This approach is much less expensive, but recovery takes more time than in the hot or cold site methods because damaged hardware must be repaired or replaced.

Steps in the Recovery Process

In most large organizations, the disaster recovery process follows a number of predictable steps. These steps include the following.

- *Step 1: Respond.* Activate the disaster plan and notify the individuals responsible for responding to disasters (the recovery team).
- *Step 2: Restore infrastructure.* The recovery team arrives at the recovery site, assesses the situation, and begins to rebuild the network.
- *Step 3: Restore data.* Once the network infrastructure is rebuilt, the process of restoring server-based data and applications from the most recent backups begins. Depending on how long the network has been down, there may be a considerable backlog of information that must be synchronized with the data restored from backups.
- *Step 4: Return to normal operations.* During this step, the company begins to return to work at the main facility.
- *Step 5: Evaluate the disaster recovery plan.* Once business operations have returned to a normal state, the disaster recovery plan must be evaluated by everyone involved in the recovery effort. If necessary, the plan should be updated.

The Help Desk's Role in Disaster Recovery

In many organizations the help desk plays a pivotal role in a company's recovery efforts. One of the key elements of any disaster recovery plan is a list of names and numbers used to contact employees after a disaster occurs. Since employees are used to contacting the help desk with tech support questions, it is logical to use the help desk to contact employees and to respond to incoming questions about the availability of systems.

As part of the disaster recovery effort, a representative from the help desk team should be intimately involved with restoring systems to a fully functioning state.

Finally, the help desk itself should store copies of critical data off-site, including

- A master contact list of all help desk team members and their home telephone numbers, cell phone numbers, pager numbers, and home e-mail addresses to facilitate communication following a disaster.
- A CD with the most recent standard image for corporate desktop machines in the event employee PCs need to be reimaged or employees must temporarily work at an off-site location.
- Installation media for core applications.
- A database for tracking issues during the recovery process. The process of creating trouble tickets continues while the company is in recovery mode. When employees in the field attempt to connect to the network and run applications at the various stages of recovery, their issues must be tracked and worked the same way as any other user requests.

✓ READING CHECK

1. **READING REVIEW** List and briefly describe the five most common data backup methods.

2. **CRITICAL THINKING** How has the need for disaster recovery plans changed in recent years? What has caused the change?

>> Summary

The following points were covered in this chapter:

1 As the role of technology in business continues to grow in importance, technology assets have come to represent a major financial investment. As a result, the ability to manage information technology assets effectively has become a critical business capability.

2 IT assets are complex and difficult to manage in several ways. PC configurations differ, and they can change. Software use must be monitored to avoid legal problems. Organizations are continually adding new locations, rearranging office space, and changing in other ways. Technology assets are mobile, which makes them difficult to track. Still, effective asset management benefits departments throughout an organization, including the help desk.

3 Technology assets include not only physical goods but also information. Information assets can take the form of software, proprietary data, backups, manuals and other books, printouts, audit records, software distribution media, and warranties and maintenance agreements.

4 The first step in asset management is to compile an inventory of all technology assets. Auto-discovery software can speed the process by gathering information about workstations automatically. Once information about assets is collected, it is stored in a central database.

5 Integrating an asset management system with the help desk system can result in greater productivity, financial savings, and increased user satisfaction. It gives the help desk immediate access to accurate information about configurations, software usage, and other issues. Integrating asset management and technical support can also help organizations determine the total cost of owning and maintaining technology assets.

6 Computer security includes the protection of programs and data in addition to hardware. Threats to computer security come from natural events and accidents as well from intentional malicious behavior. Network security, which prevents unauthorized access to an organization's information and programs, has increased in importance with the growth of the Internet. Network security measures include the use of passwords, firewalls, cryptography, and antivirus software.

7 Securing a computer system consists of five stages: identifying assets, assessing security needs and risks, preparing, monitoring networks and their use, and responding to incidents.

8 Backups, user education, and disaster recovery plans are also security measures. Backups of data help organizations recover from security incidents. Most computer-related losses result from human behavior, so users must be educated about preventing and dealing with incidents. A disaster recovery plan spells out how an organization can minimize losses and continue to operate if a major disaster occurs.

›› Key Terms

The following terms were defined in this chapter:

- ⓐ acceptable use policy
- ⓑ asset tracking tools
- ⓒ centralized reporting
- ⓓ cold site
- ⓔ computer security
- ⓕ cryptography
- ⓖ disaster recovery plan
- ⓗ encryption
- ⓘ firewall
- ⓙ hot site
- ⓚ incident handling capability
- ⓛ intrusion detection system (IDS)
- ⓜ IT asset management (ITAM)
- ⓝ network security
- ⓞ off-site
- ⓟ packet filtering
- ⓠ physical security
- ⓡ proxy server
- ⓢ router
- ⓣ server
- ⓤ sniffer

›› Reviewing Key Terms

Write the letter of the key term that matches each definition below:

_____ ① Software applications that gather data about technology assets via the network.

_____ ② The process of planning, implementing, and verifying the protection of an organization's computer-related assets from internal and external threats.

_____ ③ The protection of building sites and equipment from theft, vandalism, natural disaster, manmade catastrophes, and accidental damage.

_____ ④ The practice of protecting and preserving resources and information on a network.

_____ ⑤ A powerful computer that acts as an intermediary between PCs on the network.

_____ ⑥ A device that links a local network to a remote network and determines the best route for data to travel across the network.

_____ ⑦ A security device that examines traffic entering and leaving a network and determines whether to forward it toward its destination.

_____ ⑧ The protection of information by transforming it into an unreadable format before it is distributed.

_____ ⑨ A process whereby a firewall examines the nature of each piece of information traveling into or out of the network.

>> **Reviewing Key Terms** *(continued)*

____ **10** A software application that acts as an intermediary between applications and servers.

____ **11** The act of encoding the contents of a message.

____ **12** A system that inspects all inbound and outbound network activity and identifies suspicious patterns that may indicate an attack.

____ **13** A type of IDS that intercepts and analyzes data packets transmitted over a network.

____ **14** The process of tracking information about technology assets throughout the entire asset life cycle.

____ **15** An incident handling system that that gives users the ability to report incidents in a convenient, straightforward fashion.

____ **16** A recovery site where servers, applications, and data are synchronized with those at the main facility, so there is no loss of processing time in the event of disaster.

____ **17** The way in which an organization responds to computer security incidents.

____ **18** A set of written security guidelines that is presented to all users.

____ **19** A document that details the plans and preparations to minimize loss and ensure continuity of critical business functions in the event of a major disaster.

____ **20** A recovery site where data, applications, and servers are not synchronized with those at the main facility but are maintained with regular updates.

____ **21** A disaster recovery approach in which only data, not hardware, is stored away from the main facility.

>> Reviewing Key Facts

True/False
Identify whether each statement is True (T) or False (F). Rewrite the false statements so that they are true.

____ **1** With ITAM, an organization tracks technology assets only for the first two years it owns them.

____ **2** The mobility of computer equipment poses a challenge for asset management.

____ **3** Asset management helps purchasing managers and accounting analysts as well as technical personnel.

____ **4** An asset tracking database should include only the hardware and software configurations and the physical locations of assets.

____ **5** An asset tracking program enables organizations to prevent technical problems from developing throughout the company.

____ **6** Asset tracking can include the detection of unauthorized software on users' computers.

>> **Reviewing Key Facts** *(continued)*

____ ⑦ Most threats to computer security come from people.

____ ⑧ he purpose of a firewall is to make sure that users back up their data.

____ ⑨ An IDS can help determine whether an organization's network is about to be attacked.

____ ⑩ A hot site provides a less expensive means of disaster recovery than a cold site.

Completion

Write the answer that best completes each of the following statements:

① The first step in the asset management process is to compile an _____ of all technology assets.

② Asset tracking tools use an organization's _____ to gather data about its technology assets.

③ Within an organization, PCs are connected to a _____ so that users can exchange and share information.

④ A _____ acts as a gatekeeper, deciding who has legitimate access to a network and what sorts of materials should be allowed in and out.

⑤ Since the _____ is already a central point of contact for users experiencing technical problems, it is a logical choice for reporting security incidents.

>> Understanding Key Concepts

Provide brief answers to the following questions:

① When does IT asset management begin and end?

② How does asset management benefit the help desk?

③ When is network security important to organizations? Why?

>> Critical Thinking

As directed by your instructor, write a brief essay or discuss the following issues in groups:

① How can asset management save money for an organization?

② Provide two examples of malicious incidents that threaten data security, and describe measures that can prevent them.

③ Describe an effective technology security policy.

Chapter 9 Review

>> Help Desk Projects

Complete the projects listed below:

1 **Note and describe the security procedures you must follow when you log onto your school's network or to another network, such as one you use at home to gain access to the Internet.** For example, do you need a password? If so, what happens if you forget your password, or if you attempt to log on with the wrong password?

2 **Interview your school's technology director about the school's network security measures.** Ask if the school's network is connected to the Internet, what the school does to protect data against viruses, and how it controls access to data, along with other questions of your own. Ask whether a serious security incident has ever damaged data or given unauthorized people access to data. If there has been a serious security incident, ask about the consequences and about how the school recovered from it.

3 **Invite a school administrator to speak with your class about how the school tracks its technology assets.** Ask the administrator what asset management tools the school uses and what benefits and costs have resulted from asset management. If the school does not use asset management, find out why.

4 **Use a Web browser to find an organization whose primary concern is technology asset management and whose members are mainly technology asset management professionals.** What are the organization's goals? How much does membership cost? What are the benefits of joining this organization?

5 **Using a Web browser, advertisements in newspapers or magazines, or any other resources at your disposal, find at least three specific openings for jobs that involve technology asset management.** What skills, experience, and educational backgrounds do the jobs require? Which of the jobs is most attractive to you? Why?

6 **Using a Web browser, find two companies that provide technology asset management services to other organizations.** What specific services do they provide? Who are their clients? What specific projects, if any, do their Web sites list or describe?

7 **Find at an article about technology asset management in an online or printed magazine.** Read the article and summarize what it says. Do you agree or disagree? Why?

8 **Use a Web browser to locate information about a recent or impending conference for technology management professionals.** What kinds of topics were (or will be) discussed at the conference? Where did (or will) the conference take place? Who do you think benefits from attending such a conference?

9 **Identify and research two different antivirus software products that are available for PCs.** Compare them in terms of their prices and features. For example, do they provide ways for users to keep up with new viruses as they develop? Do they check e-mail for viruses? What other kinds of files do they check?

>> Help Desk Projects *(continued)*

10 Using periodicals, books, or the Internet, identify an organization that lost significant technology assets in an earthquake, an attack, or some other major incident, and learn about how—or whether—the organization recovered from the disaster. Did it have a disaster recovery plan before the incident occurred? If so, what were the details of the plan? How long did it take for the company to resume normal operations? What measures could have helped it recover faster?

>> Help Desk Strategies

Review the following case studies and respond to the questions:

1 The Kress Foundation manages hundreds of millions of dollars worth of investments for a charitable trust, reviews applications from community organizers who are seeking grants, and distributes money to the those whose applications are approved. Every Friday, the foundation's network administrators back up all software and data files on the network that have changed in the preceding week. The backup files are stored on tapes that are kept in an archive in a building several miles from the foundation's offices. Only a few times in the past 20 years has the foundation needed to restore its network files from backup tapes. No incident has ever caused a significant loss of computer hardware at the foundation.

- What type of backup does the foundation perform for the files on its network. In your opinion, would another kind of backup be better? Explain the reasons for your opinion.

- What type of recovery site does the foundation use? Would you recommend that it use a different kind of recovery site? If so, which kind would you recommend, and why? If not, why not?

- If the Kress Foundation's offices were damaged by an earthquake or a terrorist attack, what security risks does it run with its present backup system? Explain your answer.

2 Eugenia works on the help desk at a market research firm called MetroMetrix, where the ITAM and technical support systems are integrated. While responding to a help request, Eugenia saw that the user's hard disk drive contained a copy of a popular word processing program that MediaMetrix had not purchased and that its employees are not authorized to use. MediaMetrix has a license to use a word processing program from a different software company, along with a spreadsheet program, a calendar program, and other applications . The user told Eugenia that he uses the other word processing software at home and had brought his own disk from home to load onto his PC at MediaMetrix because he prefers it.

- What benefits might the help desk at MetroMetrix be realizing from the integration of its systems with the ITAM system?

- Should the user be required to erase the unauthorized word processing program from his office PC? Why?

>> **Help Desk Strategies** (continued)

3 SpringView Realty has recently connected its computer network to the Internet. This provides many benefits, such as enabling prospective buyers and sellers to communicate with the agency by e-mail and view information about properties on the agency's Web site.

- What computer security threats might the agency face as a result of being connected to the Internet?

- What measures should SpringView take to protect itself against security risks posed by the Internet?

10

Help Desk Survival Guide

Objectives

After reading this chapter, you will be able to:

1. Explain the relationship between resources and demands in the creation of stress.
2. Describe the categories of common symptoms of stress.
3. Identify the primary sources of stress in the help desk.
4. Discuss the reasons people resist change.
5. List ways in which organizations and individuals play a role in creating a positive work environment.

Chapter Overview

Constant phone calls, repetitive tasks, time pressures, and upset callers are just a few of the things that contribute to stress in the help desk environment. Turnover in support positions is high—as high as 35 percent according to the Help Desk Institute—and stress is a major reason cited. To be successful in a support role, individuals must be capable of managing stress. The pace of change and the constancy of change require support specialists who can easily adapt to an ever-changing environment. This chapter presents an overview of the nature of stress, the particular sources of help desk stress, and techniques that can be used to manage stress effectively.

10.1   Stress in the Workplace

Stress is the response of the body to demands made upon it. Stress occurs when there is a mismatch between an individual's resources and the demands placed on that individual. When threatened, the body produces extra epinephrine (adrenaline), which acts to stimulate essential systems within the body. This process is known as the fight-or-flight mechanism. The heightened state created by the fight-or-flight response lasts for a brief time, just until the situation returns to normal (the food was obtained, the predator was frightened off).

Years ago, the response to stress was a matter of survival; if the body was not prepared for action, the human might not survive. The human body still uses the fight-or-flight mechanism when it perceives danger, but many of today's threats are very different from the dangers of the past. Most of the time, the events that cause stress are not a matter of life and death . However, the body still responds as if the event were life threatening by secreting hormones that increase the heartbeat and create muscle tension. If it continues over a period of time, this process begins to deplete the body's limited resources. Resources that are required to fight off perceived danger are no longer available for other activities, such as thinking and reasoning. When the demands exceed the resources for an extended period of time, the person's health begins to suffer.

Burnout

Left unchecked for a period of time, stress can lead to burnout. **Burnout** is a state of physical and mental exhaustion resulting from extended periods of stress. It may be accompanied by headaches, stomach problems, and other physical symptoms. Work habits of individuals who suffer from burnout include

- Difficulty saying no to additional commitments or responsibilities
- Working under intense and sustained pressure for a period of time
- Difficulty delegating to others because of perfectionist tendencies
- Trying to achieve too much over a sustained period of time
- Providing too much support to others for too long

Often burnout manifests itself in a loss of motivation, a lack of interest, and an overall drop in performance. Many people who experience burnout end up leaving the organization. The problems of stress and burnout are costly for businesses today not only because of the high rate of turnover among employees, but also because of the loss of productivity. In a help desk environment, stress and burnout can also result in mishandled incidents. A stressed support specialist is less likely to exhibit the patience required to work with an anxious caller. Individuals working under extreme stress are also less able to solve problems effectively because of difficulty focusing on a task or time constraints.

Responses to Stress

Everyone's tolerance for stress is different, and each person handles stress differently. Peoples' responses to stress depend, in part, upon how much and what kind of stress they experienced in the past. A history of stress or trauma can actually alter brain chemistry, leaving some individuals more susceptible to stress than others.

Another factor that influences how people respond to stress is whether they believe they have the skills, abilities, and resources to cope with the situation. Some of these resources are internal (such as a positive attitude), while others are external (such as the availability of support from coworkers, family, and friends).

The response to stress also depends on other events occurring in a person's life at the time the stress occurs. An individual going through personal stress, such as a divorce, or death or serious illness in the family, is less likely to be able to tolerate additional stress than someone who is not.

Personal characteristics and genetics can also affect the responses to stress. Some people are more susceptible to anxiety and tend to worry a great deal about events they cannot control. These individuals may experience more difficulty handling stress than people who are more self-confident.

Good Stress, Bad Stress

All stress is not created equal, and stress is not always negative. Some stress is normal, even desirable and healthy. In fact, a moderate level of stress can provide the energy and motivation to meet life's challenges. Stress provides athletes that extra "something" that makes it possible to set new world records. Stress enables students to work until 3:00 A.M. to finish a paper. Even positive life events such as a job promotion, getting married, and going on vacation create stress. If there were no stress at all, the world would be made up of very bored, unmotivated individuals. Figure 10.1 illustrates the optimal amount of stress.

Good stress is time-limited; it occurs in response to a particular event and ceases when the event is over. Bad stress, on the other hand, does not go away; its cause is ongoing. A job with continual interpersonal conflicts, a bad living situation, and the inability to pay monthly bills are examples of bad stress. The body maintains an almost constant state of alarm, with no time of rest.

FIGURE 10.1

The optimal amount of stress

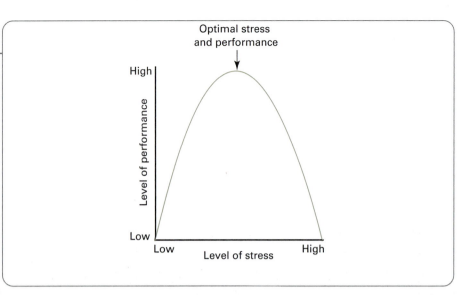

When the source of the stress cannot be eliminated, the best option is to learn to manage it effectively. This begins with learning to recognize the warning signs of stress, which take the form of physiological, psychological, and behavioral symptoms.

✓ **READING CHECK**

1. **READING REVIEW** Explain the cause of stress.

2. **CRITICAL THINKING** Why does stress affect people differently?

10.2 Symptoms of Stress

A person experiencing stress may develop numerous symptoms. These symptoms fall into three categories: physiological, psychological, and behavioral. Individual responses to stress vary, but the most common symptoms are listed below.

Physiological Symptoms

Physiological symptoms of stress are measurable changes in the body that occur in response to stress, including

- Rise in blood pressure
- Rise in perspiration
- Dilation of the pupils
- Rush of strength
- Sweaty palms

- Dry mouth
- Cold hands and feet
- Increased sweating
- Rapid breathing
- Rapid heartbeat
- Muscle tension
- Feelings of nausea
- Diarrhea

Psychological Symptoms

Psychological symptoms of stress consist of emotions experienced in responses to stress, including

- Anxiety
- Irritability
- Anger
- Mood swings
- Sadness or depression
- Low self-esteem
- Emotional withdrawal
- Hypersensitivity
- Feeling of being overwhelmed
- Impatience

Behavioral Symptoms

Changes in behavior can also occur as a result of stress. Common behavioral responses include

- Overeating or loss of appetite
- Change in sleep pattern
- Accident proneness
- Increased smoking
- Increased consumption of alcohol
- Increased dependence on drugs
- Loss of interest in sex
- Withdrawal

 READING CHECK

1. **READING REVIEW** Describe the three types of symptoms that result from stress, and give examples of each.

2. **CRITICAL THINKING** Is stress a necessary part of life, or would people be better off living stress-free lives?

10.3 Sources of Stress in the Workplace

Workplace stress often occurs when there is a conflict between the demands of the job and the amount of control an employee has over meeting these demands. In general, the combination of high demands and a low amount of control can lead to stress. Table 10.1 lists common sources of work-related stress.

Help desk staff members are particularly susceptible to stress and burnout for a number of reasons.

Time Pressure

Most help desks have service level standards such as call resolution time and time to answer a call. While standards are necessary to ensure that the help desk is performing efficiently, they create time pressures for the help desk staff. Analysts may also experience a conflict between efficiency and quality. There is constant pressure to complete calls within a specified time, but some problems require more time to resolve.

Workload

In most organizations, the help desk analyst's job is never done; that is, there are always problems waiting in the queue. To the staff, this can feel like a

TABLE 10.1

Sources of Work-Related Stress

Categories of Stress	Examples
Factors related to the job itself	Amount of control (restricted decision-making authority) Workday hours Physical environment (noise, overcrowding) Workload (too much or too little work) Length of workday Pace of work Variety of tasks Meaningfulness of work Too little or too much supervision
Role in the organization	Lack of clearly defined job responsibilities Lack of clear performance expectations and goals Conflicting demands (subordinates, coworkers, supervisors)
Career development	Promotion (too often or not enough) Job security Career development opportunities Overall job satisfaction
Interpersonal relationships	Supervisors Coworkers Subordinates
Organizational culture	Participatory or nonparticipatory Management style Communication patterns

never-ending cycle—which it is. Increased workload, long work hours, and intense pressure to perform can increase stress levels among help desk agents.

Threats to Job Security

Reorganizations, takeovers, mergers, downsizing, and other changes are major stressors for help desk employees. Advances in technology such as self-service tools may create job insecurity for staff members who fear their jobs may be eliminated. Outsourcing can have the same effect.

Interpersonal Interactions

While resolving calls successfully can result in satisfaction, a percentage of callers will be demanding, frustrated, or angry. The majority of users keep their emotions in check, but some will express these emotions during the call. Such interactions can create stress for the analyst. Negative interactions, especially when experienced without the benefit of a positive resolution, create stress for the analyst.

Workplace Environment

The nature of the job itself also adds to the stress quotient. Help desk workers are unable to move about freely, since they need to be close to a computer and a telephone to do their jobs. Most help desk personnel sit in a chair and focus on a computer monitor for hours at a time. They move about very little, and their muscles tend to stay in the same position. This results in physical as well as mental stress.

Information Overload

Help desk staff members may be overwhelmed by the amount of information they receive on a daily basis. **Information overload** is a type of stress generated by an overwhelming amount of information that requires processing. While the sheer volume of information is part of the problem, the cause of most stress and anxiety is people's inability to process it.

Did You Know?

Stress-related disorders are fast becoming the most prevalent reason for worker disability, according to the National Institute for Occupational Safety and Health.

✓ READING CHECK

1. **READING REVIEW** What are some common sources of stress for a support specialist?

2. **CRITICAL THINKING** Which of the sources of stress would be easiest to eliminate?

Keeping Current

One of the most difficult challenges of a job in the information technology field is trying to keep up with the constant change. Part of managing your career involves keeping your knowledge and skills up to date. The following strategies can be used to stay up to date on the latest innovations.

Set Aside Time for Reading

Each week, you should spend at least an hour reading about the industry and researching new trends and emerging technologies. There are many sources of information about IT available both in print and on the Internet. In your role as a support specialist, it is important to spend time reading on a regular basis.

Network with Colleagues

Talking to others in the IT field can provide valuable insight into the latest trends. Many cities and towns have technology interest groups that meet monthly to discuss new technologies in specific areas of IT. Professional organizations such as the Help Desk Institute and the Association of Information Technology Professionals (AITP) have chapters in most major cities and hold monthly meetings.

Attend Conferences

Attending professional conferences is an excellent way to stay informed about new technologies. In addition to attending workshops and conference sessions, visit vendor displays, which provide an opportunity to see demonstrations of new technologies.

Scan Newsgroups, Listservs, and Discussion Groups

There are a number of newsgroups, listservs, and discussion groups that can be of value to a support specialist. Some are specific to help desks and provide a forum to exchange ideas with other professionals in the support fields. Other groups offer valuable tips and solutions to hardware and software problems.

EXPLORING CAREERS

1. In a support position, why is it important to stay up to date with the latest technology issues and trends?

2. Use the Web, newspaper articles, magazine articles, and other resources to find information about trends in user support. What are some of the newest developments?

3. How will these trends affect the skills and aptitudes required for a job as a help desk analyst?

10.4 | The Challenge of Change

Change has always been a part of organizational life, but in recent years the pace of change has increased dramatically. New technology, new tools, and new applications are changing the way organizations do business. E-commerce is just one example of the impact of technology on business, enabling companies to buy and sell goods via the Internet. Companies continue to restructure, merge, and downsize in an attempt to remain competitive in the global marketplace. There is no escaping the rapid pace of change in the workplace.

While change may result in higher profits, it can also bring uncertainty. Today's workers may be faced with the possibility of job loss, the pressure of staying current with technology, and the demands of employers to do things better, cheaper, and faster.

Most people have some difficulty accepting change, especially when it is beyond their control. They may spend time and energy focusing on things they cannot control. This leads to frustration and anger, which in turn increases their level of stress. Table 10.2 lists some organizational events that can and cannot be controlled by individuals.

Events That Are Indirectly Affected	Events That Are Directly Affected
Company profit and loss	How we respond
Company policies and procedures	What we think
Management decisions	What we say
Staffing levels	Our performance
Coworkers' behavior	The decisions we make

TABLE 10.2

Workplace Events that are Directly and Indirectly Affected by Employees

Resisting Change

When faced with inevitable change, people's responses vary due to differences in personality, life experiences, and nature of the situation. While a few people may welcome change, most are apprehensive. Change may be viewed as threatening, especially if it is imposed from an external source. Reasons people resist change include

- Fear of the unknown
- Fear of losing control
- Threat to job or income
- Fear that skills and expertise will lose value
- Threats to power
- Failure to recognize need for change
- Threats to interpersonal relations

Viewing Change as Opportunity

Change can also be perceived as an opportunity. Expanded responsibilities on the job may require an employee to learn new skills. The acquisition of new skills enhances the employee's self-esteem and expands future career possibilities. Perhaps an employee has become bored in a position but does nothing to initiate a change because of a fear of the unknown. A change forced by an external source may provide the opportunity to restart a career.

Some people actually seek out change in order to face challenges, experience new situations, and gain new skills. Whenever a change occurs, it is helpful to consider ways in which the change may be beneficial. For example, a change could enable an employee to

- Discover unknown capabilities
- Learn about other areas of the business
- Build new skills
- Develop new relationships
- Leave an unsatisfying or unpleasant situation

While change itself may not be controllable, attitudes can be controlled. Peoples' attitudes toward change do affect their ability to handle change. Accept that all change, even good change, involves stress. No matter what the change, it will be much easier to cope with if accompanied by a positive attitude. It is not necessary to agree with the change, but a positive attitude will make it easier to accept and adjust to it.

 READING CHECK

1. **READING REVIEW** What are some reasons people resist change?

2. **CRITICAL THINKING** Is it unproductive to try to change the behavior of a coworker?

10.5 Creating a Positive Work Environment

The creation and maintenance of a positive work environment is a shared responsibility between the organization and the individual. Management is responsible for attending to issues at an organizational level, while the individual is responsible for handling issues at a personal level. In both instances, a number of actions can be taken to help create a positive work experience on the help desk.

Organizational Efforts

The organization has a responsibility to create a positive work environment for all employees, including the help desk staff. There are a number of ways this can be accomplished.

Minimize Stress

It is critical to identify the major factors responsible for help desk stress. Some organizations conduct surveys of help desk staff members to determine the major sources of stress. Once the sources have been identified, a plan is developed to minimize the negative impact . A backlog of service requests might indicate a need to rearrange schedules or hire additional staff. An interaction with a demanding user could suggest that the help desk agent requires additional interpersonal skills training, or that the user needs to be reminded of appropriate professional conduct. A problem that is difficult to solve may indicate the need to ask for additional help or escalate the problem to a higher level. The objective is to identify the causes of stress and take action to minimize or eliminate the impact on staff members.

Recognize Outstanding Performance

Employee recognition is a key factor in improving job satisfaction for help desk employees. Companies should make it a point to let help desk workers know they are valued. Some organizations present employee recognition awards on a monthly basis; others reward employees by letting them use a special parking space for a month; and still others award gift certificates to local restaurants.

Vary Job Tasks

To retain quality staff, efforts must be made to keep the work interesting and challenging. Responding to the same user problems over and over is sure to frustrate even the most dedicated analyst. Staff members should be assigned to special projects and given a variety of non-telephone tasks on a regular basis to enhance the variety in the job.

Help desk staff should also be encouraged to spend time in the business units. This will increase their understanding of how the business functions and provide the opportunity for analysts to develop a relationship with the user base. If the organization has multiple locations, specialists could move to a different site for a few weeks.

Provide Career Opportunities

One of the most common reasons for leaving the help desk is the lack of opportunity for career advancement. Perceiving no place to go within the department, employees may leave the company. To prevent turnover, the organization needs to provide avenues for promotion within the department. In addition, help desk staff members possess technical and interpersonal skills that could be of value to many departments within an organization.

Ergonomics

Support specialists are at risk for work-related injuries if the work environment is not properly designed. Most agents spend the majority of their days using computer keyboards to enter call data and speaking on the phone with users. The work also requires sitting at a desk or keyboard for large amounts of time.

The repetitive movements, combined with the limitations on moving about, can lead to a variety of conditions if proper work habits are not practiced. Repetitive strain injuries (RSI) are caused by excessive and repetitive use of the upper extremities. The most common RSI is carpal tunnel syndrome, characterized by numbness or tingling of the fingers, hand, or wrist.

The majority of these injuries can be prevented by the use of appropriate furniture and equipment and the practice of proper work habits. Ergonomics is the science and practice of designing jobs or workplaces to match the capabilities and limitations of the human body. The following guidelines describe the proper use and placement of furniture and equipment in the help desk environment.

Chair

The backrest of the chair should fit snugly against the back. The seat tilt should be adjusted so an agent is sitting upright with the feet firmly on the floor. If the feet do not reach the floor, a footrest should be used.

Monitor

The recommended viewing distance for a monitor is about one arm's length away from the screen. The top of the screen should be at about eye level or slightly lower. Monitors should be positioned away from light sources to reduce glare and reflection.

Keyboard and Mouse

The mouse should be at the same height as the keyboard and within easy reach. The wrists should be kept as straight as possible, and the forearms should be parallel to the floor. A wrist rest provides a comfortable position for the wrists when not using the keyboard. Resist the temptation to rest the wrists when you are typing, however, since that could promote RSI.

Telephone

Whenever possible, a headset should be used instead of a telephone receiver.

These preventative measures can reduce the incidence of repetitive strain injuries and improve the comfort and productivity of help desk agents.

APPLYING SKILLS

1. Explain why support specialists may be susceptible to work-related injuries.

2. How would you convince a company to invest in new workstations and chairs for their help desk employees?

Provide Competitive Salaries

Salary obviously affects job satisfaction. It is also an important indicator of the value the organization places on the help desk. If the help desk is not viewed as important, this will be reflected in salaries. If help desk staff members feel undervalued, they will leave for internal positions or jobs with an external company.

Create a Pleasing Physical Work Environment

The physical environment in which help desk agents work is critical, since most staff members do not leave the work area on a regular basis. The health and well-being of agents is dependent upon a comfortable and safe work environment. Consideration must be given to sound, lighting, furniture, and placement of equipment. If attention is not given to the physical environment, staff members are unlikely to stay on the job for any significant length of time.

Offer Training and Education

Training is another imperative when it comes to the help desk staff. Investment must be made in regular training for new employees and also for existing staff. Training should be viewed as an investment in human capital. All staff members should be given the opportunity to learn new things and to keep existing skills and knowledge up to date. In addition to technical training, staff should receive training in interpersonal and communication skills.

Provide the Latest Tools

Finally, management must provide the help desk staff with the best available tools to do the job. This includes everything from telephone headsets to sophisticated knowledge bases and call tracking systems.

Individual Efforts

The organization is responsible for creating an environment in which help desk agents can thrive. Even in the best organizations, the help desk staff will not be without stress. It is up to employees to manage stress in a way that does not interfere with their on-the-job performance or their general health and well-being. The following techniques may be effective in developing and maintaining a positive work experience.

Manage Time Effectively

A great deal of stress is the result of time pressure. In a help desk position, there are usually calls waiting in the queue and problem resolutions that must be recorded. Help desk staff members have little or no control over the flow of incoming requests. It is generally not practical to try to plan an entire day in a busy help desk environment, when a priority call may come in at any moment.

While the support staffs' first priority is responding to users, most support personnel also perform other tasks on a regular basis, such as preparing reports or writing problem solutions. Work on these assignments must be done when call volume is low. This can be challenging, since the amount of time available on any one day is unpredictable, and because these times are not without interruption from occasional calls. This requires flexibility on the part of the support specialist.

Assign Priorities

When working on tasks other than user requests, the first step is to assign priorities to each task. While it may not be possible to schedule an exact time to work on the assignment, knowing which task has priority ensures that when time becomes available, the most important task is at the top of the list. If the assignment is a larger project, break it into a number of smaller, more manageable jobs. Assign priorities to the individual jobs, and set a timeline for completion.

Take Regular Breaks and Vary Activities

Taking a break from an activity can provide a necessary change of pace. Retrieving a document from the printer, using the copy machine, and walking down the hall to confer with a colleague are simple, productive ways to break up routine computer tasks. Short breaks are also one of the most effective ways to minimize the discomforts of prolonged computer use.

Learn to Relax

The regular use of a relaxation response such as deep breathing or progressive relaxation can reduce the effects of stress. In almost all methods of stress reduction, one of the first techniques taught is effective breathing. When the body is under stress, breathing patterns change. Proper breathing is essential for good mental and physical health. Progressive relaxation involves tensing individual muscle groups for several seconds and then releasing the tension. This allows the muscles to gradually relax, and can reduce pulse rate and blood pressure.

Exercise Regularly

Making time for regular exercise may make it easier to cope with the demands of the job. Regular exercise has been found to be effective in maintaining physical and mental well-being. Activities such as walking, running, working out, aerobics, dancing, and swimming lower blood pressure and cholesterol levels, and provide effective relief from stress. Getting adequate sleep and eating a balanced diet are also important components of a healthy lifestyle.

Talk to People

Talking about work-related stresses with other people can have a positive effect on a person's ability to handle stress. The experience of verbalizing a problem with another person often results in a more objective view of the situation, and may also uncover possible solutions. Discussing concerns with an empathetic individual also allows the individual to express feelings and receive emotional support. Be sure to keep the conversations constructive and positive. Discussing problems with coworkers who are not part of the problem or the solution can result in low morale and disloyalty.

Balance Work and Play

Many people experience burnout as a result of an imbalance between work and nonwork activities. To prevent this from occurring, allow plenty of time for family, friends, and activities that are enjoyable. Humor is also a great stress reliever, both on and off the job.

 READING CHECK

1. **READING REVIEW** Why is it difficult to manage time effectively in a help desk position?

2. **CRITICAL THINKING** Why is the physical environment of the help desk such an important factor in the job experience?

Techniques for Managing Stress

After reading each section, write a brief statement that reflects how well you are using this stress management technique.

1. **Take a Positive Approach**
   - There is always an effective way to deal with each situation.
   - Problems always have solutions, even if the solution is not immediately apparent.
   - It is not always easy, but it will always be possible to do something to address the problem.

2. **Set Realistic Expectations**
   - Don't expect too much of yourself.
   - Set realistic goals.
   - Don't expect to always be right.

3. **Be Flexible**
   - If the first solution doesn't work, try again.
   - Look at mistakes as learning experiences.

4. **Be Objective**
   - Step back and look at your life situation as if it were someone else's.
   - What could this person change to reduce stress?
   - What would he or she have to accept to minimize stress?

5. **Become Aware of Your Internal Resources**
   - Assess your strengths and weaknesses for coping with stress.
   - Notice areas that could use improvement.

6. **Seek Out Other People**
   - Assess your support network.
   - Discuss your difficulties with family, friends, or colleagues.

7. **Resist the Urge to Control Everything**
   - Accept that there are many life situations you cannot control.
   - Practice accepting the things that cannot be changed.

8. **Recognize Stress Warning Signs**
   - Pay attention to yourself and notice whether you are exhibiting any of the warning signs of stress, such as difficulty sleeping, feelings of anxiety or irritability, or overeating.

9. **Maintain Physical Health**
   - Maintain sensible eating and sleeping habits.
   - Get plenty of physical exercise.

10. **Spend Time Relaxing**
    - Schedule regular relaxation activities.
    - Take vacations.

Your Response:
Did you find that you already use most of the techniques? If you feel you are not using a resource as much as you could, write down ways in which you could develop your capacity to use this approach effectively in the future.

Stress Self-Assessment Quiz

DIRECTIONS: To determine how well you handle stress, complete the quiz below, marking each statement *true* or *false*:

STATEMENT	TRUE	FALSE
1. When I feel frustrated because of normal everyday problems, I am usually able to put these events out of my mind and get through the day.	_____	_____
2. I have been told by a physician that some of my medical problems may be caused partially by stress.	_____	_____
3. I recognize when a situation is beyond my control and do not spend time trying to change it.	_____	_____
4. When unexpected problems arise on the job, I may panic for a moment or two; then I settle down and focus on what I can do to solve the problem.	_____	_____
5. If I have had a bad day at work, I have a hard time leaving it behind when I get home.	_____	_____
6. I can usually see the humorous side of a stressful situation and may make a joke to lighten my spirits and make others laugh.	_____	_____
7. Although I sometimes worry about problems, I can usually stop myself from dwelling on things that I can't control.	_____	_____
8. If too many problems happen at once, I tend to get flustered and have trouble concentrating.	_____	_____
9. When I find myself becoming stressed from working hard, I recognize this and take steps to reduce the stress.	_____	_____
10. When under pressure at work, I am usually able to stay calm and focus on what needs to be done.	_____	_____
11. I frequently get myself upset worrying about what might happen in the future.	_____	_____
12. Day-to-day problems at home and work don't really bother me that much, and I usually take things in stride pretty well.	_____	_____

SCORING: For every *true* response you gave to questions 2, 5, 8, and 11 add five points, for every *true* response to questions 1, 4, 6, 7, and 9 add three points. (Items 3, 6, 10, and 12 are not counted.) Total your score.

WHAT THE SCORING MEANS: Scores between 0 and 10: You handle most problems and stressors in a cool, calm, and collected manner. You are able to see the humorous side of most stressful situations and generally keep yourself from taking things too seriously.

Scores between 11 and 22: You probably cope with stress as well as the most people do. While you sometimes feel overwhelmed by unexpected problems, you are usually able to collect yourself, regroup, and get on with the tasks at hand. You might benefit from practicing stress management techniques on a regular basis.

Scores between 23 and 32: You find unexpected problems and heavy workloads difficult to handle. When you get home from work, you have trouble leaving the day's problems behind you. You may be experiencing stress-related symptoms and would likely benefit from a stress management course.

Chapter 10 Review

>> Summary

The following points were covered in this chapter:

1. Stress is the response of the body to demands made upon it. Stress occurs when there is a mismatch between an individual's resources and the demands placed on that individual.

2. Symptoms of stress can be categorized as physiological, psychological, and behavioral.

3. The primary sources of stress in the help desk include time pressures, workload, threats to job security, interpersonal interactions, workplace environment, and information overload.

4. People may resist change for a variety of reasons. Some people resist change because they see no need for the change. Sometimes a person's fears are an issue, especially fear of the unknown, fear of losing control, and fear of losing value to the organization. Other reasons for resistance include the possible loss of job, income, power, and interpersonal relationships.

5. The creation of a positive work environment requires efforts from the organization and the individual. The organization is responsible for creating an environment in which employees are able to perform at their best. The individual must manage time effectively, prioritize tasks, and take the necessary steps to manage stress.

Help Desk Simulation

The Help Desk Simulation requires you to apply the knowledge and skills learned throughout the book to actual help desk situations. The Simulation contains three parts.

Part I, "Larkspur Technologies Help Desk Manual," covers the company's basic policies, and procedures.

Part II, "Larkspur Technologies Help Desk Service Level Agreement," provides information about the support that is provided by the help desk, such as the hours of the help desk, a list of departments supported by the help desk, service request priorities and response times, and a list of software that is supported.

Part III, "On the Job," consists of a series of tasks to be completed using HelpSTAR, a software program that automates many help desk activities. Using HelpSTAR, you will perform a variety of tasks, such as:

- Entering new service requests from users
- Assigning priority levels to requests
- Moving requests from dispatch to queues
- Searching a knowledgebase for solutions
- Creating new solutions and adding them to a knowledgebase
- Adding new users to the database
- Creating basic help desk reports.

To begin, read through Parts I and II of the Simulation. Then, study the material in the Appendix, "Introduction to HelpSTAR." You must be famililar with the information contained in all of these sections to successfully complete the hands-on activities in Part III. Once you have finished reading these three sections, begin the activities in Part III of this Simulation.

Larkspur Technologies Help Desk Manual

Mission

The purpose of the Help Desk is to provide, through a single point of contact, prompt and professional hardware and software technical support. We achieve this mission through a variety of activities:

- Installing and supporting specific software applications.
- Troubleshooting computer problems over the telephone and through site visits.
- Performing minor hardware upgrades and repairs.
- Providing information to assist users in using technology and solving problems on their own.

Essential Qualities of a Help Desk Analyst

The best help desk analysts are not necessarily those with the highest level of technical skills. Whatever your technical expertise, it is even more important that you possess these attributes:

- A willingness to take initiative and learn continuously
- A friendly customer-service attitude
- A mature and professional approach to the job

Job Classifications and Duties

Three job classifications currently exist at the Help Desk: Junior Analyst, Analyst, and Senior Analyst.

Junior Analyst
- Answer phone, collect and forward information
- Accompany and assist Analysts on with site repairs
- Learn technical skills and procedures
- Organize files and information
- Resolve basic service requests

Analyst
- Answer phone as needed
- Schedule and carry out (assisted or unassisted) service visits
- Undertake special projects as assigned

- Develop new technical skills to match the most commonly encountered requests
- Organize files and information
- Resolve more complex requests

Senior Analyst

- Answer phone as needed
- Schedule and carry out advanced service visits
- Undertake special projects
- Develop documentation and employee training materials
- Develop technical skills in specialized areas
- Resolve most complex requests
- Assist others in development of key technical skills
- Recommend upgrades, training, etc.

Larkspur Technologies Help Desk Support Staff

Support Rep	Job Title
John Keyser	Senior Help Desk Analyst
Beth Markham	Help Desk Analyst
Sandra Liu	Help Desk Analyst
Sanjay Shah	Junior Help Desk Analyst

Larkspur Technologies Help Desk Staff Skill Matrix

Support Rep	Skill Areas
Beth Markham	Applications (Software)
	Internet
	Network
	PDA
	PCs
	Windows OS
John Keyser	Applications (Software)
	Email
	Internet
	Network
	PCs
	PDA
	Printers
	Windows OS
	Wireless Networking

Support Rep	Skill Areas
Sandra Liu	Applications (Software)
	Email
	Internet
	Network
	PCs
	Printers
	Windows OS
	Wireless Networking
Sanjay Shah	Applications (Software)
	Email
	Internet
	Printers
	Windows OS

Evaluations

All employees will submit, at the start of their employment, a self-rated evaluation of their own job skills, interests, and objectives for the future. The Help Desk manager will then meet privately with each employee to discuss these self-evaluations.

Please note that the self-evaluation is for your own growth and development and is not used as a performance evaluation. Promotions and pay raises will instead be based largely on the following criteria:

- How well you've demonstrated a friendly and professional customer-service attitude
- The amount of initiative you've demonstrated in seeking out new projects, goals, and tasks
- Your adherence to announced policies and procedures
- Your continued development of new skills and knowledge
- Your overall job performance as measured by direct observation and customer satisfaction ratings

Personnel Policies

Because the policies and procedures contained in this handbook are crucial to the success of the Help Desk, they must be reviewed carefully and agreed upon by each member of the Help Desk team. All employees will be asked to sign a statement indicating that they have read, understood, and agree to abide with the policies below.

Evaluation Period

All new employees of the Help Desk are hired with the understanding that their employment is on a conditional basis for the first six weeks.

Attendance

If you wish to be paid, it is critical that you make appropriate use of the Help Desk electronic time-clock application. Be sure that you clock in and out of the computer upon arrival at work and when you leave, and be sure that the correct time is represented whenever you do so. Please check your recorded hours prior to the end of each pay period to make sure they are correct. If your hours for a day you worked are not correct, you may not get paid for that day.

We depend upon your prompt attendance. If you will be late or must miss a day of work due to illness or emergency, advise the manager by calling as soon as possible. If you have not specified a block of time for which you expect to be gone, you must notify the Help Desk *each day* you will be absent. More than three absences or three late arrivals (more than 30 minutes late) without notice may be cause for immediate dismissal.

Work Schedules

The Help Desk is open Monday through Friday from 7:00 A.M. to 4:00 P.M. Your work schedule will consist of 40 hours per week.

Food and Drink

Food and drink, although allowed at the Help Desk, should be handled carefully to avoid damage to the equipment.

Attire

Please dress in a comfortable but neat and professional manner.

Personal Items

Do not work on personal projects while clocked in except with the permission of the Help Desk manager. There should always be work-related tasks available for you to do. Checking your e-mail is fine (in fact, there may be mail you need to see) but do not spend more than a few minutes each day reading or replying to personal mail.

Personal phone calls should be kept to a minimum. Cellular phones may be used for personal calls, but should be set to vibrate mode so that incoming rings are not audible.

All personal items should be neatly placed out of the way while you are working. The Help Desk is to be kept neat and clean at all times. Do *not*

- Enter a request title
- Enter a description of the problem
- Forward the request to dispatch

Assigning Requests to Queues

Typically a single support rep will be given the responsibility of dispatching requests to the appropriate queues. This action changes the request status from 'In Dispatch' to 'In Queue'. Support reps assigned to the queues are responsible for accepting the requests from queue (i.e. putting them 'In Service').

When a request is assigned to a queue, it is also given a priority level of critical, high, medium, or low. Priority levels must be assigned in accordance with the definitions in the current Service Level Agreement.

Accepting Requests from Queues

Each support rep is assigned to several queues, depending on his or her particular skills and experience. View the requests in your assigned queues. In general, calls with the highest priority and that have been open for the longest time should be worked on first. When a request is accepted from a queue, its status changes from 'In Queue' to 'In Service'.

Working on 'In Service' Requests

Requests that are 'In Service' are actively being worked on by support reps. After reading the description of the problem, a support rep searches the database of standard solutions and historical service requests (the knowledgebase) to see if an answer to the problem already exists. If it does, the rep can use this information to fix the problem.

The request is then updated to reflect the activity that has taken place. Efforts made to find a solution are noted. If the problem was solved with a standard solution, the solution reference number is entered, along with a brief statement such as "problem solved—solution #29".

If there is no existing solution, the rep will engage in problem solving techniques to arrive at a solution. If the rep is unable to solve the problem within the time limits specified in the Service Level Agreement, the request must be forwarded (escalated) to a rep at a higher level.

Closing Requests

Once a solution is provided to the user and noted in the service request, the request is closed. Be sure to provide information detailing how the request was resolved as this data will become part of the knowledgebase.

Other Tasks

If you have no specific task to perform, check that the following activities have been completed:

Follow up on service requests.

Remain aware of all open requests in your assigned queues and check each one to be sure that appropriate actions are being taken. Every action should be recorded in the request.

Clean the Help Desk area.

Clean up scraps of paper and place them in the recycle bin. Organize folders, materials, pens, and office supplies in the drawers and places provided.

Learn new applications and skills.

Do a computer-based tutorial, study a manual or book, or research support resources on the Internet. Practice software installations or hardware repairs on surplus computers available for this purpose.

Make suggestions.

When you see a way to improve the quality or efficiency of our services, let the Help Desk manager know.

Larkspur Technologies Help Desk Service Level Agreement

Who Is Supported Under This Agreement

This agreement is intended to cover the entire organization, including the following:

- Finance
- Marketing
- Information Technology
- Sales
- Human Resources

Methods of Contact

The Help Desk acts as a central point of contact for all technical support, including hardware and software questions, installations, network connection requests, and troubleshooting. Requests can be submitted by telephone, e-mail, fax, or via our support website.

Telephone: 408-555-1000
E-mail: helpdesk@larkspurtech.com
Fax: 408-555-2000
Website: www.larkspurtech.com

Hours of Operation

Assistance will normally be available from 7:00 A.M. to 4:00 P.M., Monday through Friday, except when the office is closed due to holidays.

Responsibilities of Those Making a Request

Whenever possible, callers should contact the Help Desk while in front of the affected computer. Callers to the Help Desk will be expected to be able to provide the following information when making a request:

- Complete contact information (first and last name, department, and phone number)
- A clear and specific description of the problem or request

Supported Software

Fully Supported
The Help Desk will install (often at no charge from a site license) and troubleshoot the following applications:

- Windows 98/NT/2000/XP
- Microsoft Office 2000, 2002, and XP

Larkspur Technologies Help Desk Service Level Agreement

- Microsoft Outlook
- Netscape (browser only)
- Internet Explorer (browser only)
- Norton Antivirus

Not Supported

The Help Desk will *not* assist you in installing, using, or troubleshooting products that are not on the fully supported list, for example:

- WordPerfect
- Microsoft Works
- Non-instructional games of any sort
- Screensavers
- Non-instructional audio

Priorities and Response Times

The help desk will use the following guidelines in prioritizing requests and will strive to resolve problems within the target timeframe. Actual resolutions may be shorter or longer depending on the volume of requests at any one time. However, a minimum of 80% of all requests will be satisfied within the target periods.

Level	Criteria	Target Response
Critical	Affects more than three individuals, no workaround available. Example: Work stoppage because network is down.	Will call or page technicians for immediate response.
High	Affects one to three individuals, no workaround available. *Example*: Computer containing critical data won't boot.	Initial response within 1 working hour.
Medium	Affects fewer than three people, workarounds available. *Example*: Can't check e-mail from one computer, but could use another.	Initial response within one working day.
Low	No affect on productivity, or unsupported software. *Example*: Monitor showing b/w instead of color.	Best effort as time allows. No guarantee of response.

You are taking the role of Beth Markham, Help Desk Analyst for Larkspur Technologies. You are just starting your shift for the day. The first task is to start the HelpSTAR software and review the requests in dispatch and determine the priority level of each one. Be sure to read the information noted in the Details window of each request.

Job #1

Forward each request that is in Dispatch to the appropriate Queue. If appropriate, select a Priority level and Problem Type and save your work. Verify that the requests have been sent to the appropriate Queues by viewing 'All Requests – In Queue' and clicking the Find button.
    Note: Remember to use the 'Refresh' button to update the preview pane.

Job #2

View the requests in your assigned queues.
    Accept the request (into your service) that has the highest priority and that has been open for the longest amount of time.
    Read the request details, then search for a resolution in the Standard Solutions or Historical Service Requests.
    Once a solution has been found, update the request, recording the standard solution or historical service request reference number in the memo field.
    Close the service request.

Job #3

You just ended a call with Charlotte Geitz of the Finance Department. She reports that when she opens a Crystal report, the report displays the first page but the other pages are not displayed.
    Enter the request in HelpSTAR. Note: By now you should be familiar with entering service requests. Do not use the 'New Request' wizard for the remaining jobs. Because no relevant Problem Type exists, you will need to create a new one.
    Once the new Problem Type has been created, continue entering the new request. Enter the Problem Type, Request Title, and a description of the problem (in the Memo field).
    Save the request.

Job #4

Human Resources has provided a list of new employees. Enter the employees in the database.

Name	Jane Ranjit
User Type	Internal
Department	Finance
Telephone	408-555-1000
Extension	61
Location	Floor 1
Workstation ID	WKST0061
Network Address	0060BFD61
Internet Address	111.22.33.61
Logins	Enabled
Password	Leave blank to default to *helpstar*
Email	Enabled
Email Address	jranjit@larkspurtech.com

Name	Randy Stein
User Type	Internal
Department	Sales
Telephone	408-555-1000
Extension	62
Location	Floor 3
Workstation ID	WKST0063
Network Address	0060BFD62
Internet Address	111.22.33.62
Logins	Enabled
Password	Leave blank to default to *helpstar*
Email	Enabled
Email Address	rstein@larkspurtech.com

Job #5

You just received a phone call from Adriana Rivera in the Human Resources Department. She is very upset that no one has responded to her request—reference no. 21. She is unable to open an attachment that she received via e-mail. The file contains the details of a severance package that is being offered to an employee who is being terminated this afternoon. She demands to speak with someone at a higher level.

Using the reference no., locate and open Rivera's request. As standard practice, enter a description in ther Memo field. Forward the request to John Keyser, the Senior Help Desk Analyst.

Job #6

Angela Psaris of the Marketing Department called to say that her PDA would not switch on today. She said that there have not been any recent changes to her PDA and she needs some urgent information from the PDA that is due to her manager by noon, and is feeling stressed.

Create a new service request. You will need to create a new Problem Type. Remember to enter a description of the problem in the Memo field.

Forward the request to a queue. Note: when you attempt to forward the request to a queue, you realize an appropriate queue does not exist. Create a new queue, and assign the queue to support reps based on the Support Rep Skill Matrix in the Help Desk Manual.

Job #7

You just got off the phone with Carl Molinari from the Finance Department. He received our e-mail notice about the new klez worm virus. He said that he opened an e-mail attachment yesterday that had the same name as the file in the e-mail warning. He is worried that his computer may have been infected with the virus.

Create a new service request.

Forward the request directly into your service (by Forwarding to 'Myself').

Search for a standard solution or historical (request) solution. Because no solution exists, you research the virus on the Internet and discover that the latest version of the anti-virus software is capable of removing the virus. You call Carl back and walk him through the steps required to install the latest virus definitions.

Create and publish a new standard solution for the problem. Be sure to add a keyword to the Solution.

Update and close the request.

Job #8

Your manager, Ron, stopped by and asked you to run several reports. Ron would like to know which problem type(s) have been occurring most often, and which department(s) have submitted the greatest number of requests.

Generate a Line Item Summary Report sorted by problem type. Accept the default entries in the Date Range box. Review the report. What problem type was reported most often?

Generate a Line Item Summary Report, filtered by Department. Accept the default entries in the Date Range box. Review the report. What department submitted the most requests?

Introduction to HelpSTAR

HelpSTAR is a software package used in a help desk environment to automate and optimize the administration of end user support. Help-STAR provides the ability to record, track, and solve service requests from the moment they are created until they are closed.

HelpSTAR also provides for knowledgebase creation and retrieval, as well as reporting and analysis functionality—two very important require-ments for an efficient help desk.

A copy of HelpSTAR Learning Edition is provided on the CD-ROM that accompanies this book. In addition, to get more information about HelpSTAR and download the latest version of the software, browse to http://edu.helpstar.com.

If you can't wait to get started using HelpSTAR, refer to the Quick Start guide at the end of this appendix (this document is also available at http://edu.helpstar.com and on the CD-ROM that accompanies this book).

A.1 How HelpSTAR is Organized

HelpSTAR is structured around the following types of data:

- Service Requests (also known as work orders, calls, or trouble tickets)
- Users
- Problem Types
- Queues
- Standard Solutions

Service Requests

Service requests are the foundation of all HelpSTAR activity. A new service request is created for each new issue or call undertaken by the help desk. Each service request is associated with a specific user (the originator of the request).

Users

In HelpSTAR, the term *users* refers both to the end users experiencing problems and the support reps who resolve them.

Problem Types

Each request is assigned a problem type. Problem types are used to categorize service requests and are very useful for searching and reporting purposes. Analysis of past requests by problem type may reveal areas where additional resources or training should be deployed. Each help desk will define problem types based on its own particular needs. Examples of problem types include:

- Printers
- Network
- Software—Microsoft Office
- Email

Queues

Queues are temporary holding areas for service requests, organized around the skills required to resolve them. Each support rep is assigned to queues based on his specific skill set and level of expertise. A rep is normally assigned to several queues, and each queue may have several reps assigned to it. When a support rep is added to HelpSTAR, a support rep–specific queue is automatically created for him. Support rep–specific queues allow you to forward a request directly to a support rep if required; however it is preferable to utilize generic queues whenever possible. Utilizing generic queues helps in optimizing support rep workloads, as well as the level-of-service provided. Each help desk will define generic queues based on the type of support it provides. Examples of generic queues include:

- UNIX
- Windows—Tech Support Level 1
- Windows—Tech Support Level 2
- Application Support, etc.

Standard Solutions

Many of the requests received by a help desk have previously been reported by other users and have known solutions. These known resolutions can be documented as *Standard Solutions* and made available to both end users and support reps (or support reps only).

Encouraging end users to look up Standard Solutions before calling the help desk can save both time and resources.

A.2   Logging into HelpSTAR

1. Start HelpSTAR by double-clicking its shortcut icon on the Desktop or by selecting *Start > Programs > HelpSTAR* from the Start menu.

2. In the login box that appears, HelpSTAR will display the name of the last user who logged into HelpSTAR on your computer.

3. Enter your password (when new users are created, the default password is "helpstar").

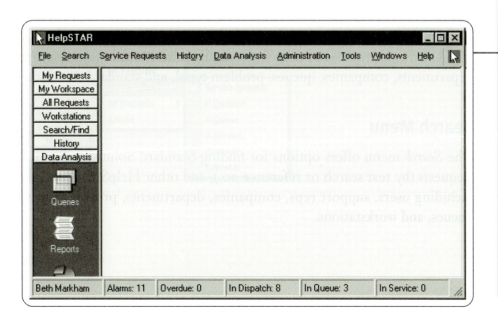

FIGURE   A.1

HelpSTAR Main Screen

All Requests

The *All Requests* submenu allows senior support reps to view all requests in the database, whether open, closed, or assigned to another support rep, etc. This section also allows senior support staff to view timesheet information to keep track of the issues that help desk employees have been working on.

All Requests
submenu options

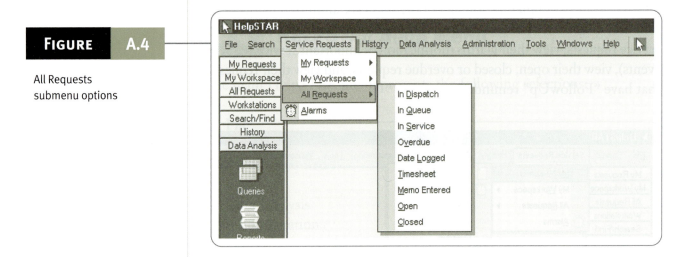

Alarms

HelpSTAR provides alarms to notify the appropriate personnel when certain events occur. For example, when a request is dispatched to a queue, all support reps assigned to that queue will receive an alarm notifying them of the new request. The *Alarms* menu selection generates a list of a support rep's outstanding alarms. The details of a request can be viewed by double-clicking on its line item in the "Alarms" list. A table detailing the events that generate alarms is located at the end of this introductory section.

Alarms window

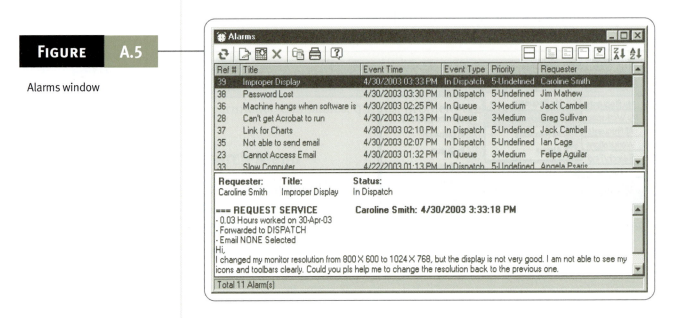

History Menu

The *History* menu generates lists of past requests filtered by *Requester*, *Support Rep*, *Company*, or *Department*. This can be used to examine problems that were experienced in the past. When generating a list of historical requests the rep will be prompted to select a time period.

Data Analysis Menu

The *Data Analysis* menu is used to create queries, reports, and charts using information stored in the HelpSTAR database.

- Queries provide information about service requests and workstations that can be filtered by various criteria. HelpSTAR provides a set of standard queries and also allows for the creation of custom queries.
- Reports offer detailed information about all aspects of the help desk, from efficiency to customer satisfaction. The Standard Reports options are: 'Detailed Work Report', 'Line Item Summary', 'Summary', 'Timesheet', 'Listing', 'Efficiency', 'User Satisfaction', 'Billing' and 'Overdue'
- Charts display HelpSTAR data in graphical format.

Administration Menu

The *Administration* menu is used to add, edit, and delete objects in Help-STAR, including companies, departments, users, queues, and problem types. This menu also provides options for assigning support reps to queues, associating users with workstations, administering standard solutions and configuring system-wide options.

Tools Menu

Options under the *Tools* menu are not used in the exercises in this text. For further information, please refer to the HelpSTAR help file.

Windows Menu

The options under the *Windows* menu are used to switch between active windows, tile open windows, and cascade open windows.

Help Menu

The *Help* menu provides a number of choices for HelpSTAR support:

- *Help Topics*—launches the built-in Help file.
- *Wizards* are aids used in creating new service requests or users, setting user privileges or assigning queues to support reps.

- *HelpSTAR.Com on the Web* (requires internet connection) provides options for accessing the HelpSTAR.com home page or support section.
- *About HelpSTAR* shows details about the installed version of Help-STAR, current usage and licensing.

A.5 The Service Request Workflow

In HelpSTAR, workflow refers to the steps that a service request follows from its initial submission until its resolution. When a new service request is entered into HelpSTAR by an end user it is automatically forwarded to 'Dispatch'. In dispatch, the nature and priority of the request are considered by the dispatcher and the request is then forwarded to the appropriate queue. The request remains in the queue until it is accepted into service by a support rep. The support rep then works on the request (updating the request with relevant information) and closes it once work is completed.

Request Status

At any given time, a service request can be in one of the following states:

- "In Dispatch" (waiting to be assigned to a queue)
- "In Queue" (waiting to be accepted by a support rep)
- "In Service" (actively being worked on by a support rep)
- "Closed" (problem solved, user satisfied)

FIGURE A.6

Typical Workflow of a Request

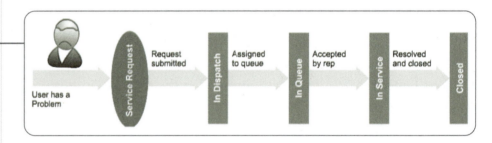

Submitting a New Request ("In Dispatch")

Service requests submitted by end users are automatically forwarded to 'Dispatch'.

Dispatching a Request to Queue ("In Queue")

The next step in the workflow is forwarding the request from dispatch to a queue. A dispatcher will examine the request, assign a priority level and a problem type, check the title (to ensure that it is relevant to the problem) and then forward the request to the appropriate queue. Requests are forwarded to queues based on the type of request and the skill set and level of expertise required to resolve it.

Accepting a Request ("In Service")

Once a request has been assigned to a queue, a support rep can accept the request into service (the electronic equivalent of grabbing the work-order). At this time, the support rep will begin working on a solution to the problem. The first step usually requires searching a knowledgebase for a solution (HelpSTAR's 'Standard Solutions'). If a solution cannot be found, the rep will use problem-solving skills to determine the actions required to fix the problem.

Updating a Request ("In Service")

Once the problem solving process begins, all actions taken by a support rep to diagnose and solve the problem should be recorded in HelpSTAR. A separate memo is created each time the request is updated by the requester or rep. The individual memos are time stamped, and trace memos provide an audit trail showing the changes made to the request.

Closing a Request ("Closed")

Once a solution has been found, it must be communicated to the requester. When a solution resolves the problem and the user is satisfied, the request can be closed.

A.6 Working with Service Requests

A new service request is created for each new job, call, or activity that is undertaken by the help desk.

Step 1: Creating A New Request

New service requests can be created by end users, or by support reps on their behalf. To create a new request, select *File > New > Service Request* from the main menu. The 'New Request' window will be displayed.

When an end user opens a new request, the following fields must be completed:

- Request Title
- Memo (all relevant details of the problem)

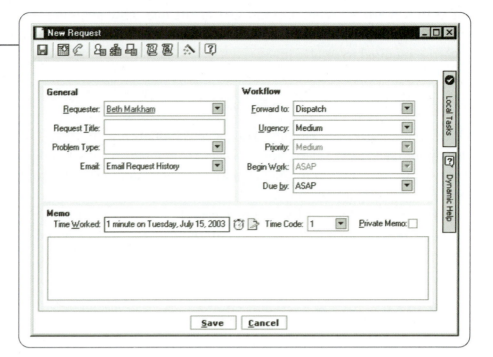

The end user may also specify an 'Urgency' and a 'Due by' date, or can simply accept the defaults of 'Medium' and 'ASAP' respectively.

When a support rep opens a new service request on behalf of an end user, the following fields must be completed with the appropriate information:

- Requester (name of user requesting service)
- Problem Type
- Request Title
- Memo (all relevant details of the problem)

Requester (Name of User Requesting Service)

The requester field is for the name of the user who is requesting service. It displays the name of the current user by default. If a support rep is opening a new request on behalf of an end user, clicking the arrow at the end of this field displays the 'Find a User' window, and the end user can be selected by double-clicking the user name.

Note: to be automatically prompted for the user name each time you open a new request, check the 'Launch Find a User Screen' option under the *Tools > User Options > Auto Launch* tab.

Problem Type

Problem types are used to categorize service requests and provide support reps with an immediate indication of the kinds of concerns they are dealing with. Problem Types are used in filtering searches for historical requests and are very important for reporting analysis, providing essential classification of the issues being managed by the help desk.

Request Title

The Request Title is a short description of the problem/request. The Title can be changed at any time when updating a request.

Memo

The Memo field is used to enter a detailed description of the problem and the efforts undertaken to resolve it. Every time a request is updated the rep should enter a memo to record the work that was performed. Each memo is automatically time-stamped, and the amount of time spent working on the request ('Time Worked') is also recorded (either manually or by the default stop-watch). Important trace information (such as changes in service request status, priority, etc.) is automatically recorded when a request is updated.

How to Create a New Service Request

1. Select *File > New > Service Request* from the main menu.
2. The 'New Request Wizard' will open to guide you through the process, along with the 'New Request' form that is usually displayed when entering new requests.
3. Follow the Wizard instructions to enter new requests until you become comfortable with the process. The Wizard can be set to not appear again by checking the "Don't show this wizard next time" check box.
4. The information entered in the Wizard fields will simultaneously appear in the 'New Request' form.
5. Use the 'Next' and 'Back' buttons to move through the Wizard screens. Note: accept the default dispatch option in the 'Forward To:' field.
6. When all of the information has been entered and the request is saved, a reference number for the request will be displayed
7. To verify that the request has been added, select *Service Requests > My Workspace > In Dispatch* from the main menu. The 'All Requests—In Dispatch' window will be displayed.
8. Confirm that the new request appears in the list.

Note: when logging a request on behalf of an end user you should inform them of the reference no. for the request. Should they need to contact the help desk again they can provide this number to allow a rep to quickly lookup the request. To locate a request by the reference no., go to *Search > Request by Ref#* and enter the relevant request no.

Step 2: Dispatching a Request to a Queue

The next step in the workflow is dispatching the request to a queue. Support reps who have been granted the 'Dispatch' privilege can view a list of requests currently 'In Dispatch' by selecting *Service Requests > My Workspace > In Dispatch* from the main menu. To dispatch a request, select it and either click on the 'Update Service Request' button or right-click the mouse and select 'Update Service Request'. The 'Update Request' window will be displayed.

A Dispatcher normally does the following:

- Categorizes the request by selecting a 'Problem Type'
- Selects a 'Priority' for the request
- Forwards the request to the appropriate queue

The dispatcher may also specify a 'Due by' date, edit the 'Title' (if it is not appropriate), enter a 'Memo' if he has additional information about the problem, and close the request if he is able to resolve the issue immediately.

Forward to:

The "Forward to:" field provides five options:

- Dispatch
- Myself
- Another Rep
- Queue
- Close

Forwarding to Dispatch

There are several situations in which a request would be forwarded to Dispatch. For example:

- A support rep is given an inappropriate service request and wishes to send it back to Dispatch for re-assignment.
- A support rep about to go on vacation may wish to send an "In Service" request back to Dispatch if it cannot be resolved before he leaves.

Forwarding to Myself

Forwarding to 'Myself' allows a rep to update a request and forward it into his own service in one step.

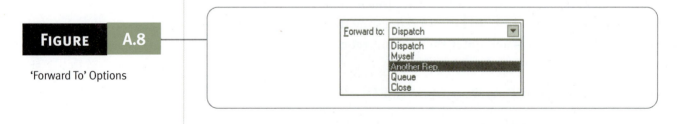

FIGURE A.8

'Forward To' Options

Forwarding to Another Rep

Forwarding to 'Another Rep' is appropriate in situations where queues are not utilized or an urgent request must be routed directly to a rep for immediate action (so that the request does not have to wait 'In Queue').

Forwarding to Queue

A request should be forwarded to a queue, based on the nature of the request and the type and level of expertise required to resolve it. If required, a service request can be routed to a particular support rep by placing it in that rep's "support rep-specific queue".

Forwarding to Close

Once work on a request is completed, the request should be closed. When closing a request, it is important to enter information stating how the problem was resolved. This will assist in developing a good knowledgebase for other/future support reps.

Priority

Requests are prioritized based on the significance of the problem and help desk practices. HelpSTAR offers four levels of priority: 'Critical', 'High', 'Medium' and 'Low'. Priority can be modified at any time by updating the request.

Priority is set by help desk personnel as a guide to the severity of the issue. This is not the same as 'Urgency', which is set by the end user submitting the request (new requests created by end users have no priority).

Note: the priority of a service request cannot be set until a queue or support rep has been selected in the "Forward to" field of the 'New Request' window.

A request's priority determines its sort order in a list of 'In Queue' requests. By default, requests are listed in order of priority and then within each priority level by "time logged" (oldest request first).

How to Dispatch a Request to a Queue

1. Select *Service Requests* > *My Workspace* > *In Dispatch* from the main menu.
2. Select a request and click the 'Update Service Request' button (🖹).
3. Select a 'Problem Type' for the request.
4. In the 'Forward to:' field, select 'Queue', and choose the appropriate queue from the list that appears (double-click on the queue name to select it).
5. Assign a 'Priority' to the request.
6. Click the 'Save' button.
7. A message will appear reminding you that you have not entered a memo for the request. Click the 'Yes' button to save the request.

8. Verify that the request is in the queue. Select *Service Requests > All Requests > In Queue* from the main menu.

9. Click the 'Find' button.

10. A list of all requests in all queues is displayed. Verify that the request just forwarded to queue appears in the correct queue.

Step 3: Accepting a Service Request from a Queue

When a support rep accepts a request from a queue, it is taken out of the queue and is put "In Service" with the rep. As previously mentioned, this is the software equivalent of the rep 'grabbing the work-order' so that he can start working on it.

Follow these steps to accept a service request from a queue:

1. Select *Service Requests > My Workspace > In Queue* from the main menu.

2. The 'My Workspace—In My Queues—All' window will be displayed.

3. Click the 'Find' button.

4. A list of all requests in the queues that you are assigned to will be displayed.

5. Select a request and click the 'Accept the Request' button (🗹) on the toolbar (or right-click on the request and select this option from the popup menu). The request will no longer be shown in the listing as it has been placed in your service.

6. Confirm that the request is in your service.

7. Select *Service Requests > My Workspace > In Service* from the main menu.

8. The 'My Workspace—In Service (I'm the Support Rep)—All' window will be displayed.

9. Click the 'Find' button.

10. Ensure that the request appears in the list of your 'In Service' requests.

FIGURE   **A.9**

Accepting a Service
Request from Queue

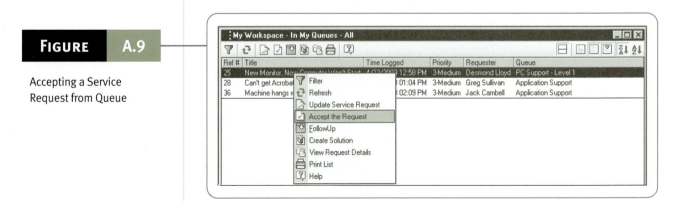

Step 4: Searching for a Standard Solution

When a support rep accepts a request from queue, one of the first steps taken to begin work on the problem is searching the HelpSTAR knowledgebase for a "Standard Solution". There is no need to conduct an elaborate problem solving session if a solution already exists.

Here's how to search for a standard solution:

1. Select *Search* > *Standard Solutions* from the main menu. The 'Text Search—Standard Solution' dialog box will be displayed.

2. Review the data fields in the dialog box, and then type "email" in the 'Search Phrase' field. Notice that the options are set to search in 'Solution Title' and 'Problem Description'. Click the 'Find' button.

3. A list of standard solutions containing the term "email" in the title or problem description will be displayed. Double-clicking on a solution will display the content of the solution. Notice that a reference number is listed for each solution. These reference numbers can be used to refer to a solution when updating a service request. For example, a request memo could read "Problem corrected, Solution #29".

Please note the following search phrase rules that apply when searching for information in HelpSTAR:

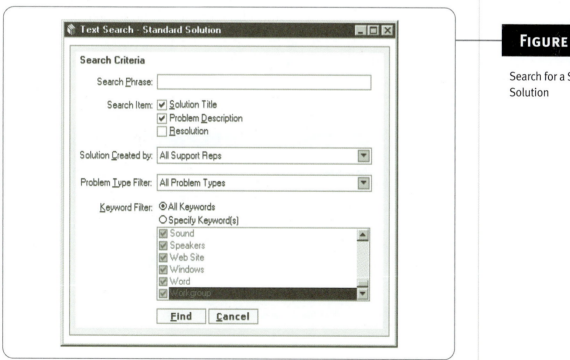

FIGURE A.10

Search for a Standard Solution

- Searches are not case sensitive
- AND, OR, and NOT Boolean operators may be used (e.g. email AND attachment)

- Multiple word phrases must be enclosed in double quotes (e.g. "MS Word")
- One word phrases do not require double quotes (e.g. PrintShop)
- Comma separators are not supported

Step 5: Searching for a Historical Request

If a resolution is not found in the Standard Solutions then the next step is to search the historical requests in the HelpSTAR database. This allows the support rep to search all requests (open and closed) for keywords in the request titles and/or memos.

Note that for the knowledgebase to be effective, the titles entered for service requests should be informative and relevant to the problems experienced, and include any error message numbers.

To search for historical service requests, follow these steps:

1. Select *Search > Service Requests* from the main menu. The 'Text Search—Service Request' dialog box will be displayed.

2. Review the data fields in the dialog box, and then type "email" in the Search Phrase field. Notice that the Search Items option is set to search in 'Title Only' (it is possible to search just the 'Memo' or both 'Title and Memo'). Click the 'Find' button.

3. A list of service requests containing the term "email" in the title will be displayed. Double-clicking on a request will display the request details. Notice that a reference number is listed for each request. These numbers can be used to refer to historical requests when updating a service request. For example, a request memo could read "Problem corrected, based on Request #9".

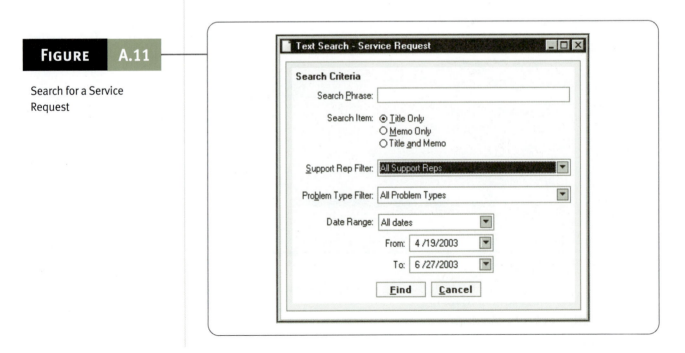

Step 6: Updating a Service Request

Service requests should be updated whenever a support rep performs work on a problem. If additional information is gathered from a user, it should be entered in the Memo field of the request. Each action the support rep takes toward solving the problem should also be recorded in the Memo field. Other fields such as Problem Type and Priority can be changed if necessary.

A support rep is permitted to update
- Any request that he is currently responsible for ('In Service' requests where he is the designated support rep)
- Any request that is currently waiting in any of his assigned queues

Follow these steps to update a service request:

1. Select *Service Requests* > *My Workspace* > *In Service* from the main menu.
2. Click the 'Find' button.
3. The 'My Workspace—In Service (I'm the Support Rep)—All' window will show a listing of all requests in your service.
4. Select a request you wish to update and click the 'Update Service Request' button (🖉). The 'Update Request' window will open.
5. Update the necessary fields.
6. Click the 'Save' button.
7. Click the 'Refresh' button (🔁) to update the preview pane (displays the details of the selected request) below the request listing.

Step 7: Closing a Service Request

When work on the request is completed (i.e. the problem has been resolved), the request can be closed. Requests should not be closed until the end user who submitted the request is satisfied with the resolution.

Here's how to close a service request:

1. Select *Service Requests* > *My Workspace* > *In Service* from the main menu.
2. Click the 'Find' button.
3. The 'My Workspace—In Service (I'm the Support Rep)—All' window will show a list of all requests in your service.
4. Select the request and click the 'Update Service Request' button (🖉).
5. In the 'Forward to': field, select the 'Close' option.
6. Enter a brief memo and update other fields as necessary.
7. Click the 'Save' button. The dialog box will close.
8. Notice that the request is still listed as being "In Service".
9. Click the 'Refresh' button (🔁).

10. The request will disappear from the "In Service" list.

11. Confirm that the request has been closed.

12. Select *Service Requests* > *All Requests* > *Closed* from the main menu.

13. The 'All Closed Requests—All' window will appear.

14. Click the 'Find' button.

15. The 'Date Range' dialog box will be displayed.

16. Accept the default dates or change as necessary.

17. Click the 'OK' button.

18. A list of closed requests will be displayed.

19. Locate the desired request (you can sort the list by clicking on a column heading).

A.7 HelpSTAR Administrative Tasks

In addition to working with service requests, senior support reps may also be required to perform administrative functions, such as adding new problem types when necessary. Administrative tasks are performed by selecting options from the *Administration* menu.

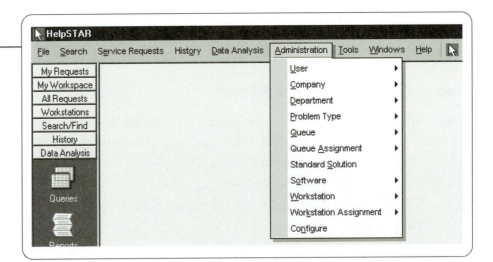

FIGURE A.12

Administration Menu

Adding a New User

All individuals who interact with the help desk, whether end users or support reps, must be added to HelpSTAR. New employees can be added to HelpSTAR as required. Users should also be added (if they do not already exist in HelpSTAR) even if support reps are creating requests on their behalf.

All users must have a unique name. HelpSTAR uses a single field for the entire user name. In the exercises in this book, names are entered in "Firstname Lastname" format in the 'Name' field (i.e. "John Smith").

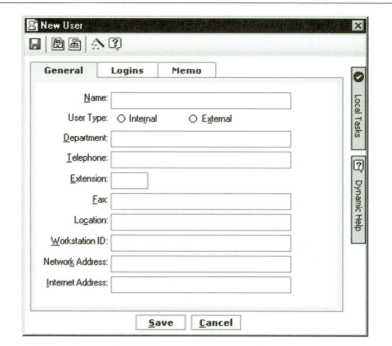

All users must be designated as either internal (to the company) or external (belonging to a different company such as a client, supplier, vendor, etc.). Internal users are associated with departments. External users are associated with companies. This book uses only internal users.

When users are added to the database, their HelpSTAR 'Logins' and 'Email' options can be enabled. With Logins enabled, a user can login to HelpSTAR from a Windows client. With Email enabled, a user can submit service requests by sending an email to the designated HelpSTAR email address (configured in the StarWatch utility). Any email received from this user will then be automatically imported into HelpSTAR as a service request.

Users who have their Logins and/or Email enabled are known as interactive users.

Follow these steps to add a new user:

1. Select *Administration > User > New User* from the main menu.
2. The 'Add User Wizard' will be displayed to guide you through the process, along with the 'New User' dialog box that is usually displayed when adding new users.
3. Follow the Wizard instructions to enter new users until you become comfortable with the process. The Wizard can be set to not appear again by checking the "Don't show this wizard next time" checkbox.
4. The information entered in the Wizard fields will simultaneously appear in the 'New User' dialog box.

5. Use the 'Next' and 'Back' buttons to move through the Wizard screens.

6. When finished entering the user, verify that he or she has been added to the database.

7. Select *Administration > User > List Users > All Users* from the main menu. The 'List All Users' window will be displayed.

8. Confirm that the new user appears in the list.

Creating a New Problem Type

Whenever a support rep opens a new request on behalf of an end user, a problem type must be specified. Occasionally, it is necessary to add a new problem type to the database. Both service requests and standard solutions are categorized by problem type. This can be a very useful filter while searching for standard solutions or historical requests. In addition, categorizing each request by problem type allows for more detailed reporting on the kind of problems experienced by end users or the help desk.

To create a new problem type, follow these steps:

1. Select *Administration > Problem Type > New Problem Type* from the main menu. The 'New Problem Type' dialog box will appear.

2. Enter the name of a problem type in the 'New' field.

3. Click the 'Save' button. A message will indicate that the problem type has been added.

4. Click 'No' when prompted to add another problem type.

5. Confirm that the new problem type has been added.

6. Select *Administration > Problem Type > List Problem Types* from the main menu. The 'List All Problem Types' window will be displayed.

7. Locate the newly added problem type in the list.

Creating a New Queue

At times it may be necessary to add new queues to the database. This may be needed when a new product is introduced (hardware or software) or another area/level of technical expertise is required, creating the need for a new 'holding area' to which support reps with the required skills can be assigned.

Here's how you would create a new queue:

1. Select *Administration > Queue > New Queue* from the main menu.

2. Enter a queue name in the 'New' field.

3. Click the 'Save' button.

4. A message will appear indicating that the queue has been added.

5. Click the 'OK' button.

6. A message will appear asking if another queue is to be added.

7. Click the 'No' button.

8. Confirm that the queue has been added.

9. Select *Administration* > *Queue* > *List Queues* from the main menu.

10. The list of queues will be displayed.

11. Locate the newly added queue in the list.

Assigning a Queue to Support Reps

Once a new queue has been added, the queue must be assigned to one or more support reps. These reps will be responsible for accepting requests from the new queue. Follow these steps to assign a queue to a support rep:

1. Select *Administration* > *Queue Assignment* > *Queue to Rep* from the main menu.

2. The 'Assign Queues to Support Rep' dialog box will be displayed.

3. Select the new queue from the drop-down list.

4. The left side of the dialog box will list the available support reps.

5. The right side of the dialog box will list any support reps who have been assigned to the queue.

6. To assign a rep to the queue, select the rep's name and click the 'Assign' button. The rep's name is removed from the 'Available' list and now appears in the 'Assigned' list.

7. When the assignment of reps is complete, click the 'Save' button. A message will appear stating that queue assignments have been updated and the dialog box will close.

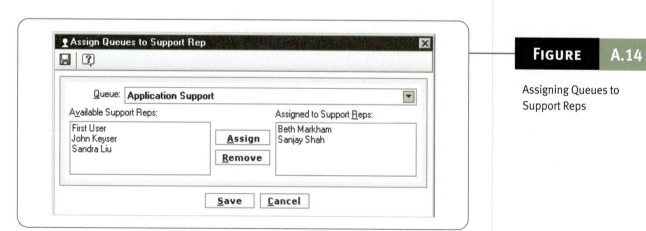

FIGURE A.14

Assigning Queues to Support Reps

Creating a New Standard Solution

Standard Solutions allow the help desk to build a database of resolutions to known/common problems. End users and support reps can search this database as a first step in solving problems that arise. The Standard Solutions database should contain concise answers to specific problems.

There are two types of standard solutions: 'Draft' and 'Published'. Draft solutions are only available to support staff and will contain resolutions to known/common problems that are not appropriate for end users to try (e.g. changing registry or BIOS settings). Published solutions are available to end users (as well as support staff) and provide a self-help solution.

When creating a Standard Solution it is important that the title is descriptive of the problem (and includes any relevant error numbers); this will allow for easier searching of the solutions database. It is also important that the resolution is described in a clear and concise format so that it is easily understood. For complex resolutions, numbered steps are recommended for clarity.

Support reps can also create Standard Solutions from existing service requests (by clicking the 'New Standard Solution' button (⬛) on the toolbar of any request listing window).

How to Create a New Standard Solution

1. Select *Administration > Standard Solution* from the main menu. The 'List of Standard Solutions' window will be displayed.

2. Click the 'New Standard Solution' button (⬛). The 'Create a New Standard Solution' window will appear.

3. Enter a concise title into the 'Title' field.

4. Select an appropriate Problem Type.

5. Click the 'Add' button next to the 'Keywords' field if you wish to add keywords to the Standard Solution. Keywords may be used to narrow the search criteria when searching for Standard Solutions.

6. In the 'Problem Description' field, enter a detailed description of the problem.

7. In the 'Resolution' field, enter the steps required to resolve the problem.

8. After you have entered all of the information for the Standard Solution, click the 'Save' button.

9. A message will appear stating that the solution has been added as a 'Draft' solution (only accessible by support reps). To confirm that the solution is 'Draft', click the arrow at the end of the 'Published List' field (at the top-left of the Standard Solutions listing) and select 'Draft List'. Only the solutions in draft mode will be shown.

10. To publish the new Standard Solution, select it in the draft list and click the 'Publish' button ( ) on the toolbar. The solution will disappear from the draft list (as it has been moved to the list of published solutions).

11. To verify that the solution has been published, click the arrow at the end of the 'Draft List' field and change the display from 'Draft List' to 'Published List'.

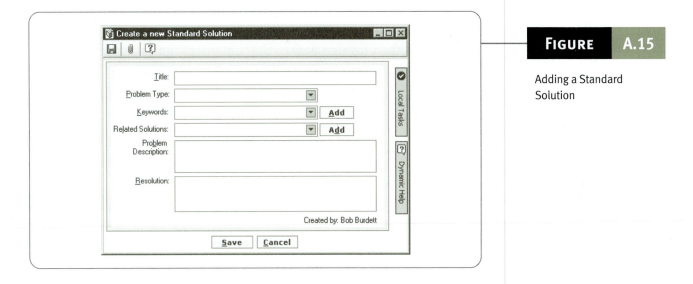

FIGURE   A.15

Adding a Standard Solution

A.8   HelpSTAR Reports

A major feature of any help desk package is the ability to create reports. Help desk performance can be monitored regularly using data collected by the software. HelpSTAR provides a number of pre-defined 'Standard Reports'. In this text, 'Line Item Summary' Reports will be used.

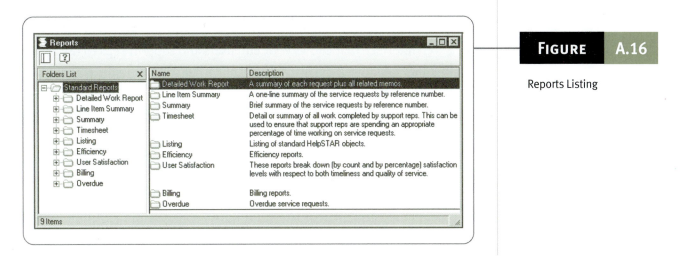

FIGURE   A.16

Reports Listing

Creating a Line Item Summary Report

Line Item Summary Reports provide one-line summaries of all service requests within a selected date range. Using these reports, it is possible to determine at a glance the kinds of problems your help desk is managing.

Here's how you would create a line item summary report:

1. Select *Data Analysis* > *Reports* from the main menu. The 'Reports' window will be displayed.

2. Click the plus sign next to the 'Line Item Summary' folder to display its contents. Five subfolders will be shown.

3. Click any subfolder. The 'Date Range' dialog box will appear.

4. Enter the desired dates for the report.

5. Click the 'OK' button. The report will be displayed. To move to other pages of the report, use the right and left arrow buttons at the top of the report window.

6. To print the report, click the 'Print' button located at the top of the report window.

A.9   Additional Notes

HelpSTAR provides many other important features that are not described in this text, including the following:

- StarWatch—This utility monitors the HelpSTAR database and generates alarms for the appropriate help desk personnel whenever a request reaches its scheduled or due-by date. In addition, this utility will monitor a technical support email account and automatically import email into HelpSTAR, creating/updating service requests based on the email.

- Web Interface (Not included in Learning Edition)—HelpSTAR offers a web interface that allows your end users and support reps to use a web browser (such as *Microsoft's Internet Explorer*) to login and submit new requests, check on the status of existing service requests, search for standard solutions, etc. Additional information is available at:

  http://edu.helpstar.com

Privilege	Rights Granted
SUBMIT	Users can open service requests on behalf of end users. This privilege is NOT required for an interactive end user to enter requests on his own behalf.
DISPATCH	Users can assign incoming service requests to queues and prioritize them.
PASS DIRECT	Users can assign service requests directly to support reps, thus bypassing queues.
ADMINISTER	Users can perform administrative functions such as adding/editing/deleting queues and problem types, adding support reps and assigning them to queues, etc.
REPORT	Users can view other service requests in addition to their own. Also, they can generate reports on other users' service requests, queue status, support rep status, etc.
AUTHORIZE	Users can grant and add privileges to others.
APPROVE	Users can designate service requests as 'complete' by providing approval ratings (after the requests are closed), even if other users requested the services.
EDIT MEMOS	Users can modify historical memos (text, time worked) and delete requests.
UPDATE ALL	Users can update requests even if they are not designated support reps.

TABLE A.1

HelpSTAR User Privileges

There are two additional privileges that can be granted only to Support Reps:

Privilege	Rights Granted
AUTO ACCEPT	Reps allowed to open and accept request into his service in one step.
QUICK FIX	Reps allowed to open and close request in one step.

TABLE A.2

Events that Trigger Alarms

Note that 'Support Rep' is in itself a privilege. Support reps are able to accept service requests from their assigned queues and close the requests when they have finished working on them.

Event Type	Alarm Received By
New service request arrives in dispatch.	All users with the dispatch privilege.
Service request is placed in queue.	All support reps assigned to the queue.
Service request passed direct to a support rep.	Support rep receiving the request.
Service request updated by another support rep in 'update all' mode, or by end user who initiated the request.	If request is in service: currently designated support rep. If request is in queue: all reps assigned to the queue. If request is in dispatch: all dispatchers.
Service request is not closed when its due date arrives.	If request is in service: currently designated support rep. If request is in queue: all reps assigned to the queue.
Service request is resumed when its scheduled date (Begin Work date) arrives.	If request is in service: currently designated support rep. If request is in queue: all reps assigned to the queue.
Service request is suspended.	NO ALARM IS GENERATED
Service request is closed.	End user who initiated the request.

Automatic Notification

Whenever you log into HelpSTAR, your outstanding alarms are automatically displayed in the 'Alarms' window. While you are logged onto HelpSTAR, the system will periodically notify you when new alarms arrive. When a new alarm is generated, the HelpSTAR icons on the main task bar and in the upper left-hand corner of the main HelpSTAR window will flash. The current number of alarms is also displayed in the bottom of the main window. The notification frequency can be controlled by specifying the 'Scanning Interval' in your personalized 'User Options.'

A Logging a New Service Request

Support reps and other help desk staff use the following form to submit service requests.

1. Select a Requester **B**.
2. The Title should be meaningful and concise to facilitate historical solution searches.
3. Problem Type classification is used for reporting and analysis.
4. Email the current memo or the request history to the requester.
5. A request can be forwarded to the dispatcher, to yourself (Auto Accept), another rep, a queue, or closed altogether.
6. The end user's stated Urgency is used as an input in determining the actual priority.
7. The actual Priority, based on stated Urgency and overall help desk workload determines when the request will be processed, and how it will be escalated.
8. The start date for working on this request (if not ASAP).
9. The deadline for completion of this request (optional).
10. A Stopwatch calculates the time worked (can be manually overridden).
11. Allows you to bill clients for support at different charge rates.
12. If checked, only the support staff can view the memo.
13. A full description of the problem. You may press <F7> to spell-check your text.

Service Request Toolbar
(left to right)

- Log (save) the request.
- [Standard] used in conjunction with user defined fields **U**.
- Create a FollowUp reminder **E**.
- Attach a file **D**.
- Dial requester's phone number.
- View requester's User Details.
- View requester's Department (or Company) Details.
- View requester's Workstation Details
- View requester's service request history.
- View the request history of the requester's department (or company).
- Run a Wizard to guide you through filling out the request.
- Help.

B Selecting a Requester

1. Enter the first few letters of the user's name.
2. Click the 'Find' button to display a list of names matching the selection.
3. Highlight the desired name and double-click on it.

See **R** : Finding HelpSTAR Objects / Advanced Search

C Service Request Groupings

Use the main menu or the outlook style quickbar on the left to display service requests grouped by:

My Requests
Requests where you are the requester.
My Workspace
Dispatchers - view a listing of requests in dispatch.
Support reps - view listings of requests in your assigned queues or in your service.
All Requests
Intended for a help desk manager - requests are grouped by state (in dispatch, in queue, in service, overdue, etc.) or by date.

D Attachments / Encryption

Users can attach files to service requests and any other HelpSTAR objects. Files can be attached when creating or updating the objects.
Attachments can be encrypted to prevent unauthorized access.

Plaintext

🔓 **Encrypted**

E FollowUp Reminders

All HelpSTAR users can set automatic reminders for themselves when logging or updating service requests. Privileged users can also schedule FollowUp reminders for other support reps.

F Paging

HelpSTAR can be configured to send email messages to your pager when service requests are entered or updated, and in response to events as depicted in the screen shot.

G Workflow Basics

1. When a new service request is logged into HelpSTAR it normally gets forwarded to 'Dispatch'.

2. From there, a dispatcher (usually a support rep or an administrator) assesses the nature and priority of the request and forwards it to the appropriate queue.

    HelpSTAR uses queues and support reps to organize the workflow of service requests. A queue is a temporary holding area for requests grouped by a particular skill set required to resolve them.

3. A support rep is assigned to queues based on his specific skill sets. A rep is normally assigned to several queues. Each queue, in turn, may have several reps assigned to it.

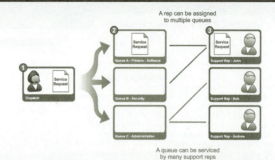

A rep can be assigned to multiple queues

A queue can be serviced by many support reps

H Workflow Example

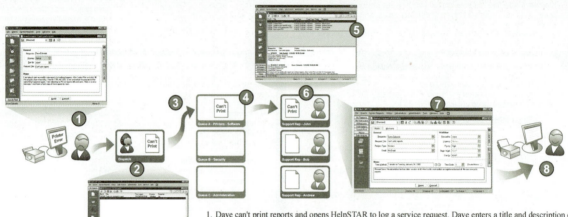

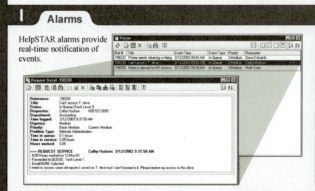

1. Dave can't print reports and opens HelpSTAR to log a service request. Dave enters a title and description of his problem, and he designates his urgency as critical.

2. When Dave submits his request, it automatically goes into 'Dispatch' and the dispatcher is notified. The dispatcher selects Dave's request to view its details in the bottom panel.

3. The dispatcher forwards the request to the "Printers - Software" queue.

4. Alarms are automatically generated for all support reps assigned to the "Printers - Software" queue. John just happens to be finishing up another request and when he closes it he checks his alarms.

5. Requests in queue are presented to support reps in order of priority (and chronologically by time logged within priority, with the oldest first). Dave's printer problem is the highest priority request in John's queues, so John will work on it next.

6. John takes the request into service by forwarding it to himself. By doing so he prevents another rep from accidentally working on it at the same time.

7. John can enter multiple memos as work progresses on the service request. Once he has solved the problem he can update the request again. He enters a memo describing the work he has performed, selects a "Time Worked" for his time spent solving the problem and closes the request.

8. Dave automatically receives notification once service on his request has been completed.

I Alarms

HelpSTAR alarms provide real-time notification of events.

EVENT TYPE	ALARM RECEIVED BY
New service request arrives in dispatch.	All users with the dispatch privilege.
Service request is placed in queue.	All support reps assigned to the queue.
Service request passed direct to a support rep.	Support rep receiving the request.
Service request updated by another support rep in 'update all' mode, or by end user who initiated the request.	If request is in service: currently designated support rep. If request is in queue: all reps assigned to the queue. If request is in dispatch: all dispatchers.
Service request is not closed when its due date arrives.	If request is in service: currently designated support rep. If request is in queue: all reps assigned to the queue.
Service request is resumed when its scheduled date arrives.	If request is in service: currently designated support rep. If request is in queue: all reps assigned to the queue.
Service request is suspended.	NO ALARM IS GENERATED
Service request is closed.	End user who initiated the request.

J Working with Service Requests

A support rep should 'accept' a request before working on it. This ensures that other reps (who are assigned to overlapping queues) don't inadvertently work on it at the same time.

To accept a request, select *My Workspace/In Queue* to list all requests in your assigned queues, highlight a request (usually the top request) and click the 'Accept' button.

Service Request (in queue) Listing
The list is sorted in descending order by priority, and then by time logged. This is the order in which requests should normally be worked on.

Preview Panel
This shows the details of the selected service request.

K Privileges

User privileges determine the type and scope of functions that a given User can perform within HelpSTAR.

Two additional privileges are specific to support reps:

- AUTO ACCEPT allows reps to open and accept requests in one step.
- QUICK FIX allows reps to open and close requests in one step.

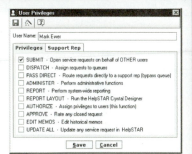

L Priority Escalation

The request's priority determines when it will be processed and how (or if) it will be escalated.

If the help desk is experiencing a heavy workload, it is possible that a request submitted under low or medium priority will stay unattended indefinitely.

HelpSTAR provides a facility for automatically escalating a request's priority after it has been left unattended for a long time. The escalation table is based on the request's initial priority, and on how long it has been left unattended.

M StarWatch

StarWatch monitors HelpSTAR events and conditions in the background, and responds accordingly.

If a monitoring activity stops running, an Alert message will be displayed to all privileged users logged onto HelpSTAR's Windows interface.

1. Three functions must be configured via their Options buttons before they can be run:
   - Priority Escalation
   - Mail Sentry
   - Pager

2. The polling interval is the time period that StarWatch waits before scanning for events or conditions that require response.

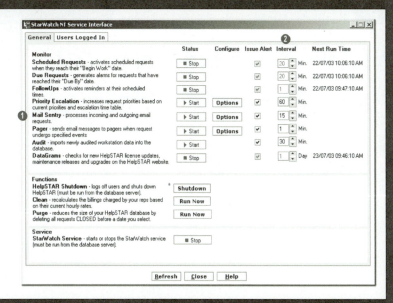

N Hardware/Software Auto Discovery

HelpSTAR provides a utility to gather inventory data about the workstations on your LAN.

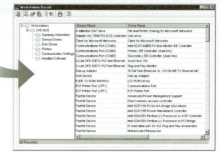

Login Script

Workstation

Hardware and software scanning occurs as a low priority background process. Therefore, it is transparent and completely unobtrusive to the end user.
Automatic periodic scanning of networked workstations is enabled through the login script.

Workstation Information

O Viewing Workstation Details

Information scanned through Auto Discovery **N** can be viewed by selecting *Data Analysis/Queries* from the quickbar.

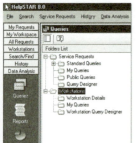

Workstation details can be viewed by workstation name, by the user to whom the workstation has been assigned, or by the last user to log into the workstation.

This example depicts summary information collected through Auto Discovery for the workstation.

Additional hardware information is grouped by:

- Device Drivers
- Disk Drives
- Printers
- Communication Settings
- User Defined Fields (if created)

HelpSTAR's Auto Discovery utility also enables you to collect information on any software you wish to audit.

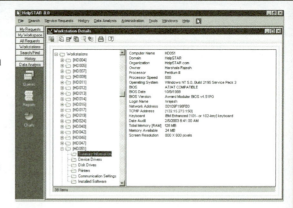

P Knowledge Management - Standard Solutions

Statistics indicate that 80% of service requests relate to recurring questions or problems.

HelpSTAR's Standard Solutions database ensures that search results are focused and comprehensive. Standard Solutions enable access to resolutions for known, recurring questions.... significantly reducing support costs!

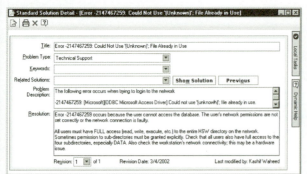

End users and support reps can search this database as a first step in solving problems that arise.

Q Searching Historical Solutions

Because users often have problems similar in nature to those previously handled by the help desk, you may be able to find the solutions in past requests.

Tip: Service Request Titles
You should strive to make the titles as descriptive as possible so that the appropriate requests can be found in a 'Title Only' search. Key information such as error numbers and the syntax of error messages should also be placed in the request title for maximum search efficiency.

R Finding Objects/Advanced Search

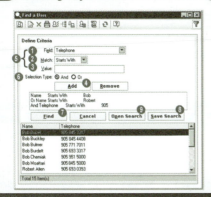

Advanced Search is accessed by clicking the "Advanced" button on the basic search form.
1. Select a 'Field' to search on.
2. Select a Match criteria (starts with, contains, etc.).
3. Enter a search 'Value' (phrase, number, etc.).
4. Click 'Add'. This will append the current criteria to the search specification.
5. Repeat Steps 1-3 to add another search criteria.
6. Choose whether to OR or AND the criteria.
7. Click 'Find' when you have finished adding criteria.
8. 'Save Search' allows you to name and save this search for future use.
9. 'Open Search' allows you to run a previously saved search (your own or Public).

S Standard Reports

HelpSTAR contains a library of Standard Reports which allow you to:

- Examine the current state of your help desk
- Measure performance, and
- Identify trends

Detailed Work Report - shows details of service requests and related memos in chronological order.
Line Item Summary - shows one-line summaries of service requests in chronological order.
Summary - the same as a detailed work report but without the memos.
Timesheet - shows detailed or one-line summaries of the work completed by your support reps.
Listing - shows all instances of the selected object in the HelpSTAR database (i.e. company, department, user, support rep, queue, problem type or workstation).
Efficiency - shows one-line summaries of closed requests. Support rep efficiency shows statistics (displayed in %) for support rep efficiency and the time in suspense ratio. Queue efficiency shows, by priority level, the average time periods that requests are in dispatch and in queue.
User Satisfaction - is based on approval ratings given to requests. You can filter by queue, problem type or support rep.
Billing - shows summaries of time worked and the related charges, based on the hourly rates individually assigned to your reps.
Overdue - shows details, with related memos in chronological order, of all service requests that are past their due date.

T   Queries / Query Designer

Queries allow you to filter and view service request and workstation information. HelpSTAR provides Standard (pre-defined) queries and also enables you to design your own custom queries.

Designing a Service Request Query
When you select the Query Designer, a new window will appear with the left side showing a treeview of the database fields that are available.

1. Check the fields you wish to display (or use as selection filters).
2. Selected fields are added to the grid on the top right.
3. You can refine your selections by clicking on the Criteria for the appropriate field. Input the appropriate filtering (selection) criteria.
4. As you design your query, you can test it by clicking the 'Execute' button. The results will be displayed in a listing below the field selection grid.
5. You may name and save your custom query for future use.

Workstation Queries
The Workstation Query Designer allows you to create queries based on the data captured through Auto Discovery 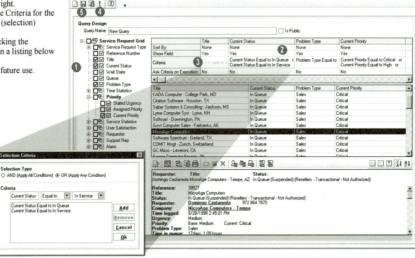.

U   User Defined Fields

HelpSTAR's Database Administration Tool allows you to create user defined fields for service requests, as well as users, departments, companies, queues, problem types, standard solutions and workstations.

The example below shows:

1. six new fields being defined (created) for an internal user.
2. the resulting fields on the *Internal* tab of the New User form.

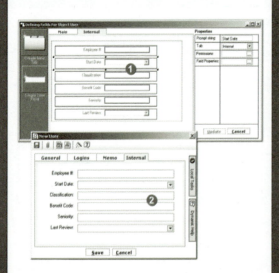

V   Index / Glossary

HelpSTAR.com

http://edu.helpstar.com/support

Glossary

acceptable use policy	A set of written guidelines pertaining to technology usage
action plan	A plan that lists the steps required to solve a problem as well as a timetable for implementation
active communication style	A communication style in which individuals are genuinely interested in understanding other people and frequently check the accuracy of their understanding
analysis	Taking the user's description of the problem, reasoning how to further test and confirm what the problem is, and determining the most effective resolution
asset management	The process of collecting and maintaining data about a company's technology assets
asset tracking tools	Software applications that gather data about technology assets via a network
attentive communication style	A communication style in which individuals are genuinely interested in hearing and understanding the other person's point of view, and as such, they prefer to let others make decisions and feel that others generally know more than they do.
authentication	Establishing whether or not a request falls within the help desk's domain
auto attendant	A phone system that answers calls with a recorded message
automated call distributors (ACDs)	Telephone systems that route calls, prioritize calls, and play recorded messages
Automatic Speech Recognition (ASR)	Computer software that recognizes human speech and translates it into instructions that computer programs can process
auxiliary time	The amount of time each help desk analyst is unavailable to receive calls because he or she is performing non-phone support tasks
available time	The amount of time each help desk analyst is logged into the automated call distributor (ACD) system waiting to take inbound calls
average abandon rate	The percentage of calls that come into the help desk but are not answered by the support staff
average handling time (AHT)	The time it takes a support rep to resolve a user problem
average hold time	The average time callers are on hold before their calls are answered

The average amount of time each caller waits before his or her call is answered	**average speed to answer (ASA)**
The amount of time a support rep spends out of the queue performing work required to complete a call after hanging up the telephone	**average work time (AWT)**
A group technique that results in creative solutions to a problem	**brainstorming**
The capability to send messages to a large number of people, whether or not they are using the same device to communicate	**broadcast messaging**
A state of physical and mental exhaustion resulting from extended periods of stress	**burnout**
A way of organizing a help desk into groups based on the business units they support	**business model**
The process of observing and evaluating agent performance for quality assurance and training purposes	**call monitoring**
The use of various technologies to record actual help desk calls for later analysis	**call recording**
A state that exists when a solution is implemented that results in the elimination of the problem	**call resolution**
Identifying and collecting information to be included in a knowledge base	**capturing**
A method of reasoning that uses past cases to solve new problems	**case-based reasoning (CBR)**
A single physical location within an organization that provides support to all users	**centralized help desk**
The ability to report incidents in a convenient, straightforward fashion	**centralized reporting**
A pool of telephone lines leased at the phone company's central office	**Centrex**
The process of measuring and evaluating an individual's knowledge and skills in a particular area	**certification**
Questions that can be answered with a simple answer or a yes or no	**closed-ended questions**
A disaster recovery approach in which data, applications, and servers are maintained on a standby basis with regular updates	**cold site**
The particular way a person communicates	**communication style**

competitive communication style	A communication style in which people like to be right, feel that they know more than most people, and that people should follow their directions
computer security	The process of planning, implementing, and verifying the protection of an organization's computer-related assets from internal and external threats
computer telephony	Tools that combine telephone and computer technology into one system
computer telephony integration (CTI)	The integration of telephone and computer-based systems
cost per call	The average cost of each call coming in to the help desk
cryptography	A method of protecting information by transforming it into an unreadable format before it is distributed
customer satisfaction	A customer's perception of the service that is being provided
customer service	The process of satisfying customers
database administration	The area within Information Technology (IT)that develops, implements, updates, tests, and repairs databases
decentralized help desk	A help desk structure in which multiple support sites are located throughout an organization
decision making	The process of choosing among a number of alternatives
decision tree	A series of questions that guide an individual to relevant solutions based on his or her responses
diagnostic programs	Software that collect PC configuration information, analyzes the diagnostic data, and troubleshoots problems, all from a remote location
diagnostic tools	Tools used by support specialists to assist in identifying the source of a user's problem
dispatch structure	A help desk structure in which the first-line personnel act as dispatchers, taking just enough information to refer the question to the appropriate group
disaster recovery plan	A detailed plan designed to minimize loss and ensure continuity of critical business functions in the event of a major disaster
discussion forums	Online message boards in which individuals post and respond to text messages

A performance management event that occurs when a manager overhears an agent's phone conversation with a user while passing by and stops to provide feedback	**drive-by**
The act of encoding the contents of a message before it is distributed	**encryption**
User satisfaction measured by a one-time survey completed soon after a service encounter	**event-based satisfaction**
A program that simulates the interaction a user might have with a human expert to solve a problem	**expert system**
Information that can be expressed using language and that can be easily transmitted among individuals	**explicit knowledge**
A help desk in which the main focus is on supporting external clients	**external help desk**
A list of frequently asked questions (and answers) about a topic	**FAQ**
A security device that examines traffic entering and leaving a network, and determines whether to forward it toward its destination	**firewall**
The percentage of incidents that are resolved by a help desk on the initial contact	**first call resolution (FCR)**
A graphic representation used to identify all possible causes of a problem	**fishbone diagram**
A system of logic that creates rules that use approximate or subjective values and incomplete or ambiguous data	**fuzzy logic**
A single point-of-contact in an organization that provides support to individuals who use technology to perform their jobs	**help desk**
A disaster recovery approach in which servers, applications, and data are maintained in real-time synchronization with the main facility	**hot site**
The process of evaluating each possible solution to a problem through testing	**hypothesis testing**
The way in which an organization responds to computer security incidents	**incident handling capability**
The process of receiving, processing, and resolving user problems	**incident management**
The data required for the proper interpretation of how to implement a solution and for understanding why and how the solution functions	**information**

information overload	A type of stress generated by an overwhelming amount of information that requires processing
intelligent escalation	The capability of identifying problems that are beyond the scope of the knowledgebase and bringing them to the attention of the help desk
intermittent problems	Problems that occur occasionally but not all the time
internal help desk	A help desk in which the main emphasis is on supporting individuals within the organization
Interactive Voice Response (IVR)	Telephone-based systems that allow individuals to interact with a telephone using the buttons on the telephone keypad
Internet Protocol (IP) telephony	A technology that allows voice calls to be routed over the Internet or a corporate intranet
intranet	A network similar to the Internet, except that the information is accessible only to employees within an organization or others who have been granted access rights
intrusion detection system (IDS)	A security system that inspects all inbound and outbound network activity and identifies suspicious patterns that may indicate an attack
IT asset management (ITAM)	The process of tracking information about technology assets throughout the entire asset life cycle, from initial purchase to retirement
keyword search engine	A search method in which users enter several key words and press a key to begin a search
knowledgebase	A database of related information used as a resource by help desk personnel and end users
knowledge	Information that can be applied by people in a useful manner
knowledge management	The process of collecting, organizing, analyzing, and distributing information
left brain	The side of the brain that excels at rational and analytical thinking and also processes language
logging	The process of recording information about a call
method structure	A structure in which help desks are organized by the manner in which support is provided

Quantitative measures of the efficiency of the help desk — **metrics**

Software that connects two or more otherwise separate applications across a computer network — **middleware**

A problem-solving method that involves replacing computer components that might be the cause the problem — **module replacement**

Systems that evaluate words based on their positioning in relation to each other — **natural-language processing systems**

Building and maintaining the technology that supports user applications — **network engineering**

The process of managing and controlling the network configurations within the organization — **Network management**

The practice of protecting and preserving resources and information on a network — **network security**

The process of informing others about a problem — **notification**

A disaster recovery plan in which data are stored off-site, but no hardware is located off-site — **off-site approach**

Documents such as user manuals, installation instructions, and training materials that are available online — **online documentation**

Questions that cannot be answered with a yes or no; an explanation is required — **open-ended questions**

The process of using an external company to perform a job that was previously performed by internal staff — **outsourcing**

User satisfaction that is determined through ongoing surveys, conducted at regular intervals, and annual surveys — **overall satisfaction**

Taking responsibility for a problem and seeing it through until it is resolved — **ownership**

A process in which a firewall examines the nature of each piece of information traveling into or out of the network — **packet filtering**

The monitoring of help desk services to determine compliance with a Service Level Agreement (SLA) — **performance measurement**

The protection of building sites and equipment from theft, vandalism, natural disasters, manmade catastrophes, and accidental damage — **physical security**

private branch exchange (PBX)	An internal telephone network in which users share a certain number of lines for making telephone calls outside the company
pool structure	A help desk structure in which all support staff members support the same technology, serve the same customers, and perform the same job duties
position certification	A statement that an individual has the skills and abilities to perform the duties associated with a specific position
prioritizing	the process of determining both the timing and the level of support that will be provided
proactive knowledge management	the process of building knowledge before it is needed
problem data	information about the problem itself, such as a description of the component affected, the symptoms, the date and time the problem first occurred, and a description of the problem
problem management	the process of receiving, monitoring, and resolving problems that are reported to the help desk
problem management tools	Tools used to log, track, route, and record information about problems reported to the help desk
problem resolution tools	Tools used to determine the causes of users' problems and develop effective solutions
problem solving	A process used to arrive at a solution to a difficult or disruptive situation
product certification	A statement regarding a person's competencies in a particular product area
product model	A structure in which the help desk is divided into a number of groups, each responsible for supporting a specific product group
proxy server	A software application that acts as an intermediary between applications and servers
quality assurance (QA)	The area of the Information Technology (IT) department that is responsible for ensuring that a company's technology products are free of errors before they are released and marketed
reactive knowledge management	The process of capturing new knowledge after a problem occurs and a solution is found
real-time remote monitoring	A method of measuring performance in which a manager listens to calls without being present at the agent's workstation

Software programs that allow support personnel to take over and manage users' PCs without leaving the help desk	**remote control programs**
The process of deliberately taking steps to recreate a problem	**replication**
The process of responding to user requests for hardware, software, or services	**request/change management**
The specific answer and response that eliminates the user's problem	**resolution**
The amount of time that passes until a call is answered	**response time**
A measure of the cost of providing support as compared to the value of a support group's services	**return on investment (ROI)**
The side of the brain that processes incoming colors, sounds, and patterns; it processes incoming information in a holistic manner	**right brain**
The restoration of a program or computer to an earlier configuration that is known to work effectively	**rollback**
A process that can be used to identify the underlying factors that are causing a problem	**root cause analysis**
A device that links a local network to a remote network and determines the best route for data to travel across the network	**router**
A concise description of a set of conditions and a set of actions to take if the conditions are true	**rule**
An expert system that uses a set of rules as its knowledge base	**rule-based expert system**
Information about a caller that appears on the call recipient's computer screen at the time of the call	**screen pop**
The process of gathering information about a problem so that problem solving can begin	**screening**
The process of providing and maintaining security for an organization's assets	**security management**
Software programs that automatically restore desktop applications to their original state by reinstalling components that have been damaged, removed, or modified	**self-healing programs**
Tools that provides users with the resources to solve their own problems	**self-help technology**

self-service support	Assistance that enables users to solve problems on their own, through the use of a support Web site
server	A powerful computer that acts as an intermediary between PCs on a network and provides a large volume of disk storage for shared information
Service Level Agreement (SLA)	A formal, quantitative statement of the scope and level of services provided by a help desk
service-level management	The set of people and systems that allows the organization to ensure that SLAs are being met and that the necessary resources are being provided efficiently
side-by-side monitoring	A method of reviewing performance that takes place at an agent's workstation
situation	The context of a solution
skill-based routing (SBR)	A routing method in which calls are routed to the agent who can best handle the request, with the goal of solving the problem as efficiently as possible
sniffer	Software that intercepts and analyzes data packets transmitted over a network
software engineering	The group within the Information Technology (IT) department that designs, develops, and revises the software used by the company and/or its external customers
specialized structure	A help desk structure in which support is provided based on the product or the business unit
speech authenticator	A biometrics-based system that provides secure access to a company's telephone and computer resources
standards	Policies that specify the acceptable use of both software and hardware and that define standard software and hardware equipment
stress	A mismatch between an individual's resources and the demands placed on that individual
structuring	The process of indexing, categorizing, and classifying information

An individual who exhibits the highest level of expertise in performing a specialized job, task, or skill within the organization	subject-matter expert (SME)
Knowledge that is part of a person's individual experience and is not easily communicated to others	tacit knowledge
services that enable individuals and businesses to effectively use technology	technical support
A standard in which the physical connection between the computer and the telephone system is made at the desktop level	Telephony Application Programming Interface (TAPI)
A standard in which the telephone system is physically connected to a server on the network, which in turn is connected to a user's PC	Telephony Services Application Programming Interface (TSAPI)
A structure in which the help desk is divided into several groups, each providing a higher level of support	tiered structure
The amount of time that passes until a problem is resolved	time to resolution
The number of calls received in a fixed period of time	total number of calls
A form of processing messages that enables agents to access all messages and requests in a single location, regardless of whether they were originally sent via voice, fax, e-mail, or pager	unified messaging
A queue system through which all incoming requests pass, regardless of their origin	unified queue
Information about a user, such as the user's name, title, department, and hardware and software configuration	user data
People who perform tasks with the aid of technology	users
Testing a solution to determine if it resolves the problem	validation
Determining whether a user is eligible to receive support	verification
Technologies that make it possible for users to interact with the help desk by speaking their requests rather than entering them using the telephone keypad	voice application
A technology that allows voice calls to be routed over the Internet or a corporate intranet	Voice over IP (voIP)

Index

Certification, 41–43, 47–48
   defined, 41
   position, 42
   product, 42–43
Certified Help Desk Analyst (CHDA), 42
Certified Help Desk Professional (CHDP), 42
Certified Novell Administrator (CNA), 43
Certified Novell Engineer (CNE), 43
Change, 285–286
   keeping current, 284
   as opportunity, 286
   resisting, 285
Change requests, 255
Clarifying statements, 79
Clarity of communication, 79
Closed-ended questions, 94–95, 116–117
Closing calls, 119
Cold site, 268
Collect caller information, 140–141
Communication skills, 11, 68–83
   barriers, 80–83
   communication style, 72–74
   guidelines, 76–79
   help desk challenges, 70–75
   language differences, 75
   listening, 11, 68–77
   responses to avoid, 80–83
   telephone versus face-to-face, 71
Communication style, 72–74
   appropriate, 74
   language differences, 75
   self-assessment test, 72–73
Competitive communication style, 72–74
Computer security, 255–256. *See also* Security
   management
Computer Technology Industry Association
   (CompTIA), 42–43
Computer telephony, 129–151
   automated call distributors (ACDs), 132–135
   defined, 17–18
   Interactive Voice Response (IVR), 136–144
   need for, 130–131
Computer telephony integration (CTI), 144–150
   advantages, 150
   automatic display of caller and call details,
     145–146
   data analysis and reporting functions, 149–150
   defined, 144
   delivery of automated responses, 149
   features and benefits, 145–150
   retrieving messages from single location, 148–149

   routing messages into unified queue, 146–148
   widespread availability, 144–145
Concentration, 77
Configuration management, 104, 251–252
Continuous improvement, 218
Cost per call, 205–208
   determining operating costs, 206–207
   interpreting, 207–208
Cryptography, 260–261
Customer satisfaction, 20, 32, 199–201
   communicating results, 200
   defined, 199
   determining, 119, 200
   improving, 201
   measuring, 200
Customer service
   defined, 12
   measuring, 19–20

D

Dantz, 21
Database administration, 47
Database software, 5
Data collection, 92–93
   data types, 92–93
   ruling out the obvious, 93
   skill-based routing (SBR), 135
Decentralized help desk, 29
Decision making, 105
Decision trees, 232–233
Defensiveness, 81
Delayed assisted support, 171–174
   described, 165
   discussion forums, 173
   e-mail, 171–173
Diagnostic programs, 171
Diagnostic tools, 18
Difficult users, 113–118
Disaster recovery plan, 267–269
   help desk role, 268–269
   steps, 268
Discussion forums, 173
Dispatch structure, 30–31
Distractions, 70
Diverse user base, 75, 106
Documentation
   benefits, 121–122
   online, 169
   user call, 121–122
   See also Reports and reporting
Drive-by monitoring, 204

I

IC³ (Internet and Computing Core Certification), 42
Impatience, 78
Incident handling capability, 263–264
Incident management, 55–128
    communicating with caller, 75, 78–79
    communication barriers, 80–83
    defined, 56
    difficult users, 113–118
    documenting calls, 121–122
    listening, 68–77
    processing incidents, 92–112
    receiving incidents, 56–68
    resolving calls, 119–120
Information
    knowledgebase, 224–225
    knowledge versus, 121
Information overload, 283
Information technology (IT)
    career paths, 18–22
    See also IT asset management (ITAM)
Interactive Voice Response (IVR), 136–144
    assistance to people with motor skills impairment, 141–142
    Automatic Speech Recognition (ASR), 140
    collect caller information, 140–141
    described, 136
    Internet Protocol (IP) telephony, 139–140
    making most of, 137
    speech-to-text technology, 140
    status of most recent request, 142–144
    verifying callers, 144
    voice applications, 138–139
    voice over IP (voIP), 139–140
Intermittent problems, 97
Internal help desk, 4
Internet Protocol (IP) telephony, 139–140
Interpersonal interactions, 283
Interpreting messages, 69
Interrupting, 78, 82
Intranets, 167
Intrusion detection system (IDS), 263
Intuit, 21
Inventory data, 249–250, 253
IT asset management (ITAM), 248–255
    asset inventory, 249–250, 253
    benefits, 249
    challenges, 248–249
    common IT assets, 248
    defined, 248
    help desk responsibilities, 251–255

J

Jargon, 82
Java Script, 161–162
Job security, 283

K

Key business initiatives, 64–65
Keyword search engine, 173, 231
Knowledge
    defined, 121
    different levels of, 70–71
    explicit, 221
    information versus, 121
    reviewing knowledge, 228–229
    structuring, 227–228
    tacit, 222, 223
Knowledgebase, 18, 167–168
    characteristics of effective, 218–219
    components of solutions, 221–225
    defined, 15
    maintenance, 218, 229
Knowledge management, 215–241
    barriers to effective, 238–239
    benefits, 216–218
    careers, 237
    components of knowledge-based solution, 221–225
    defined, 15
    effective knowledgebase, 218–219
    knowledgebase search methods, 231–235
    metrics, 235–236
    proactive, 220–221
    processes, 226–229
    reactive, 219–220

L

Language differences, 75
Left brain, 100
Listening, 11, 68–77
    active, 74
    angry callers, 113–114
    challenges, 70–75
    guidelines, 76–77
    hearing versus, 68–69
    listening cycle, 69
Live chat, 165, 170
Local area networks (LANs), 45, 258
Logging calls, 60–61

M

Maintenance information, 255

INTERNATIONAL CONTACT INFORMATION

AUSTRALIA
McGraw-Hill Book Company Australia Pty. Ltd.
TEL +61-2-9900-1800
FAX +61-2-9878-8881
http://www.mcgraw-hill.com.au
books-it_sydney@mcgraw-hill.com

CANADA
McGraw-Hill Ryerson Ltd.
TEL +905-430-5000
FAX +905-430-5020
http://www.mcgraw-hill.ca

GREECE, MIDDLE EAST, & AFRICA
(Excluding South Africa)
McGraw-Hill Hellas
TEL +30-210-6560-990
TEL +30-210-6560-993
TEL +30-210-6560-994
FAX +30-210-6545-525

MEXICO (Also serving Latin America)
McGraw-Hill Interamericana Editores S.A. de C.V.
TEL +525-117-1583
FAX +525-117-1589
http://www.mcgraw-hill.com.mx
fernando_castellanos@mcgraw-hill.com

SINGAPORE (Serving Asia)
McGraw-Hill Book Company
TEL +65-6863-1580
FAX +65-6862-3354
http://www.mcgraw-hill.com.sg
mghasia@mcgraw-hill.com

SOUTH AFRICA
McGraw-Hill South Africa
TEL +27-11-622-7512
FAX +27-11-622-9045
robyn_swanepoel@mcgraw-hill.com

SPAIN
McGraw-Hill/Interamericana de España, S.A.U.
TEL +34-91-180-3000
FAX +34-91-372-8513
http://www.mcgraw-hill.es
professional@mcgraw-hill.es

UNITED KINGDOM, NORTHERN,
EASTERN, & CENTRAL EUROPE
McGraw-Hill Education Europe
TEL +44-1-628-502500
FAX +44-1-628-770224
http://www.mcgraw-hill.co.uk
computing_europe@mcgraw-hill.com

ALL OTHER INQUIRIES Contact:
McGraw-Hill Technology Education
TEL +1-630-789-4000
FAX +1-630-789-5226
http://www.mhhe.com/it
omg_international@mcgraw-hill.com